THE PSYCHOPATH EPIDEMIC

Why the World Is So F*CKED UP and
What You Can Do About It

CAMERON REILLY

Health Communications, Inc.
Boca Raton, Florida

www.hcibooks.com

Library of Congress Cataloging-in-Publication Data
is available through the Library of Congress

© 2019 Cameron Reilly

ISBN-13: 978-07573-2360-7 (paperback)
ISBN-10: 0-7573-2360-X (paperback)
ISBN-13: 978-07573-2361-4 (eBook)
ISBN-10: 0-7573-2361-8 (eBook)

Publisher: Health Communications, Inc.
    1700 NW 2nd Avenue
    Boca Raton, FL 33432

This book would not be possible without Publishizer, *www.Publishizer.com*

Cover design by Cameron Reilly
Interior design and formatting by Lawna Patterson Oldfield

*For Chrissy, Hunter, Taylor, and Fox,
so they can stop asking me, "When are you
going to finish that book?"*

*And to my friend Tony Kynaston,
who suggested I write this book, and
patiently guided its progress over many years,
providing invaluable suggestions and
criticism, all of which improved
the final product.*

CONTENTS

PREFACE

Every day in the news we hear about people in positions of business, political, and religious leadership doing deplorable things—sexual harassment, polluting the environment, lining their own pockets at the expense of their employees and customers, raping children, and covering up crimes. The common explanation is that they are just "bad eggs"—normal people who have gone astray for reasons unknown. However, I believe there is a better explanation.

Psychiatrists estimate that 1 percent of the adult population are psychopaths—people physiologically incapable of empathy, who crave risk, are often charismatic, and who possess an extreme desire for wealth and power. In the United States, this 1 percent would be nearly two million adults. Where might these people be hiding?

The premise of this book is that these psychopaths are quite possibly to be found occupying senior management positions in many of our institutions and organizations, wielding enormous power. In other words, our economy is run by psychopaths. If that is true, then we need to build systems that protect us from their behavior. This book examines the evidence and then suggests solutions for saving us all—from the psychopaths who are literally right in front of us, who are literally hiding in plain sight, or who are in the next office, the Oval office, or the office down the street.

INTRODUCTION

*"The greatest trick
the Devil ever pulled was convincing
the world he didn't exist."*

—Kevin Spacey,
The Usual Suspects

don't know if you've noticed, but the world is in a bit of a fucking mess right now. Our political leaders continually fail us. Our business executives fail us. Our religious leaders fail us.

Almost every day we hear about people in positions of business, political, and religious authority, who should know better, doing horrific things.

There's an old saying: "Power corrupts; absolute power corrupts absolutely."

What if we have it backwards? Maybe it should be: "The corrupt seek power; the absolutely corrupt seek absolute power."

The central premise of this book is simple: The world is in a fucking mess because we have allowed too many psychopaths to rise to positions of power. The cultures of many of our largest organizations—business, political, military, law enforcement, and religious—attract and reward psychopaths. They prosper and rise into management positions, where they contribute to increasing the toxicity of the organizational culture. Combined, these toxic organizations pose an extraordinary danger to society. We are facing an epidemic of psychopaths.

Psychiatrists estimate that psychopaths (or, as they prefer to call them, people suffering from Antisocial Personality Disorder) make up something like 1 to 2 percent of the adult population—or maybe even as high as 4 percent.[1]

The condition seems two or three times more prevalent in men than women.[2]

Despite what Hollywood might have told you, psychopaths (that's what I'm going to continue to call them for the sake of brevity, and it includes sociopaths) aren't all serial killers. Psychopathy is actually much more common than most people assume.[3]

In fact, according to criminal psychologist Robert Hare, only about 15 to 20 percent of a typical prison population are psychopaths.[4]

So, if psychopaths aren't all serial killers or criminals, what are they?

Let's start with a definition. According to the FBI:

Many psychopaths exhibit a profound lack of remorse for their aggressive actions, both violent and nonviolent, along with a corresponding lack of empathy for their victims. This central psychopathic concept enables them to act in a cold-blooded manner, using those around them as pawns to achieve goals and satisfy needs and desires, whether sexual, financial, physical, or emotional. Most psychopaths are grandiose, selfish sensation seekers who lack a moral compass—a conscience—and go through life taking what they want. They do not accept responsibility for their actions and find a way to shift the blame to someone or something else.[5]

In this book, I'm going to make the case that many of the behaviors that come naturally to psychopaths—the lack of empathy combined with a high appetite for risk, lack of conscience, the ability to fake charisma, and an intense desire for power—make them attractive to organizations. Think about your colleagues and managers for a second—do you know anyone who fits that description?

I believe a relatively small group of these "garden-variety psychopaths" end up in management positions in many of our business, religious and political organizations. Most of them, however, do not. They lack the IQ or the motivation to climb the ladder. In some cases, they have both of those but burn too many bridges early on in their careers, scaring people with their intense raw ambition and cold glare.

Martha Stout from the Harvard Medical School, author of *The Sociopath Next Door*, suggests "most of them are obscure people, and limited to dominating their young children, or a depressed spouse, or perhaps a few employees or coworkers."[6]

Some, however, have the right combination to climb the ladder. Enough, I believe, to cause society enormous problems.

Reasonable people can do bad things from time to time. We can be cruel, insensitive, selfish and thoughtless. But nature has imbued us with a degree of empathy. We feel remorse, guilt, and regret when we hurt others. While we will all do horrible things from time to time, we don't go out of our way to do them, and we feel bad afterward. Psychopaths, on the other hand, have no conscience. They don't feel bad; they feel like winners. And they try to convince the rest of the world that if we want to be winners, too, we should be more like them.

One percent of the adult population of the United States is roughly two million people—two million psychopaths. A percentage of them are undoubtedly already in the prison system. Some are sitting at home, drinking beer while their wives go out to work. Some might be sitting in the big corner office in your building. Some might be working inside the White House, Downing Street, the Vatican, and the Pentagon.

Collectively they wield enormous power over society. If I am right, we need to build systems that protect us from their worst instincts.

Throughout the book, I'm going to examine psychopaths in more detail and explore the various ways that different kinds of organizations develop toxic cultures.

In the final chapter, I suggest a range of things we can all do to stop psychopaths from ruining our organizations and society and how we can protect ourselves from them as individuals.

Psychopaths, like redheads, have probably always been with us. But modern capitalism has given them access to more power than they might have had two hundred years ago.

I want to convince you that this epidemic of psychopaths in positions of power is the biggest problem facing the world today. It's bigger and more pressing that climate change, Brexit, wars, and offshore tax shelters—because these issues are all caused, or worsened, by the fact that unchecked psychopaths are in power. Remove the psychopaths from the world's boardroom tables and we could probably solve all of these issues a lot faster.

For the sake of society we need to better understand them, their role in society, and how to stop them from exercising their worst impulses.

CHAPTER ONE

GARDEN-VARIETY PSYCHOPATHS

The smiling assassin. That's how I remember him. He was a boss of mine for a year or so. I don't want to say where, because I'm not keen on a lawsuit. I'll just call him Fred. He became my manager's manager at a large company I worked for in my younger days and, at first, I liked him. Fred smiled a lot and seemed very charming and personable.

It didn't take long for me to learn there was another side to his personality. My immediate manager started to tell me stories about his interactions with Fred. How he would say one thing to someone's face and then the opposite behind their back.

When my manager had enough, he quit the company, and I reported directly to Fred. Although Fred assured me that everything was copacetic between us, that he liked me and thought I was a valuable member of the team, my colleagues started to whisper in my ear that Fred was out to get me. He was fishing for stories that he could use against me. There weren't any such stories—but that was beside the point. When I took my concerns to the HR department, they did nothing to stop Fred. When I took my concerns to the managing director of the company, he did nothing to stop Fred. So, like my manager before me, I also quit the company.

Back then I thought Fred was just a bully. Today I realize he was probably my first corporate psychopath.

LET'S TALK MORE ABOUT PSYCHOPATHS

The majority of people have pretty simple needs and wants. They just want to live their lives, fall in love, knock out a few kids, get laid regularly, stay well fed, entertained, see some sights, and die peacefully, surrounded by the people they love.

For some people, however, that's not enough. They want to own *everything*. They want to control *everything*. Enough is never enough. They have a winner-take-all attitude. Dog eat dog. Law of the jungle. Kill or be killed. People like that are often going to end up on top—because the rest of us let them. We don't want to be on top enough to do the things that need to be done. We can't sleep at night if we have to lie and cheat and steal and screw our way to the top. But psychopaths don't lose a wink of sleep. On the contrary, they sleep *better* knowing they are #WINNING!

You know what I'm talking about. You know this kind of person. You've worked for this kind of person. Chances are you probably work for someone like this right now.

When discussing the diagnostic features of people with "antisocial personality disorder," the current edition of the *Diagnostic and Statistical Manual of Mental Disorders* (aka DSM-5) says:

They are frequently deceitful and manipulative in order to gain personal profit or pleasure (e.g., to obtain money, sex, or power). The essential feature of antisocial personality disorder is a pervasive pattern of disregard for, and violation of, the rights of others that begins in childhood or early adolescence and continues into adulthood. This pattern has also been referred to as psychopathy, sociopathy, or dyssocial personality disorder.

Because psychopaths don't care about the feelings or rights of others, they are willing and ready to do the things other people won't to succeed. This makes them think of themselves as superior. They are the alpha males and females. They think of themselves as the winners. And therefore, in their minds, they deserve more power. For some, the way to get maximum power is to run a large organization.

It appears they have always been with us. I've spent the last fifteen years recording hundreds of hours of detailed podcasts about some of the "Great Men of History"—Alexander the Great, Julius, Augustus and Tiberius Caesar, Cosimo de' Medici, Napoleon Bonaparte, Churchill, Stalin, Roosevelt—and one of the questions I'm always asking myself is, "Was this guy a psychopath?"

They appear frequently in Roman and Greek mythology, in the Old Testament, the writings of Cicero, *The Annals of Tacitus*, *The book of One Thousand and One Nights* and in Shakespeare. In his Renaissance masterpiece *The Prince*, Niccolò Machiavelli wrote:

If you only notice human proceedings, you may observe that all who attain great power and riches, make use of either force or fraud; and what they have acquired either by deceit or violence, in order to conceal the disgraceful methods of attainment, they endeavor to sanctify with the false title of honest gains. Those who either from imprudence or want of sagacity avoid doing so, are always overwhelmed with servitude and poverty; for faithful servants are always servants, and honest men are always poor; nor do any ever escape from servitude but the bold and faithless, or from poverty, but the rapacious and fraudulent. God and nature have thrown all human fortunes into the midst of mankind; and they are thus attainable rather by rapine than by industry, by wicked actions rather than by good. Hence it is that men feed upon each other, and those who cannot defend themselves must be worried.

But it wasn't until the German psychiatrist Julius Ludwig August Koch invented the term "psychopath" in 1888 that humans started to think about this as a psychiatric disorder. It was further developed as a field of study by American psychiatrist Hervey M. Cleckley in 1941 when he identified the major traits of a psychopath.

Unfortunately, when many people today think about psychopaths, they still think of serial killers, mafia dons, and ranting dictators—Ted Bundy, Al Capone, and Joseph Stalin. They don't think of their local priest, CEO, their favorite politician, or police captain.

In every society, since the dawn of time, there has been a relatively small percentage of the population who feel it is their destiny to control as much power as possible. This is the primary goal of their lives, and they will do anything it takes to achieve it—fight, steal, murder, lie, cheat, bribe, fuck, and burn.

Many studies suggest they make up about 1 percent of the population but other experts go further. Psychiatrist Donald Black, co-author of the *Introductory Textbook of Psychiatry* and author of *Bad Boys, Bad Men: Confronting Antisocial Personality Disorder*, suggests the number of psychopaths in the adult population might actually be as high as 4.5 percent.[7]

Something about their brains is abnormal, and they are either born that way (a psychopath) or something happens to them when they are young kids that makes them that way (a sociopath).

They will sacrifice their loved ones and their friends to end up on top—the top of the company or just the top of the household, depending on their level of ambition. Most people aren't built that way; we are happy to live simple lives, raising a family, enjoying our weekend, and smelling the roses. And this just makes it easier for the power-hungry people, the 1 percent, to hack and slash their way to the top.

In millennia gone past, some psychopaths, typically those born into aristocracy, probably ended up as kings and queens; warlords, emperors, popes, and cardinals; prophets, lords, and dukes; and the landed gentry. And there wasn't much that the masses could do about it. They just accepted it as "the way things are." The lower classes stayed in their village, in their poverty, and tried hard to survive and keep their children alive. The nobility, a fancy name for the richest 1 percent and their descendants, fought for power among themselves, while the other 99 percent quite often found themselves as battle fodder.

We have capitalism to thank for making it easier than ever before for more psychopaths to leverage themselves into positions of power.

In feudalist societies it would have been much harder for the garden-variety psychopath to rise to elite positions. Unless you were born into the nobility, it was pretty tough to get out of your class circumstances and engineer yourself into a place where you could rise above.

Until the Industrial Revolution, if you were a psychopath, but not a member of the aristocracy or nobility, let's say you were the son of a blacksmith, what could you do? You didn't have much chance of putting together an army or rising above your station in terms of wealth creation opportunities.

If you were born a plebeian in the Roman Republic, your chances of rising to power were kept in check by the tools of the aristocracy — the Senate, the army, and paid mobs. During the Roman Empire, a small number of plebeians rose through the ranks to become generals and even emperors, but they were few and far between. Some centurions of plebeian extraction were rewarded with property by Augustus Caesar, after his civil war with Mark Antony; they suddenly found themselves as the nouveau riche with a seat in the Senate — but again, these stories were extremely rare.

If you were a Hun in the 5th century, you could brawl it out with some other guys to see who the king of the tribe would be, but by the Middle Ages, these opportunities were scarce. There were rare people like the condottiere Francesco Sforza who, in the early 1400s, managed to use his father's private army of mercantile soldiers to become the Duke of Milan — but again, those accounts are quite uncommon.

In theory, you could enter the Catholic Church and rise through the ranks to become a wealthy archbishop, cardinal, or even pope—and a few people did manage that—but these titles were typically reserved for people from wealthy families who could buy their way in by filling the coffers of the church.

For most of human history, if you were of humble birth, you stayed that way.

So, if 1 percent of the population were psychopaths, and 99 percent of the population were commoners, it stands to reason that 99 percent of the psychopaths probably stayed poor and, while they may have caused trouble for their immediate family and village, they usually never went further than that.

Then the Industrial Revolution came along and we entered the rise of modern capitalism. Now those 99 percent had a much better shot at unleashing their psychopathy on the world. They could get an education, get a job, and use their inherent tendencies to climb the ladder of power inside an organization—business, political, religious, academic, or military. Suddenly, after one thousand years of being trapped in their villages, the psychopaths had a ladder to affluence and dominance unlike anything before.

Studies show that most people who are born into modest circumstances continue to stay poor.[8] But we live in a world where the psychopaths who are born underprivileged, and have no qualms about fucking over other people in their march toward power—who care as much about committing an unethical act as you or I do about what we ate for breakfast a week ago—have an open playing field.

Capitalism has unleashed an epidemic of psychopaths on the world.

CHIEF EXECUTIVE PSYCHOPATH

What makes me think psychopaths run our organizations?

Well, for a start, there is the obvious overlap between the traits of a psychopath and those of many cold-blooded, remorseless, empathy-lacking, power-seeking, charismatic modern managers. The presence of psychopaths in senior management might explain why our political, business, and religious leaders often make decisions that seem to willfully destroy economies, the environment, families, and, sometimes, especially during times of war, entire nations.

Then it's just a question of the numbers.

Psychiatrists estimate that psychopaths make up about 1 to 4 percent of the adult population. Assuming this is correct, and taking the lower number, then Australia has roughly 184,000 adult psychopaths running around. The U.S. has about 2.3 million and the UK has five hundred thousand.

The global psychopath population would be in the vicinity of 60 million. SIXTY. MILLION. PSYCHOPATHS.

Let that sink in a minute. I'll wait.

Australia had 1,123 opioid drug-related deaths in 2018 and that gets called an epidemic. What do we call 184,000 psychopaths on the loose?

And what are they all doing?

The Australian Bureau of Statistics reports that there were roughly 43,000 inmates in Australian prisons at 30 June 2018.[9] Even if they are all psychopaths (and, according to psychiatrists, it's more likely that only 20 to 50 percent of them are), that leaves roughly 141,000 psychopaths walking around.

The United States has the largest prison population per capita in the world (roughly 2.2 million people) and it includes a lot of people imprisoned for minor drug offenses, who are probably not psychopaths. But even if 50% of the prison population are psychopaths, that leaves 1.2 million of them unaccounted for.

What are all of these people doing? Where would we expect a cold-blooded, power-hungry person to end up?

It makes sense to me that a lot of them are running our organizations.

It takes a special kind of person to rise to the top of any organization. The myth, of course, is that success just takes a combination of hard work, intelligence, dedication, and loyalty. Anyone who has worked inside of a significant organization, however, knows that there's another ingredient—politics. While politics isn't always Machiavellian by nature, there are always moments when you are going to have to smile while you're sliding the knife in between someone's ribs. We all know how it works—from pretending to laugh at your boss's joke even when you've heard it a hundred times before (and it wasn't that funny the first time), to playing golf with the boss or accompanying him to a seedy strip club while on a business trip. A worthy sycophant will agree with their boss on absolutely everything. To be a respectable flattering parasite, a person needs to be willing to subjugate their true feelings or opinions to curry favor with the people who can further their career. It usually involves doing whatever you can to keep yourself in their good books until they either get promoted, resign, fired—or until you finally manage to knife them when the opportune moment comes along. Et tu, Brute?

The "smiling assassin" is such an organizational archetype that they appear as stock characters in Hollywood films and TV shows, part-sycophant, part-Iago (think Dwight in the U.S. version of *The Office*), and while we may laugh at them on our screens, in real life they are far less amusing. Experts at the manipulation of others, you never can be sure of precisely where you stand with them—one minute they will treat you like a long-lost brother, and the next they will have you up against the wall down a darkened alley with a blade at your throat.

According to the *Handbook of Organization Politics*, political skill is "the ability to effectively understand others at work, and to use such knowledge to influence others to act in ways that enhance one's personal and/or organizational objectives."

There's a fine line between influencing someone by openly presenting your arguments, letting them reach their own conclusions, and manipulating them into reaching the conclusion you want them to reach.

Most of us don't like to manipulate others. We don't like to be deceitful. It goes against our grain. We would rather have an open and honest discussion about the pros and cons of an idea and let the best idea win. We're happy to state the reasons we believe in a certain idea or course of action, let others have the same courtesy, and then have an open and friendly discussion to determine which idea should be victorious.

None of us likes feeling manipulated and so, it's natural to assume, the people we work with don't like being manipulated either. This is the nature of the empathic response—if I don't like something, I can understand that someone else probably won't like it either. Empathy is the capacity to understand or feel what another person is experiencing from within the other person's frame of reference, that is, the capacity to place oneself in another's point of view. So manipulating others to do what you want them to do requires a certain dampening or rationalizing of our empathic response.

Under the right circumstances, if we feel like our lives or

livelihoods are being threatened, all of us can probably dial down our empathy. There are some people, however, for whom empathetic feelings aren't a problem—the psychopaths.

Psychopaths care only about their power and success. They care only about #WINNING.

I remember seeing Oliver Stone's film *Wall Street* when I was in my early twenties and not being sure whether I despised Gordon Gekko or admired him. That's probably a sign of excellent writing and acting. I think most men have a natural, biological, grudging respect for the alpha male (thanks a lot, evolution), the guy who is all balls and bravado, who can talk his way in or out of most situations, the guy with the fierce laser eyes and the killer smile who first gets the money, then the power, and then the woman (a line from a different Oliver Stone film). As he recently told an Australian audience of finance industry workers, Stone didn't mean for Gekko to be a role model for the audience:

> *"Gordon Gekko was an immoral character that became worshipped for the wrong reasons."*[10]

Gekko, the ultimate 1980s capitalist, the "greed is good" guy, was a psychopath. He didn't care about the harm his financial wheeling and dealing did to others—the jobs that were lost, the careers that were ruined, the investments that disappeared. He just cared about his profit, his success. Unfortunately, it seems like many people, especially in the finance sector, missed the point. They thought Gekko was a hero. Stone himself says that Wall Street culture is much worse today than it was when he made the original film in the mid-eighties. Maybe many of the people who went into finance missed the point of the film—or maybe they were unable to understand it. Like Gekko, many of them care only about money and power.

According to Lawrence McDonald, a former vice president at Lehman Brothers, who wrote a book about the firm's 2008 collapse, Gordon Gekko's "greed is good" ethos pushed Wall Street heavy hitters into taking greater and greater risks, which lead to the 2008 global financial crisis.

"There were Gordon Gekko types in all of these banks."[11]

And they aren't just in finance. Gekko types can be found in every industry. They don't care about people's feelings or society in general—they only care about power. In their minds, that makes them a winner.

It turns out that I'm not alone in believing that psychopaths end up in management.

Martha Stout believes that "the higher you go up the ladder, the greater the number of sociopaths you'll find there."[12]

Robert Hare, the inventor of the Psychopath Checklist, argues that while "serial killers ruin families.... corporate and political and religious psychopaths ruin economies. They ruin societies."[13]

Christopher Bayer, a psychologist who provides therapy to Wall Street professionals, believes that the rate of psychopaths in the financial services industry might be 10 percent—or even higher.[14]

This apparently isn't a new idea—and yet I don't see anything being done about it. When was the last time you heard the media or the HR department referring to a senior executive, politician, or cardinal as a psychopath?

Over the last couple of years, we have all heard a lot about the 1 percent and the 99 percent, mostly due to the Occupy Movement.[15]

The basic idea is that a minute percentage of people in developed countries control the majority of the wealth—the rest of us live on the leftovers.

In the late eighteenth century, the richest 1 percent of U.S. households held only 8.5 percent of total income. In 2018, the richest 1 percent have *20 percent* of total income.[16] This means the top ranks of the elite in the U.S. today are roughly 250 percent better off, in terms of their share of the total income, than their predecessors were just after the American Revolution.

In January 2013, a report by Oxfam noted that the 100 richest people in the world earned enough in 2012 to end the extreme poverty suffered by the poorest on the planet four times over. According to the report, the richest one percent of the world's population had increased its income by 60 percent in the last twenty years. And, thanks to the revelations of the Panama Papers, we now know that the rich have hidden their wealth away from taxation and oversight in offshore tax havens.

> *No one knows for sure how much money is stashed offshore, but economists estimate it's $5 trillion to $32 trillion, or more than a third of the entire global domestic product.*[17]

In the United States, "a family in the top 1 percent nationally received, on average, 26.3 times as much income as a family in the bottom 99 percent."[18]

Of course, wealth disparity isn't a new situation. Since the dawn of recorded history, society has been made up of the "haves" and the "have nots." Even in our relatively small experiments with democracy and human rights, wealth typically ends up concentrated into the hands of the few.

Some argue that this is the natural order of things. I've often heard it said that if you took all of the money in society and distributed it equally, within a couple of years we would end up with the same situation—1 percent of the people controlling 99 percent of the wealth. Perhaps that is true, or perhaps it is just a myth perpetuated by the 1 percent to justify their actions—but even if it is true, it doesn't justify the situation. The 1 percent will argue that they have accrued their wealth by simply working harder or being luckier or by taking risks that paid off, and some of this is true.

But psychiatrists estimate that 1 percent of the population are psychopaths and 1 percent of the population also control most of the power. I have to wonder if there is some overlap.

So why should the rest of us care that some people have more wealth than others? Are we just jealous? Are we lazy bums who don't want to work, who just want handouts from the government with money derived by unfairly taxing the rich?

There will be some people who feel this way, certainly. But mostly this is propaganda, designed to push the blame away from the psychopaths and onto the public. It's a version of "blame the victim."

There are genuine concerns we should all have about the 1 percent situation.

The primary problem inherent in capitalism is this: with enormous wealth comes enormous influence. With enormous influence comes the ability to unfairly manipulate the economic, legal, and political systems in a democracy in order to make sure that your power will increase.

Here's how one person explained it:

Private capital tends to become concentrated in few hands, partly because of competition among the capitalists, and partly because technological development and the increasing division of labor encourage the formation of larger units of production at the expense of smaller ones. The result of these developments is an oligarchy of private capital the enormous power of which cannot be effectively checked even by a democratically organized political society. This is true since the members of legislative bodies are selected by political parties, largely financed or otherwise influenced by private capitalists who, for all practical purposes, separate the electorate from the legislature. The consequence is that the representatives of the people do not in fact sufficiently protect the interests of the underprivileged sections of the population. Moreover, under existing conditions, private capitalists inevitably control, directly or indirectly, the main sources of information (press, radio, education). It is thus extremely difficult, and indeed in most cases quite impossible, for the individual citizen to come to objective conclusions and to make intelligent use of his political rights.

Who do you think said that?

Was it:

a) Che Guevara?

b) Fidel Castro?

c) Vladimir Lenin?

d) Noam Chomsky?

e) Julian Assange?

Need to phone a friend?

It was none of the above, actually.

It was…Albert Einstein.[19]

I was shocked and surprised in my early twenties when I first read that quote. I had, up until that time, believed that capitalism was a benevolent force for good and that Western democracies were free, fair, and "by the people, for the people." The fact that one of the most celebrated intellects of the twentieth century cast doubt on capitalism rattled me. Of course, being a brilliant physicist doesn't mean you are necessarily right about everything, so I decided to learn more about what makes the world tick, to try to get to the bottom of things and find out if I agreed with Albert. As it turns out, I now do.

Most of us want to protect what we have. Nobody wants to lose their home, their savings, and their lifestyle. But a certain kind of person is more willing to cross over ethical norms in order to achieve their personal success.

One of the major issues with capitalism is that it inevitably concentrates the power into the hands of a relatively small number of people. This becomes an even bigger problem if those people with the power are psychopaths.

PSYCHOPATH VERSUS SOCIOPATH

Are you confused about the difference between a psychopath and a sociopath? If so, you aren't alone. The literature on the topic is also more than a little bewildering. Some sources claim they are very similar, while others argue they differ quite a bit.

According to Dr. Xanthe Mallett, senior lecturer in forensic criminology at University of New England and author of *Mothers*

Who Murder, they have a lot in common, including a lack of empathy and remorse. Both are manipulative and accomplished liars. Mallett believes psychopaths engage in more careful planning of their crimes whereas sociopaths are more spontaneous.[20]

Dr. John Grohol, the founder and editor-in-chief of Psych Central, lumps them both together, saying that "psychopath and sociopath are pop psychology terms for what psychiatry calls an antisocial personality disorder (ASPD)."[21]

Other experts disagree. Robert Hare and Paul Babiak, in their book, *Snakes in Suits*, claim that "sociopathy is not a formal psychiatric condition" and that sociopaths in fact have a "normal capacity for empathy, guilt and loyalty."[22]

Another way I've heard it explained is that psychopaths are *born that way*, but sociopaths are *made that way*. The former come out of the womb with an empathy center that is broken, but the latter experience something devastating in their childhood that breaks theirs. It appears that there is some debate over the differences, so let's not dwell on it. For the purposes of our model, let's talk about psychopaths.

THE PSYCHOPATH CHECKLIST

So what makes someone a psychopath? According to Robert Hare's widely used Psychopath Checklist test (known as the PCL-R),[23] psychopaths tend to display many of the following traits:

- ✓ Glib and superficial charm
- ✓ Grandiose (exaggeratedly high) estimation of self
- ✓ Need for stimulation

✓ Pathological lying

✓ Cunning and manipulativeness

✓ Lack of remorse or guilt

✓ Shallow affect (superficial emotional responsiveness)

✓ Callousness and lack of empathy

✓ Parasitic lifestyle

✓ Poor behavioral controls

✓ Sexual promiscuity

✓ Early behavior problems

✓ Lack of realistic long-term goals

✓ Impulsivity

✓ Irresponsibility

✓ Failure to accept responsibility for own actions

✓ Many short-term marital relationships

✓ Juvenile delinquency

✓ Revocation of conditional release

✓ Criminal versatility

When sitting the PCL-R test, a subject is ranked against each of the twenty characteristics. They get a score of 0, 1, or 2, based on how much they display each characteristic. The higher the score, the more likely the subject is a psychopath.

Why the lack of empathy? According to recent fMRI studies on the brains of psychopaths, their inability to empathize with others seems to result from a problem with the amygdala, the part of the brain that deals with emotions, memory, and decision-making. Instead of the amygdala lighting up when a psychopath imagines causing someone else pain (as it does when they consider their own pain), there was an increased response in the ventral striatum, part of the brain that manages our "reward system." In other words, when thinking about causing others pain, a psychopath might feel pleasure instead of remorse.[24]

Other long-term studies on children indicate that these malfunctions in the brains of future psychopaths can be detected as early as three years of age, suggesting psychopaths are born and not made.[25]

Now, of course I don't want to imply that *all* managers or business owners are psychopaths. That would be ridiculous. There are obviously some "very fine people" in the ranks of the elite.

So how do we tell the very fine people from the psychopaths? I think it comes down to looking at their behavior and the actions of the companies they run. If we see evidence of psychopathic behavior, e.g., a lack of empathy towards customers and staff and society as a whole, a desire for power, criminal activity without remorse, the failure to accept responsibility, then we have good reason to suspect psychopaths are involved.

It's hard to deny that the character traits of psychopaths—in particular the charm, the grandiose self-opinion, the willingness to lie, the cunning, the lack of remorse and guilt, and the failure to accept responsibility (blaming problems on other departments, or on previous management, or their own staff, etc.)—might help them climb the ranks inside certain organizations. People who have a more realistic appreciation of their own weaknesses and are willing to admit them, who aren't willing to lie and don't like making decisions that hurt other people, probably aren't going to climb the ladder as easily.

And if some managers *are* indeed psychopaths, it makes sense that society needs to be protected from their worst instincts.

What's worse than your garden-variety psychopath? A garden-variety psychopath with a huge bank account and plenty of power. That is a combination that could be incredibly destructive.

That said, we probably don't want to remove psychopaths from power altogether. I have no doubt that there are positive contributions that psychopaths can make to an organization and to society—for example, innovative vision, a disregard for old ways of doing things, massive amounts of drive, etc.—but it is still necessary for us to protect ourselves from the negative aspects of their personalities.

There is a certain ruthlessness that is required to be a "master of the universe." You have to be able to hold the lives of people in the palm of your hand and be willing to manipulate them as necessary. Not everybody has the stomach to fire thousands of people the week before Christmas or to pocket a salary that is fifty times what your employees take home (the average salary of an Australian Top 100 CEO in 2018 was $4.5 million—fifty times the salary of an average worker).[26]

In the United States, CEO pay has risen 300 percent since 1990—three times more than the profit of the companies they run! In this time the minimum wage has actually *declined* 9 percent.[27]

How many of us would feel comfortable taking home 300 times the salary of our colleagues at work? It takes a special kind of person to accept that their value is 300 times that of most of the people they work with. It takes a sense of grandiosity, an unrealistic sense of superiority, a sustained view of oneself as better than others. It takes a narcissist psychopath.

Of course, psychopaths genuinely think that they deserve

these benefits. They have a thousand different ways to justify it to themselves.

"I worked hard to get where I am."

"I made my own success."

"I did things that others were not willing to do in order to succeed."

And while some of these things might be true, it still belies an underlying narcissism.

The "I made it to the top all by myself" rationale, what we might call the "Ayn Rand Model," after the Russian-American author of *The Fountainhead* and *Atlas Shrugged*.

THERE IS A WAR

One downside of being a psychopath today is that, since the rise of modern mass media in the twentieth century, it has become harder for the 1 percent to get away with certain kinds of behavior. Even if they control more power than the rest of society, there are always ninety-nine of us to every one of them, so they need to play their cards carefully. Gone are the days when they had private armies and fortified castles to hide in. The people's revolutions around the world during the eighteenth, nineteenth, and twentieth centuries were examples of what can happen when the majority of the population get fed up with being oppressed by a wealthy minority.

Why do we let them get and stay in positions of power? Why don't we—the 99 percent—do a better job of preventing these psychopaths from taking power?

The method they use to get and stay on top of the power pyramid is by fighting a war. It's not the "War on Terror," the "War on Drugs," or even the "War on Christmas." There's a much more significant war going on, but it doesn't get talked about in polite company because, like *Fight Club*, the first rule of this war is that you don't talk about it. If the general public became too aware of it, it would stop being effective. Instead, our leaders distract us by focusing our attention on the other wars, real and imaginary. They distract us with televised sport, reality shows, presidential tweets, celebrity gossip, and two-year-long election circuses. They won't talk about this other war because it isn't in their best interests to make the public aware of it.

This other war has been going on, in its present form, since the rise of modern democracies, and billions of dollars are spent on it every year—yet it gets almost zero coverage in the nightly news or from our elected leaders.

The war I'm talking about is the "Propaganda War." It's a war on your mind, a battle to control how you think, feel, and act regarding the political and economic issues of the day. It is being fought daily on the battlegrounds of television, talk-back radio, newspapers, films, magazines, books, and, now, the internet.

Or course the psychopaths weren't going to just give up their power. They had to find new ways of staying in control of how the masses think.

In days gone by they used religion to control the masses— wealthy clergy (to get high ranking clerical jobs in the Middle Ages you often had to buy your way in) preaching from the pulpit that being poor was God's will and the people should just suck it up and wait for their rewards in the afterlife.

When that slowly stopped working around the time of The Enlightenment, and revolutions started breaking out all over the place, the elite became experts at manipulating our thinking with political propaganda and distraction theatrics. We've been exposed to propaganda for so long that many of us aren't even very conscious of it. It's just part of the background noise that we've grown up with.

Think of it like the laugh track on a sitcom—it's always been there, telling us when to laugh and what to think, how to vote and why we should go to war, what to focus on and what to ignore. Most of us are so used to it, we don't even notice, let alone think much about it, and that's precisely what the establishment are counting on—that you'll accept their conditioning without questioning it or fighting it. They are counting on the fact that the average person is too tired after working a long day or feeling too helpless to take back control of their thinking. They are counting on us just sitting in front of the television (or Netflix or Fortnite) and letting it wash over us, every night and every day, for the rest of our lives. They will tell us how to think, how to vote, what to buy, and constantly keep us scared about the enemy du jour who is coming to destroy our way of life, or about looming pandemics, natural disasters, and our financial future.

Therefore, the psychopaths who make up the ruling class stay dominant and prosperous and in control of the engines of our economies. Thanks to a century of propaganda, we call them "capitalists," "titans of industry," or "CEO" instead of psychopaths—because it sounds far more respectable.

Capitalism may have lifted the standard of living of millions of people around the world, but it has also caused its share of damage. It's not a binary situation; capitalism doesn't have to be either all good or all bad. The same is true, by the way, of socialism,

Christianity, and Hollywood films. Most things lie on a spectrum, providing both positives and negatives. There is even some good country music (but you have to search hard to find it). Hopefully, they provide a net positive, but sometimes it's difficult to tell, especially when the media provides a constant narrative that only focuses on one side of the equation.

As I live in a country that is a capitalist democracy, I think it's vital to understand the weaknesses as well as the strengths of our socioeconomic model, especially in terms of how easy it might end up run by people with psychopathic tendencies.

In Western countries, the forces of capitalism, controlled by psychopaths, keep the majority of the population distracted, broke, scared, and politically disempowered. That prevents them from launching a revolution or agitating for political and economic reform.

Through a simple framework of overlapping interests, capitalism allows a small number of psychopaths to maintain control over the rest of the population, creating a series of rippling negative effects.

Over the course of the book I'll tell some stories about corporations, governments, and religions making horrible decisions that damage the lives of individuals, families, the environment, and economies and ask, "Would someone who is *not* a psychopath have allowed this to happen?"

Hardly a day goes by when we aren't presented with evidence that another influential organization has led us astray in one way or another. Like the lies of Donald Trump, it's hard to keep up with them all.

They lied about weapons of mass destruction in Iraq. They lied about the war in Vietnam. About child molestation in the ranks of their priests, bishops, and cardinals. About the cause of the global financial crisis. About recording our private telephone calls and reading our emails. About hacking our voicemails. About manipulation of election results. About deleting their private emails. About their dealings with Russia. About promises they made in their last election campaign which were broken as soon as they got into power. The list often seems endless.

When someone in the past has proven to be a habitual liar, would you implicitly trust everything they say in the future? Unfortunately, that's the situation we now find ourselves in when it comes to the governments, corporations, intelligence agencies, religious organizations, and media companies in Western democracies. If someone has lied to you repeatedly in the past, isn't it natural to keep a healthy distrust about everything they say afterward? Does it make you a "conspiracy theorist" to suggest that these organizations might not always be telling us the truth about their actions and statements?

Today, perhaps more than ever before, we have proof that the Powers That Be are deceiving us. According to Edward Snowden:

> *"Western intelligence agencies are attempting to manipulate and control online discourse with extreme tactics of deception and reputation destruction, using what they call 'The Four D's'— Deny, Disrupt, Degrade, Deceive—to mislead the general public and destroy not only the efforts of political activists but also their personal reputations, should cause even the most conservative member of the public to reconsider what kind of democracy—and how much of it—we have."[28]*

Too often, when such behavior is exposed, such as when companies are caught dumping toxic waste[29] or when the Vatican gets an average of one credible rape complaint a day[30] or when politicians are caught misleading the public,[31] the suggestion is that it's either the behavior of "a few bad eggs" or that some otherwise decent people made an unfortunate mistake—chalk it up to "bad intel." This "few bad eggs" or "bad intel" theory of explaining organizational malfeasance is, I suspect, another deliberate attempt to mislead us from the truth.

Like the sugarcoated appellation "captains of industry," the "bad eggs" euphemism is used to distract us from the fact that this kind of terrible behavior is actually a natural result of psychopathic organizational cultures.

That isn't to suggest that all organizations are inherently psychopathic—on the contrary, organized efforts by significant groups of people are central to any significant undertaking. But I do want to propose that the survival instincts of organizations often provide them with an incentive to promote people who have no ethics and are willing to do anything for power.

Over the course of the book I will explore the kinds of personal behaviors that organizations tend to encourage, how they map conveniently to those that come naturally to psychopaths, and how the correlation of those two is destroying society.

Once you make the conceptual leap from "bad eggs" to understanding that it is often in the best self-interests of organizations to deceive us, it fundamentally changes the way you interpret the daily news—and suddenly things start to make a lot more sense.

By the end of this book, you'll understand that you are being deceived by organizations on a regular basis and that this is *precisely* what you should expect from psychopathic cultures.

In order to understand how psychopaths end up on top of the power pyramid, we need to understand how organizational cultures have themselves become psychopathic.

To protect themselves from the possibility of another revolution, psychopaths have built themselves protective structures —organizations of scale and influence that are "too big to fail," armed with PR departments and legal teams to deflect attention and threaten critics. They also spend enormous amounts of money on propaganda, waging a war on the minds of the public, trying to convince us that the psychopaths are actually "winners," to be admired and put on the front cover of business magazines, while the rest of us are losers because we aren't willing to go to the same lengths to gain power that they are. They invest heavily into political campaigns to ensure the politicians who agree with them get elected and enact laws that continue to protect them and stop the masses from threatening their power. And they invest in religions that will tell people not to worry about it, to have faith and wait for their rewards in the afterlife.

CHAPTER TWO

PSYCHOPATHIC ORGANIZATIONS

To begin to understand the extent of the damage that psychopaths can do, we first need to appreciate how and why they end up running organizations. We need to examine the fundamental nature and purpose of organizations to try to understand what drives them, what makes them tick.

And the first thing to understand is that, just like psychopaths, organizations are also driven by the need for power, whether they are a business, a government, an army, a police force, a school, or a religion. To serve its purpose, an organization needs to survive and grow. And to accomplish those things, it requires power, which comes in the form of wealth and influence.

Of course, not *every* organization fits into this model. There are rare varieties that don't want to grow. For example, old hippies running a small cafe selling hemp cookies and soy lattes might be completely content to keep their business small. There may even be organizations that don't want to survive. For example, a short-term fund-raising committee to build a new wing on a hospital has a limited lifespan by design. But these are exceptions to the rule, and such small and short-term organizations don't play a significant role in determining the direction of society.

Psychopaths are attracted to power. They may sometimes seek this in smaller organizations, like a small business, a local parish, or the local police force. The ones we should be most concerned about, however, are those that influence society, the most significant organizations, the ones that try to shape public policy and public opinion. Therefore, from now on, when you read the word *organizations* in this book, please assume I mean the "significant and powerful" kind.

> *"We are survival machines—*
> *robot vehicles blindly programmed to preserve*
> *the selfish molecules known as genes."*
>
> —Richard Dawkins, *The Selfish Gene* [32]

Every organization starts as a group of people with a common objective, and they are necessary for accomplishing tasks too big for a single person. There is nothing inherently wrong with the idea of people coming together to get something done. What is concerning is what happens when organizations amass a certain amount of power and become toxic. The theory that I want to explore is that this outcome (toxicity) is built into the very fabric of organizations and isn't some kind of unexpected malfunction. It's precisely the kind of behavior we should expect from organizations, especially if psychopaths run them. If we anticipate toxicity as a probable outcome, then we can prepare contingencies or, even better, engineer models to prevent it from happening as much as possible.

Although there are many different kinds of organizations, the three I will focus on are business, religious, and political—including the media, military, police, and educational organizations—as these dominate the affairs of most of the modern world.

Organizations exist to marshal human activities toward a common goal, but they also play a substantial role in our survival as individuals. In many ways, the organization acts as a giant survival machine.

Richard Dawkins, in his classic 1976 text, *The Selfish Gene*, promotes the idea that, from a biological perspective, the raison d'être of human existence is to act as "survival machines," giant-sized protection mechanisms for our much smaller, highly valuable cargo—our genes:

> *Individuals are not stable things, they are fleeting. Chromosomes too are shuffled into oblivion, like hands of cards soon after they are dealt. But the cards themselves survive the shuffling. The cards are the genes. The genes are not destroyed by crossing-over, they merely change partners and march on. Of course they march on. That is their business. They are the replicators and we are their survival machines. When we have served our purpose, we are cast aside. But genes are denizens of geological time: genes are forever.*

Dawkins makes the argument that a human being is merely a "vehicle" designed (by evolution) to safeguard and copy its precious cargo—the genetic code—and uses this model to explain the biological basis of selfishness and altruism. While you might think that the purpose of your life is to eat, drink, and be merry, or to worship this god or that, or to become wealthy and famous, Dawkins suggests that your actual purpose is to act as an incredibly sophisticated and oversized bodyguard of a microscopic collection of proteins.

Our primary purpose in life is to get laid, have kids, and protect them long enough that they can survive without us—so they, too, can get laid and continue the cycle. And to achieve these three things, we perform many elaborate tasks. We get an education so we can get a decent job. The job provides a reliable income, which means we can afford a place to live and to eat and to pay for basic health care. These things increase our chances of achieving our prime objectives—i.e., get laid, have a kid, and raise it.

Organizations help us do all of those things.

The organization acts as a new, supplemental support mechanism for our genes. It provides us, via a regular income, with sufficient high-quality nutrients and protection from the elements, increasing our chances of successful replication.

One way of looking at this is that organizations are built by humans to help themselves survive and, in turn, to pass on their genes. And in order for organizations to help its humans survive, *it's fundamental that the organization itself survives.*

Perhaps organizations are the next step in the evolutionary ladder? If a human being is designed to protect the survival of the genes, then perhaps organizations are designed to protect the human being—and, in turn, protect the genes? The organization is like a suit of armor wrapped around the human, providing it with wealth and power (at varying levels, depending on your position inside the organization) and therefore allowing the genes inside those humans to stand a better chance of surviving.

A suit of armor is actually a decent analogy because when you take the human out of a suit of armor, it continues to exist and can be worn by another human. If you take some or all of the humans out of an organization, it, too, may continue to exist and can be inhabited by other humans. Take, for example, IBM. Charles Ranlett Flint, who founded the company in 1914 (although at the time it was called the Computing-Tabulating-Recording Company), died in 1934. It's reasonable to assume that nobody who worked at the company in 1914 is still there today, and yet the company survives. The Catholic Church has been around for 1700 years and is still going strong (despite some recent and inconvenient attention to its history of turning a blind eye to child rapist priests).

Although organizations are created by humans to achieve larger objectives, to give them more power to shape the world around them, at the most basic level they exist to help us enhance our individual lives. Business organizations are formed to create wealth. Political organizations are constructed to create political influence. Religious organizations are invented to influence what people think. All of them involve power of some kind. They shape how people in the society around them live.

The people who work in organizations believe they will be a vehicle to make their own lives better—monetarily, politically, or religiously—and, sometimes, all three. They are all designed to increase money and power ("social capital") for their founders. There is nothing inherently wrong with that ambition—unless the organizations become toxic, which, unfortunately, they often do.

Organizations exhibit other biological attributes. They merge through acquisitions, in a similar way to plasmodial slime mold, which live freely as single cells but aggregate together to form multicellular reproductive structures in times of food shortages (or, in business terms, economic downturns).

They form alliances and partnerships, symbiotic relationships with other organizations whereby each benefits from its relationship to the other.

Organizations even have their own version of chromosomes—a board and management team. Each organization is usually governed by less than a couple of dozen people. They make the decisions that determine how the organization looks and acts. Change one of those key players, like altering a chromosome in a living organism, and it slightly changes the behavior of the organization.

The organizations we create are programmed from birth to survive and grow. Instead of existing to build new copies of themselves like biological organisms, organizations exist to grow more social capital. With greater social capital comes the ability to survive and thereby protect the genes of the people inside the organization. They do whatever they can to manipulate their environment to engineer survival.

From a distance, when we see an organization choose its survival over doing the right thing, it appears to be a moral lapse. After all, what does it matter if the organization survives or fails? In theory, the death of the organization isn't the end of the people inside it. It's just a construct, a paper dragon, a logo, a decent idea while it lasted. But remember—organizations are survival machines, and they aren't going to go down without a fight. And if I make the connection between the survival of the organization and the survival of the genes of the people inside it, it becomes clearer why the people at the top of the organization feel compelled to do whatever it takes to keep it alive.

So organizations continually fight to survive. Every organization invests enormous amounts of time, effort, and money to perpetuate its existence. They fight off predators and hoard resources.

RED IN TOOTH AND CLAW

Organisms have sophisticated biological mechanisms for filtering out rogue cells that are threatening their health—organizations do, too. They are called "performance reviews."

Darwinism suggests that organisms evolve through the natural selection of small, inherited variations that increase the individual's ability to compete, survive, and reproduce.[33]

Organizations also survive by increasing their ability to compete, survive, and reproduce (they reproduce capital); they are "red in tooth and claw" as Tennyson put it.

This is what I call "Organizational Darwinism." Survival of the fittest, when it comes to organizations, means the one that can amass the most social capital (power) will usually survive.

Utopian views of capitalism suggest that only the businesses that best serve the needs of the market will survive. This might be true in a market where a level playing field exists, but when enterprises control enormous amounts of power, there isn't a level playing field. The power differential between well-funded Company A and start-up Company B means the playing field is tilted dramatically in Company A's favor. All too often, these businesses will do whatever they can to destroy their competition by means fair and foul. For example, they might use their influence to try to coerce the compliance of politicians to introduce laws that favor the older, richer company, through the employment of lobbyists, promises of campaign funding, and hints of post-government jobs. Or they might use their army of lawyers to negotiate their way around existing legislation. They might use their influence with the media, due to their advertising budget, to spin positive stories about the company's actions and negative stories about their competition for as long as they possibly can.

For example, in 1888, Westinghouse started selling a cheaper AC electricity delivery system developed by Nikola Tesla that threatened the dominance of Edison Electric's DC system. In response, Edison published an 84-page pamphlet titled "A Warning from the Edison Electric Light Company" and sent it to newspapers and companies that had purchased or were planning to purchase electrical equipment from Edison competitors. The pamphlet warned them that the AC system was dangerous and subject to patent disputes that could find customers ending up in court at a future date.[34] They didn't say, "May the best product win—that's how capitalism works." They tried to exterminate the competition.

I once heard a senior executive at Australia's largest telecommunications company, Telstra, refer to the practice of putting start-ups out of business as "killing the baby in the crib." There are lots of ways that significant companies go about killing start-ups. Some classic tactics include launching spurious lawsuits against them; betting that the start-up will run out of money paying for lawyers and subsequently go out of business; and acquiring them with promises of new markets and better funding, only to shut them down with claims of "shifting priorities." This happened a lot during the early days of the internet industry. Look at the lengths the taxi industry has gone in trying to stop competitor Uber from getting a piece of their action.[35]

If we get back to the idea of protecting the genes, the leaders of these businesses almost *have* to destroy their competition. It's incumbent upon them to do whatever is necessary to dominate; otherwise, they risk losing their job and, with it, their substantial salaries and reputations. *If I don't survive in my position, what will friends and family think of me? Will my wife and children still love me if I am not a winner? And if I don't do what's required, won't I just be replaced by somebody else who will?* These fears tie directly into Maslow's hierarchy of needs, e.g., our ability to provide for our families and to be loved. These fundamental human needs are often, subconsciously, at the heart of much of our behavior— along with the prime objectives mentioned earlier.[36]

This kind of behavior is also true with non-business organizations. Political parties want to destroy their competition—at the ballot box, with intrigue, or with guns. There are plenty of examples throughout history of domestic political parties going to war with each other for domination. Revolutions, such as the American and the Russian, are simply wars between political parties.

Civil wars fall into the same category.

The Russian Revolution was a civil war between the Royalists and the Socialists, who themselves fractured into the Bolshevik and the Menshevik factions and fought each other, mostly nonviolently, for control.

Even during peacetime, political parties are always fighting to survive. They struggle to get more campaign contributions, to get more positive press coverage, and to get more votes. They will sometimes do sneaky things to damage their opponents, such as gerrymandering or launching fake news campaigns. In years gone by in countries like America, political machines like the infamous Tammany Hall would use fraud, bribes, and hired groups of thugs to get their preferred candidates elected.

Australians might recall the efforts of Tony Abbott and the Liberal Party (Australia's largest conservative party) in the late 1990s to crush Pauline Hanson's new One Nation party, which was threatening to win too many votes in the Liberal Party's base. He established a secret "slush fund" by which he funded political attacks against One Nation, while simultaneously adopting many of their far-right policies.[37]

In the early twentieth century on the left side of politics, there were desperate efforts of political parties in various democratic countries to shut down communist parties who posed a similar threat to their own voter bases.[38]

Religions also have a long and bloody history of battling it out for supremacy, even within the same belief system. In the late fourth century, the Emperor Theodosius was blackmailed by Bishop Ambrose of Milan into banning nearly all religions and philosophies that competed with his preferred sect of Nicene Christianity. They were exterminated—temples were destroyed, sculptures were torn down or defaced, scriptures were burned, and philosophers, like Hypatia of Alexandria, were torn to shreds. Competing versions of Christianity, such as the Arian sect, were declared heretics and forced to convert to the only allowed version. Freedom of religion was banned under a Christian theocracy.

A few decades later, the Visigoths, also Christians but of the Arian variety, attacked Rome, murdering and raping their way through the Christian population. And so it went for centuries—

Christians, urged into battle by popes and bishops, attacked other Christians who didn't agree with their views on Jesus and killed Jews who they often blamed for plagues and famines; Muslims came along and fought against Christians, even though they both believed in the same Abrahamic god; Sunni Muslims fought Shi'a Muslims for supremacy, even though they both recognized Muhammad as the prophet; Christians later invaded countries in the South Pacific, who each had their own religious beliefs that were thousands (or even tens of thousands) of years old—and did their best to replace those religions with their own. In the East, Hindus persecuted Buddhists, who fought against Taoists. Christianity eventually turned on itself again, with Catholics and Protestants killing each other for centuries—because that's how Jesus would have wanted it.

Organizations always fight to survive. But there should be a line they don't cross. There's no reason why an organization can't fight within the rules. No reason why they can't fight and remain ethical.

However, if *psychopaths* are in charge of those organizations—business, political, or religious—we should expect those organizations to exhibit additional psychopathic behaviors. They will fight to protect their power, regardless of the consequences.

#WINNING

Another day, another corporate scandal. At least that's the way it seems sometimes.

Every time another scandal hits the news, the inevitable questions arise—why would they do such a stupid thing? How could they? Where did they go wrong?

But that's the wrong way of looking at it. We should *expect* organizations to build and protect their power, and, if psychopaths are in control of the culture, they will go to extreme lengths, even doing things that are unethical or illegal.

Let's take a look at a handful of recent examples of terrible organizational behavior from around the world and then ask ourselves if they could have played out differently. If a person with empathy and a conscience, (i.e., a non-psychopath) was running these organizations, how would they have managed the process?

And let me be clear about something at the outset. I am not a psychiatrist, and I am in no way accusing any of the following people of being psychopaths. Nor am I suggesting that the cultures of these particular organizations are now or have ever been psychopathic.

I'm just asking questions.

VOLKSWAGEN

One of the most significant corporate scandals in recent years was that of Volkswagen (a company created by the command of Adolf Hitler, which has a long history of alleged cooperation with dictatorships[39]) and their fraudulent diesel emission reporting.

In September 2015, it was revealed that the company had been deliberately manipulating the level of nitrogen oxide emissions that their diesel cars produced in a test environment. They used special software, designed by the company, to tell when the vehicle was being tested in a laboratory. It then fudged the emission results to make them look better than they actually were.

And not just by a little bit.

When researchers tested the cars in a real-world environment, they found that one model exceeded U.S. emissions limits "by a factor of 15 to 35" while another exceeded the limit "by a factor of 5 to 20." Eleven million vehicles worldwide are alleged to be implicated.

The company has admitted fault, and their CEO, Martin Winterkorn, stepped down. He claims that he knew nothing about the issue until just before it hit the media, and he blamed it on "the terrible mistakes of a few people." That's his version of a "few bad eggs."

As of September 2019, Winterkorn and other executives, including the former CEO of Audi, have been charged with fraud.[40] Prosecutors claim Winterkorn knew all about the scheme and failed to put a stop to it.

So let's stop for a moment. Ask yourself: if a regular person knew that their company was doing something illegal, what would they do about it? Would they admit it and fix it? What kind of person would cover it up and lie about it? The type of person who thinks "I'd rather lie and try to get away with it instead of putting my billion-dollar company into a position of having to pay some fines, re-engineer our products, and put my job on the line."

Of course, I'm not saying Winterkorn or his co-accused are guilty. I'm speaking purely hypothetically.

Sure—we all lie from time to time. Sometimes for good reasons, sometimes for selfish reasons. But we're not talking about a teenager being caught smoking a joint behind the school or a president being caught getting his jollies from an intern in the Oval Office. We're talking about a senior executive who employs thousands of people and sells millions of cars deliberately (allegedly) destroying the environment. Surely a person in that position should be expected to be honest, to do the right thing. That company can afford the fine. That CEO can afford to take some lumps. He's probably already wealthy.

Winterkorn, for example, was paid more than 15 million euros in 2014, making him the highest-paid executive out of Germany's blue-chip stocks.

ENRON — SURVIVAL OF THE NASTIEST

Another story you might have heard about is that of Enron. In 2001, it was revealed that the Texas-based outfit, one of the world's significant electricity, natural gas, communications, pulp, and paper companies, with claimed revenues of nearly $111 billion during 2000, had been systematically using accounting fraud to bolster its reputation. Business magazine *Fortune* named Enron "America's Most Innovative Company" for six consecutive years, from 1996 to 2001. Chairman and CEO, Ken Lay, who was also co-chairman of President George W. Bush's reelection committee in 1992, died of a heart attack before he could go to jail. Another key player in the scandal, former CEO Jeffrey Skilling, was sentenced to twenty-four years and four months of imprisonment (however, in 2013, ten years was cut from his sentence).

When the company went into bankruptcy, 20,000 employees lost their jobs and many of them their life savings. Investors lost billions of dollars.

Although it might look at first glance that Enron is an example of an organization most definitely *not* being a survival mechanism for the people inside of it—after all, 20,000 people lost their jobs and their life savings—remember that this only happened after the company died. Up until that time, lots of people were working inside the belly of the beast. Do you really think none of them knew that the books were being cooked? Surely at least the people working in the accounting department must have at least had an inkling. But, as far as I know, none of them spoke out about it; there were no whistleblowers. After all—why would you look a gift-horse in the mouth? Keep your head down, say nothing, and hope they keep paying you.

And we might wonder—where were the investment industry's financial analysts and financial media during all of this? Where was Wall Street? Why didn't they work out something was amiss at Enron? It wasn't until February 2001, when a journalist at *Fortune* finally asked how Enron could keep its high stock value, that the façade started to be questioned. A couple of months later, when Wall Street analyst Richard Grubman questioned Enron's unusual accounting practices during a recorded conference call, CEO Skilling replied, "Well, thank you very much, we appreciate that…asshole."[41]

That didn't win him many friends outside of the company (apparently there were plenty of high fives internally), but I have to wonder why Wall Street analysts didn't ask that kind of question years earlier. Was it because their firms had interests in the continued growth of Enron stock? The joint interests between public companies like Enron, financial analysts, and the financial media are often hard to unpack. Not to mention the various banks that were involved.

About four years after the Enron collapse, Citigroup agreed to pay $2 billion to investors who accused the bank of aiding Enron in its accounting scandal.[42] Other banks to pay settlements to Enron investors included Goldman Sachs, Royal Bank of Scotland Group Plc, Royal Bank of Canada, Canadian Imperial Bank of Commerce, Toronto-Dominion Bank, JPMorgan Chase & Co., Credit Suisse Group, Merrill Lynch & Co., Fleet Bank NA, Barclays Plc, and Deutsche Bank AG.[43]

And Arthur Andersen, the fifth-largest accounting firm in the world, was deeply involved in helping them.

Most of these external players are still around today (except Arthur Andersen, which collapsed as a direct result of the Enron debacle). If the allegations about their knowledge about Enron's actual financial situation are correct, they all played a part in choosing their corporate profits over doing the right thing.

Let's take legendary investment bank Goldman Sachs as one example. Sure, they paid a $7 million fine—a mere slap on the wrist—to Enron creditors. But Enron was just one of the scandals Goldman has been involved in over the last two decades.[44]

They have been accused by many of playing a significant role in creating (and subsequently profiting from) the global financial crisis of 2007–2008, along with a string of other controversies. How many of these scandals did they benefit from while using their political influence and an army of lawyers to avoid repercussions? Taking a $7 million slap on the wrist now and then is a small price to pay for a company that makes $7 billion in profit a year and paid out $16.7 billion in employee bonuses after a bailout by taxpayers.[45]

Rolling Stone's Matt Taibbi once characterized Goldman Sachs as a "great vampire squid" sucking money instead of blood, allegedly engineering "every major market manipulation since the Great Depression…from tech stocks to high gas prices."

What could have made Enron's Lay, Skilling, and Chief Accounting Officer Richard Causey think their plan wouldn't backfire?

Skilling, previously a consultant for McKinsey & Company, apparently believed that the only two things that motivated people were "money and fear."[46]

I don't want to accuse him of being a psychopath, but that sounds pretty psychopathic to me.

The money motivated him—in 2001 he was named CEO of Enron and handed a $132 million salary—*for a single year.*

According to *Forbes*:

> *"He fostered a culture at Enron that could be termed survival of the fittest–or the nastiest. His personnel system was known as "rank and yank." The idea was that the bottom 20 percent would be fired. The others would be rewarded lavishly. Of course, few were rewarded as lavishly as Skilling, who sold more than $66 million in Enron shares even as he encouraged others to buy. When asked about Enron's accounting, Skilling developed a standard reply: "I am not an accountant."*[47]

Psychopathic cultures tend to develop when psychopaths are in charge.

Skilling was found guilty of conspiracy, insider trading, making false statements to auditors, and securities fraud, so we can assume he knew something about accounting—and the scam that Enron was engaging in. So let's assume that he also was smart enough (McKinsey isn't known for hiring dullards) to understand what the potential consequences would be when it all came crashing down. Either he didn't care—or, more likely, he thought he would somehow get away with it.

Did he and Lay think at all about the potential consequences to their 20,000 employees or investors? It doesn't seem like it. What kind of person can put the lives of 20,000 people who work for them at the risk of losing their livelihoods and life savings?

Once the company had started to play funny business with their accounting, hiding liabilities to make their balance sheet look stronger than it actually was, they had two options: admit they had been deceiving everyone and accept the personal and professional consequences of the admission—or up the ante, get even more plates spinning. Lay and Skilling chose the latter path.

And it's easy to understand why. A confession would have meant their personal reputations, wealth, careers, and lives would have been in tatters. It might, though, have saved the company from bankruptcy and thereby saved the jobs of their employees. But instead they chose to continue the charade and see how long they could get away with it.

It's easy to judge from the sidelines and say, "I would have done things differently if I'd been in their shoes"—but would I? $132 million a year buys a lot of self-denial.

But of course, they should never have started cooking the books in the first place.

Was their behavior what we should expect from psychologically healthy people running a large company? Or is it another example of psychopathic behavior—lying, cheating, no concern for the rights of others, winning at all costs—inside an equally psychopathic culture that allowed them to get away with it for so long?

The interconnectivity of interests between Enron, accounting firms, Wall Street analysts, and the financial media must be similar to the overlapping interests in other sectors. Take, for example, the start-up industry in Silicon Valley.

THE PUMP AND DUMP

Let's imagine a start-up technology company called Bloogle whose whizz-kids have developed a fresh new product that is going to revolutionize some industry. They need investors to grow. If a venture capital (VC) firm invests in Bloogle, the VC will start talking the company up to her contacts at media companies that cover the technology industry. "Bloogle is going to be the new Google!" they might declare. The media companies then start pumping up Bloogle's prospects and the way it will revolutionize things because in doing so they create excitement—excitement leads to readers; readers lead to advertising—and advertising leads to the dark side. All of a sudden you have hundreds of start-ups trying to do the same thing as Bloogle and all of the other investors trying to find their slice of the Bloogle pie. Over the next year or two, there is a lot of heat, and frothy excitement over the space Bloogle is in—so much so, that the VC that initially invested in them can exit their investment, either with a trade sale or IPO, which involves selling off Bloogle to the market—who have been reading all of the hype about Bloogle in the tech media and can't wait to invest their life savings into the new "new thing." Whether or not the new "new thing" turns out to be a flash-in-the-pan or the real deal doesn't really matter anymore to the VC or the tech media. They have accomplished what they set out to do—make short-term money. They are on to the next thing. The new Bloogle. And—rinse and repeat. The VC and the media company understand the game; they both have vested interests in the short-term success of Bloogle but no real long-term interest in either the company, the founders, the employees, or the general public who jump on board the IPO.

Even if a journalist with some integrity does want to bust the Bloogle bubble, they might find their work cut out for them. There are too many interests invested in not seeing the hype bubble get burst.

For another example of the Silicon Valley "Pump and Dump" scheme,[48] have a look at what happened to bitcoin and related "cryptocurrency" stocks in 2017–18.[49] Lots of hype pushed the price of bitcoin from around $2000 in July 2017 to $20,000 by December. A few months later it crashed back down to $8000, and then down to $3300 by December 2018. Then, in early 2019, the hype cycle started again. Somebody, somewhere, is profiting from the boom and bust cycle.

An experienced journalist friend of mine once explained why financial journalists don't tend to ask probing questions at annual general meetings. If they do ask questions that put pressure on the board of the company, their editor gets a call immediately afterward from the CEO of the company and is told: "Pull that person into line or your paper will get shut out—no more stories and no more ad spending." The editor calls the journalist into her office, and he either gets the message and pulls his head in, or he is moved to reporting something other than finance—or, if he's particularly strong-willed and doesn't like having his integrity challenged, he can leave, and go work somewhere else. Either way, the CEO of the company wins, and the hard questions go unasked. Other financial journalists then hear that story and learn from their colleague's experience.

The same is true for journalists covering politicians. Irritate the wrong people by asking inconvenient questions, and your career could be in jeopardy. In 2018 it was revealed that high profile Australian television journalist Emma Alberici was ordered to be terminated by the chairman of the Australian Broadcasting Corporation (Australia's national broadcaster funded by the federal government) because of a complaint from then-prime minister Malcolm Turnbull. "They [the government] hate her," chairman Justin Milne, a former business partner of Turnbull (they ran an internet company called Ozemail back in the 1990s, where I was employed at the time) wrote in an email to the ABC's managing director. "I think it's simple. Get rid of her."[50]

You end up with a neutered media which is too afraid to ask questions.

CLIMATE CHANGE AND EXXONMOBIL

ExxonMobil is the largest direct descendant of John D. Rockefeller's Standard Oil Company, and, as of 2019, the world's eighth-largest company by revenue and the tenth-largest publicly traded company by market capitalization.

According to the *LA Times*, ExxonMobil was at the forefront of research into climate change in the '70s and '80s. While the company readily accepted the reality of climate change and incorporated it into their internal business models, externally they denied it, referring to the concept as "unproven" or "sheer speculation," as CEO Lee Raymond did at an annual meeting in 1999.[51]

So what should we conclude about the executives of a company like ExxonMobil? Executives who knew their business could destroy the climate but chose not only to ignore all of that in their external statements but to actively sponsor confusion?

Over the years, according to Greenpeace, ExxonMobil has spent more than $30 million on think tanks and researchers that promoted climate denial.[52]

For decades now, ExxonMobil and their colleagues in the fossil fuel industry have adopted and adapted the methods used by Big Tobacco in the '60s and '70s to cast doubt on the science that was attacking their sector. They sell DOUBT.

According to an infamous 1969 tobacco industry memo:

> *Doubt is our product since it is the best means of competing with the "body of fact" that exists in the mind of the general public. It is also the means of establishing a controversy. Within the business we recognize that a controversy exists. However, with the general public the consensus is that cigarettes are in some way harmful to the health. If we are successful in establishing a controversy at the public level, then there is an opportunity to put across the real facts about smoking and health. Doubt is also the limit of our "product."*[53]

In 1998 a leaked American Petroleum Institute memo explained how a dozen public relations professionals, think tanks, and fossil fuel lobbyists had developed a mass scale misinformation project to cast doubt on climate science. They called it their "Global Climate Science Communications" (GCSC) plan.[54] Its goal was to convince "a majority of the American public" that "significant uncertainties exist in climate science." The memo claims that "victory will be achieved when average citizens understand uncertainties in climate science and recognition of uncertainties becomes part of the 'conventional wisdom.'"

You'd think they might care enough about their own families to put stopping the destruction of the human race above corporate profits, but that doesn't appear to be the case.

A good friend of mine, Australian futurist Dr. Peter Ellyard, author of *Designing 2050*,[55] assured me back before COP 15 (the 15th Conference of the Parties held at the 2009 United Nations Climate Change Conference in Copenhagen) that world leaders on the issue would make serious progress because they now realized, he said, that their grandchildren's lives were at risk. Of course, instead of producing a legally binding treaty between all members of the UN as it had been hoped, COP 15 ended in "vague, nonbinding comments about how other people should use less fossil fuel," as one commentator said. With the presidency of Donald Trump, climate change is no longer even seen as a threat to American national interests.[56]

So much for the grandchildren.

We have to assume that the people running these fossil fuel companies all know the truth about what their companies are doing to the environment and the future of the human race. And yet they continue to fund dubious science and to bankroll the election funds of politicians who will prevent new government policies being introduced that will curb their industry.

What can we deduce about these people? They aren't just ripping off investors or automobile buyers; they are knowingly destroying the planet for the sake of short-term profits. Does that sound psychopathic to you?

What about all of the people inside their organizations who must know the truth? Are they all living inside psychopathic organizational cultures?

The urge to survive, to keep their power and position and the wealth that comes with it, is stronger than the urge to stop destroying the planet.

RICH RELIGIONS

Let's look at another kind of corporation—the religious type.

Major religions and their various churches are often also significant corporations that control incredible amounts of wealth and, usually, receive tax breaks from governments. However, unlike other forms of organizations, the religious kind will often justify their wealth not by the profit motive but by claiming they use their money to do "good works" in society.

But is that really where the bulk of church wealth goes?

According to a 2012 report by *The Economist*, the Catholic Church in the United States spends a tiny percentage of its annual revenue on charity.[57]

The Economist found that, of the estimated $170 billion spent by the church in 2010, only 2.7 percent ($4.25 billion) was spent on "national charitable activities." By the way, to put that number into some kind of comparison, General Electric's entire revenue in the same year was only $150 billion.

The magazine claims that "the finances of the Catholic Church in America are an unholy mess" and "the financial mismanagement and questionable business practices would have seen widespread resignations at the top of any other public institution."

Where did the rest of the church's wealth go? Perhaps surprisingly, given the amount of media attention it gets, only $3.3 billion of their funds over the past fifteen years has gone to settle cases over molestation and the rape of children by priests in America —"thousands of claims for damages following sexual-abuse cases, which typically cost the church over $1 million per victim."

Can you imagine what would happen to any other corporation that had paid out billions in compensation for its employees systematically raping thousands of children?

However, these penalties may rise significantly in the coming years as more attention is directed at child rape by Catholic priests and how it was deliberately swept under the rug by the church leadership.

The church also spent around $98 billion (57 percent) on health care networks, followed by 28 percent on colleges, with parish and diocesan day-to-day operations accounting for just 6 percent.

Spending nearly $100 billion dollars a year on health care is a pretty impressive feat, but as pointed out by Mother Jones: "Catholic hospitals are required to follow health care directives handed down by the U.S. Conference of Catholic Bishops—a group of celibate older men who have become increasingly conservative over the past few decades."[58]

Add to that the fact that "between 2001 and 2011, the number of American hospitals affiliated with the Catholic Church grew 16 percent, even as the number of public hospitals and secular non-profit hospitals dropped 31 percent and 12 percent," and you might start to wonder if it's a good thing that a religion that has historically turned a blind eye to child rape and condemns homosexuality and the use of condoms to prevent the spread of HIV should be responsible for a growing component of American health care. When Cardinal Timothy F. Dolan was the archbishop of the Roman Catholic Archdiocese of Milwaukee in 2007, he sent a letter to the Vatican asking permission to transfer $57 million into a cemetery trust fund to protect the assets from victims of clergy sexual abuse who were demanding compensation. In the letter, he explained that he foresaw "an improved protection of these funds from any legal claim and liability."

The Vatican approved the request in five weeks.

Dolan, who was promoted to the role of archbishop of New York, delivered a Bible reading at Trump's 2017 inauguration.[59]

Okay, let's stop again for a second. I'm going to talk more about the Catholic Church and sexual abuse later, but I need to ask right now—what kind of person hides money from the victims of sexual abuse? And what kind of organizational culture supports that kind of action?

The Vatican itself apparently controls at least $8 billion in assets, although the actual figure is probably much higher.[60] Even Cardinal George Pell's old stomping grounds, the Sydney Catholic archdiocese in Australia, controls over $1.2 billion in funds.[61] As of 2014, it had spent only $9.4 million in compensation to victims of sexual abuse.[62]

For another example, take The Church of Jesus Christ of Latter-Day Saints (the official name of the Mormon Church). According to financial information released by the site MormonLeaks in May 2018, the LDS church has a stock portfolio worth $32 billion[63] and sucks in about $7 billion a year in tithing from its members, who are coerced to donate at least 10 percent of their gross income annually if they want to stay in the church's good books.[64]

Starting in 2005, the LDS church spent an estimated $2 billion building a shopping mall, City Creek Center, which opened in downtown Salt Lake City (the location of the church headquarters) in 2012. As unseemly as a church owning a major glitzy temple to consumerism might seem, the Mormon apologetics site, FairMormon, claims it was justified as a decent investment:

> "Some have insisted that funds would be better if directed to charitable works such as feeding the poor. The Church does have an extensive humanitarian effort. Critics on this point often overlook the fact that Church funds are best managed not by sitting in a bank account, but through prudent investment. Investment in land and real estate development is often a wise and ultimately profitable investment approach. It is entirely possible that the City Creek Center Mall will eventually become a money-making venture, as the Church collects rent from mall merchants. This investment strategy would allow the Church to, over time, recoup its initial outlay or even make money that could be further dedicated to the Church's religious and humanitarian goals."[65]

However, it doesn't seem to be much of an investment, according to Keith B. McMullin, who has "for 37 years served within the Mormon leadership and now heads a church-owned holding company, Deseret Management Corp. (DMC), an umbrella organization for many of the church's for-profit businesses."[66]

McMullin explains that City Creek exists to combat urban blight, not to fill church coffers.

According to *BusinessWeek*: "Will there be a return?" he asks rhetorically. "Yes, but so modest that you would never have made such an investment—the real return comes in folks moving back downtown and the revitalization of businesses."

So what's the real reason for building a shopping mall? It may have something to do with the fact that American churches are often exempt from paying taxes on real estate properties they lease out, even to commercial entities.

DMC also runs "a newspaper, 11 radio stations, a TV station, a publishing, and distribution company, a digital media company, a hospitality business, and an insurance business with assets worth $3.3 billion."

BusinessWeek reports that:

> *According to an official church welfare services fact sheet, the church gave $1.3 billion in humanitarian aid in more than 178 countries and territories during the 25 years between 1985 and 2010. A fact sheet from the previous year indicates that less than one-third of the sum was monetary assistance, while the rest was in the form of "material assistance." All in all, if one were to distribute that $1.3 billion over a quarter-century evenly, it would mean that the church gave $52 million annually. A study co-written by Cragun and recently published in Free Inquiry estimates that the Mormon Church donates only about 0.7 percent of its annual income to charity; the United Methodist Church gives about 29 percent.*

In other words, the LDS church spent more on a single shopping mall in its hometown than it did on humanitarian aid over twenty-five years.

Many smaller churches are doing pretty well also.

Australia's Pentecostal Hillsong Church spans 12 countries

and has 35,000 members across Australia. Its founders, Brian and Bobbie Houston, apparently live like millionaires, and their empire earns $50 million a year.[67]

As has been widely reported in the Australian media, Brian's father, Frank Houston, another one of the founders of the Hillsong empire, was a confessed pedophile. When Brian found out, he failed to tell the police. His church then tried to avoid paying out compensation to one of Frank's victims.[68, 69]

Despite all of this, the current prime minister of Australia, Scott Morrison, a Pentecostal Christian, calls Brian Houston his "mentor"[70] and recently tried to take him to the White House to meet Donald Trump.[71]

I'm sure a full tally of the wealth of religious groups around the world would be stunning. In Australia alone, the federal government provides an estimated $31 billion every year in tax relief for religions—and this continues in an era where we always hear about how broke the country is and how the government needs to cut back on essential community services.[72]

Of course, there may be arguments for the amount of wealth and tax benefits that these churches have accrued, but the fact remains that they are wealthy corporations and, therefore, we should expect them to exhibit the same kind of behavior as other, non-religious organizations—self-protection at all costs. And, as such, it should not surprise us to find psychopaths running them.

We should not be surprised to learn that the UN Committee on the Rights of the Child said Catholic Church officials had imposed a "code of silence" on clerics to prevent them from reporting cases of child abuse by clergy to police and moved abusers from parish to parish in an attempt to cover up such crimes.[73]

To the average person, the idea of systematically and deliberately covering up the rape of children is disgusting and inconceivable. To people managing a religious organization that wants to protect its assets, this kind of behavior is acceptable.

Forgive me a moment while I go down a bit of a rabbit hole about the Catholic Church and sexual abuse. I promise there's a point.

Over the last decade, the Catholic Church's involvement in covering up the sexual molestation of children has become very public. In Australia, the federal government recently conducted a Royal Commission into Institutional Responses to Child Sexual Abuse.[74]

The commission held fifty-seven public hearings over five years, involving 1300 witness accounts and more than 8000 personal stories from survivors of sexual abuse, with approximately 60 percent of the total relating to religious institutions and 60 percent of the religious incidents relating to the Catholic Church. The final report concluded that thousands of children had been sexually abused in many institutions in Australia and "the greatest number of alleged perpetrators and abused children were in Catholic institutions":

> *"In many religious institutions, the power afforded to people in religious ministry and the misplaced trust of parents combined with aspects of the institutional culture, practices and attitudes to create risks for children. Alleged perpetrators often continued to have access to children even when religious leaders knew they posed a danger. We heard that alleged perpetrators were often transferred to other locations, but they were rarely reported to police."[75]*

The most high-profile case was that of Cardinal George Pell. At the time the charges were brought against him in 2017, he was the third highest-ranking official of the Vatican. In the subsequent February 2019 trial, where he was accused of sexually abusing two boys in 1996—a trial so secret that the Australian media was banned from talking about it until it had concluded—Pell was found guilty by a unanimous jury on five charges of sexual abuse. A panel of judges denied his later appeal. As of September 2019, he is appealing again, this time to the High Court of Australia.[76] He is still a cardinal, a "Prince of the Church."

Similar inquiries, particularly relating to the Catholics, have been held around the world. In May 2018 it was announced that all thirty-three bishops in Chile were resigning after a sexual abuse scandal rocked the country.[77]

How did the Catholics let this happen?

In 2001, while the future Pope Benedict XVI was still Cardinal Ratzinger and the head of the Congregation for the Doctrine of the Faith (formerly known as the Supreme Sacred Congregation of the Roman and Universal Inquisition), he authored a document entitled "De delictis gravioribus"" (Latin for "On more serious crimes"), which was then approved by Pope John Paul II.

A 2006 BBC documentary, *Sex Crimes and the Vatican*, alleges this "secret Vatican edict" instructed the world's Catholic bishops to put the Church before children's safety. The film claims Ratzinger enforced the document, which included an oath of secrecy, enforceable by excommunication, for twenty years. Ratzinger allegedly advised Church leaders not to report incidents to the police.[78]

This letter built on the existing 1962 church document "Crimen sollicitationis,"[79] which set out the process for church authorities to follow when a priest or bishop was accused of making sexual advances to a member of the church. Both documents stressed that such issues were to be dealt with internally by the church under the strictest of secrecy. No outside authorities were to be involved. Don't take it to the cops. Like La Cosa Nostra, the Vatican handles its own dirty business.

A whistleblower lawyer who was fired from the Vatican for publicly criticizing the way it handled child abuse, Fr. Tom Doyle, appeared in the BBC film and claimed that the Vatican's policy was to cover up abuse. According to Hans Kung, a Swiss Catholic priest who, along with Ratzinger, was one of the youngest theologians at the Second Vatican Council from 1962 to 1965:

> There is no denying the fact that the worldwide system of covering up cases of sexual crimes committed by clerics was engineered by the Roman Congregation for the Doctrine of the Faith under Cardinal Ratzinger (1981–2005). During the reign of Pope John Paul II, that congregation had already taken charge of all such cases under oath of strictest silence. Ratzinger himself, on May 18th, 2001, sent a solemn document to all the bishops dealing with severe crimes ("epistula de delictis gravioribus"), in which cases of abuse were sealed under the "secretum pontificium" ("the pontifical secret"), the violation of which could entail grave ecclesiastical penalties."[80]

A standard church practice around the world was to transfer priests who had been accused of sexual abuse to another parish— where they still had contact with children.

We have to wonder why an organization like the Catholic Church, which, according to the *Catholic Encyclopedia*, is "a society founded on moral principles, aiming at higher ends, and dispensing spiritual benefits," would choose to cover up allegations of sexual abuse within its ranks rather than do the moral thing and expose them? According to the report "The Nature and Scope of the Problem of Sexual Abuse of Minors by Catholic Priests and Deacons in the United States" aka "The John Jay Report," commissioned by the U.S. Conference of Catholic Bishops, one of the critical factors in the abuse not being adequately dealt with was an "overemphasis on the need to avoid a scandal."[81]

The Australian Royal Commission seems to concur:

> "Many leaders of religious institutions demonstrated a preoccupation with protecting the institution's 'good name' and reputation. Actions were often taken with the aim of avoiding, preventing or repairing public scandal, and concealing information that could tarnish the image of the institution and its personnel, or negatively affect its standing in the community."

Unlike corporations, the leaders of a religious institution (such as bishops of the Catholic Church) probably aren't worried about protecting their own personal wealth (with the exception of "megachurches"), as they tend to be on relatively small salaries, with all of their personal needs taken care of by the church. Cardinals in the Catholic Church, like George Pell, are considered a "Prince of the Church" and are rewarded with a lifetime appointment. But it does seem plausible that they might be concerned about protecting the wealth and reputation of the institution, as their career and personal reputation are tied closely to it. If you've been involved in the church since you were a teenager and spent your life rising through the ranks until you've become a bishop or a cardinal, you probably have a natural tendency to want to protect the institution—not to mention avoiding "grave ecclesiastical penalties" (which, according to the *Catholic Encyclopedia*, can involve excommunication and being banned from the sacraments). It's easy to imagine that someone who has spent their life inside the church might find excommunication and being banned from the sacraments a horrifying punishment. If the church suffers on your watch, you might also find yourself out of a job—and what does a fifty-year-old ex-bishop do for a career?

And yet I have to wonder what kind of religious people would allow harm to come to their parishioners, while systematically covering up the crime of child abuse and protecting the perpetrators? I can't imagine doing something like that, can you?

But this kind of behavior makes absolute sense for a psychopath, someone devoid of empathy, who only is concerned about protecting their power.

CHAPTER THREE

THERE IS NO "I" IN PSYCHOPATH

So we've had a look at some examples of individuals and organizations whose actions suggest somewhat psychopathic tendencies. They display an extreme lack of empathy and conscience, coupled with a desire to protect their power and a willingness to take risks in the pursuit of power.

In this chapter, I want to explore the idea that to survive and thrive inside an organization, a person's ethics and values need to map closely to the primary survival priorities of the organization. Anyone whose ethics conflict with their employer's priorities will either leave of their own volition or get pushed out, a little like how the body's immune system expels a virus. Some people will turn into whistleblowers, exposing fraud and corruption inside their place of employment. This usually doesn't end well for them.

As we've seen, organizations are driven to survive and prosper, and it stands to reason that individuals who can help organizations achieve those objectives will do well inside of them. But how does an organization know that it's on track to achieving its goals of growth and survival? Different kinds of organizations have different metrics that are of primary importance. For example, a business pays attention to parameters like revenue and profit, dividends paid out to shareholders, and market share.

Political parties care about a different set of objectives—how many seats they won in the last election, polling numbers, campaign donations, and membership numbers. Religious organizations will have other goals, which are probably a combination of the first two. They are also interested in revenue (coming partly from donations and tithing, partly from sales of religious merchandise, and partly from diversified investment portfolios in stocks, real estate, and businesses), membership numbers, and attendance levels.

At the risk of sounding obvious, any employee who isn't "on board" with delivering the objectives of the organization she works for will have a hard time getting hired in the first place. If she does manage to get in the door, she will struggle to get promoted to positions of leadership. It's the person who jumps in with both feet, who drinks the Kool-Aid, and is ready to be a good soldier without asking questions, who will succeed. Some of the most challenging situations I've had in my career involved questioning the decisions my superiors were making. I'm sure you've all had similar experiences. Nothing irks a boss more than for an underling to ask, "Should we be doing this?" It shines the spotlight back on the ethics of the superior in a way that they are likely to find irritating and discomforting, especially if they are a psychopath.

Imagine for a moment one of those wealthy, influential corporate executives that you have seen in the media—$22,000 Zegna suit, chauffeur-driven Benz 600SL, cavernous shiny office with a stunning view of the city, living in a mansion or penthouse apartment, surrounded by staff who jump at every opportunity to gain favor and a possible promotion. Imagine you are that person—a "master of the universe."

If you were that person, would you ever want to give that lifestyle up? Even if you're not a psychopath, you might do everything in your power to keep things precisely the way they are. Why not? You're on top of the pile, and life is excellent. You probably don't see anything at all wrong with wanting to stay on top. In your mind, you've worked hard and made sacrifices to get where you are. You deserve your success. People will have to pry that power out of your cold, dead hands.

What kind of corporate culture is someone like this going to propagate inside the organization they run? If the success of the organization determines their continuing personal success, then you would expect them to engender a culture that places great stock in the continued success of the organization and its executives. Of course, this is also their job.

But what if there is a conflict of interest between the continued success of the organization and reforming the organization? Let's say the organization has some fraud going on, and the CEO is made aware of it, but the scam directly contributes to the financial success of the organization and its executives.

What will this person do if they find themselves in a situation where the success of their organization, their personal success, and "doing the right thing" are mutually exclusive?

Wouldn't you expect them to put the success of the organization ahead of the reform?

If they didn't need a revolution to get to the top, it's highly unlikely they are going to start one once they get there—dramatic change produces dramatic unknowns, which creates instability, which, in most cases, makes your chances of holding on to power tenuous (although there are cases where volatility can work in your favor).

Even if this person at the top wanted to make revolutionary changes, they might not be allowed. Most significant organizations have an entire tier of senior management who, like the CEO or the president or the pope, rose through the ranks to get to where they are. The system is working out pretty well for them, too. Even if a rogue manager manages to make her way to the top of the food chain and then decides to make revolutionary changes, we should expect the rest of the management to try to stop her. Like Pope John Paul I (who died, some suspect murdered, thirty-three days after he became pope), she may find that her days of upsetting the applecart are extremely limited.

This is undoubtedly truer if her colleagues are psychopaths.

I'm not talking about making specific cosmetic changes once they get to the top—every leader wants to do that. They might have their pet projects they want to support or particular policies that will get more airtime than they have previously or specific projects their backers want to see enabled. I'm talking about massive, sweeping changes to how the system works—cleaning up corruption, draining the swamp, changing a culture, making government more transparent, or curbing the military.

HOW THEY TREAT CUSTOMERS

I think you can tell a lot about the management and culture of a company by the way it treats customers.

If you're an employee working in the customer service department, you'd better be on board with the company's policy. I once had a boss who assumed every customer was trying to rip him off. When I did my best to convince him that most people are reasonable, he accused me of being naïve. He was later accused of embezzling $500,000 out of the company he ran and disappeared to Bangkok before charges were brought against him. The company went into liquidation. I guess he presumed everyone thought like him.

If the company treats customers like disposable numbers or an unfortunate but necessary problem, but *you* care about making them satisfied, you're going to end up frustrated or fired.

There are very few businesses that make customer satisfaction a serious priority. I can't speak for the rest of the world, but whenever I come across excellent customer service in Australia, it is so unexpected, I am shocked. "Treat your customers well" doesn't seem to be a hard idea to wrap your head around. Why, then, is it so uncommon in the real world? Is it because organizations are run by people without any empathy?

Apple is one company that seems to have an excellent code of customer support. Their "Genius Bars" are always staffed by super-friendly nerds willing to try as hard as they can to resolve customer problems. I can't tell you how many iPhones I've had replaced within five minutes of walking into an Apple store to report a problem.

That attitude came from the top. One night in 2005, after watching Steve Jobs' keynote at Macworld, I posted a question on my blog asking how to get my podcasts into Apple's (then brand new) podcast directory. The next morning, I opened my email to find the answer to my question—from *sjobs@apple.com*. How did the CEO of Apple find time to write me an email to answer a question that, no doubt, many lower-level employees at Apple could have responded to just as easily? When Steve died in 2011, I heard lots of people tell stories similar to mine.

But as we all know, more often than not, trying to get decent customer support is a frustrating and maddening exercise, where companies seem to throw every possible obstacle in the way of solving their customer's problems. We've all sat on a helpline to a telco, bank, or insurance company, talking to someone on a call desk in a foreign land, who is underpaid, undertrained, overworked, and apparently incentivized by how quickly they can get you off the phone (often by "accidentally" hanging up the call). Companies hire vast teams of belligerent lawyers to write customer contracts the length of *War and Peace* that have pages and pages of fine print designed to avoid having to redress customer complaints legally. The ethics of these companies are easy to see, despite what they might claim on their websites. Saying, "We care about our customers!" isn't the same as actually *demonstrating* that care. The customer comes last, not first (which is reserved for profit). Anyone working in customer service for one of these companies who tries to insist that they should treat their customers with more respect is likely to last as long as the person at Apple who *doesn't* care about customer support.

People whose values don't map closely to those of the organization, either won't get employed in the first place, will get fired, or will remove themselves from the organization. Or they won't even apply to work for the company in the first place.

If you've ever had the experience of working in an organization where you felt compelled to challenge the ethics or values of the status quo, you might have found that your superiors and colleagues didn't always exactly appreciate your input. You might have found yourself terminated, reassigned, "managed out," or having to resign after an antagonistic relationship developed with your management. Dissent and free thinking tend not to be tolerated inside "command and control" cultures. This weeding-out process is designed to lead to a homogenous environment, where everyone thinks the same, has the same values, and stays "on message."

This can also happen in entire societies, where dissenters are deemed "un-American" or "a traitor to the glorious revolution" or "not righteous enough" and are shunned, deported, imprisoned (even for smoking a harmless joint), excommunicated, or executed. In cultures like these, it becomes increasingly difficult to change the dominant mind-set as the culture has calcified under several layers of hierarchical intransigence. Even senior executives or honest politicians, who are brought in to an organization because of a specific skill set they have or through an acquisition, can find their efforts to make a difference stymied if they don't fit well within the dominant culture.

Typically, organizations try to hire people who are judged to be a "decent fit" for the company's culture and values. The result is that very few people who *do* get hired will question the dominant cultural values, either because they naturally agree with them or because they understand the consequences of being the squeaky wheel (and it isn't getting oiled; it's getting managed out). Managers will naturally try to create a company culture that rewards certain kinds of behavior and punishes others. If you have a healthy organizational culture, this might result in creating an atmosphere where people do the best work of their lives. But if you have a toxic culture, it can mean that people will do dishonest things they wouldn't do otherwise. Of course, every organization *thinks* its culture is fine for the reason mentioned above—people who aren't a "decent fit" for the culture probably either don't get hired in the first place or leave once they figure out how toxic it really is.

So we end up with organizations with minimal internal dissent, with few left who can or will call foul if they see it going off the rails. According to academic Dennis Mumby's book, *Communication and Power in Organizations*, you typically end up with cultures where "everything from organizational symbols, rituals, and stories serve to maintain the position of power held by the dominant group."[82]

At the very least, this stifles innovation and creativity. At worst, with a psychopath at the helm, it can lead to disaster. Take, for instance, General Motors. In 2014 their recently appointed CEO, Mary Barra, confessed that the GM culture was permeated by "bureaucratic processes that avoided accountability." And she should know—Barra followed in her father's footsteps when she started working for GM in 1980, as a co-op student, when she was only eighteen years old.

She said the culture included such things as the "GM salute," which involved "a crossing of the arms and pointing outwards toward others, indicating that the responsibility belongs to someone else, not me," and the "GM nod," when everyone agrees to a plan of action after a meeting "but then leaves the room with no intention to follow through." Employees also didn't take notes at safety meetings "because they believed GM lawyers did not want such notes taken." Words such as *problem* and *defect* were banned inside the company. Instead, employees were instructed to use softer words, such as *issue, condition,* or *matter.* During her first year as CEO, General Motors was forced to issue eighty-four safety recalls involving over 30 million cars, and Barra was called before the Senate to testify about the recalls and deaths attributed to a faulty ignition switch. Thirteen deaths were ultimately blamed on the GM culture.[83]

Of course, GM mentioned none of these cultural issues on their website. A snapshot of their "Our Culture" page from April 2013 (thanks to the Wayback Machine) claims, "We believe in accountability from every member of our team, and we demand results from everyone. In short, the GM culture is all about creating excellence—and providing our team members what they need in order to contribute to that success."[84]

Rule number one of building an organizational culture should be "Thou shalt not believe one's own bullshit." Of course, as a result of that natural weeding-out process I mentioned earlier, the people who wrote and authorized that statement about accountability likely believed it was true.

Now let's compare the GM nod to reports of the culture at Apple. According to Adam Lashinsky's book *Inside Apple,* the company uses a management technique called DRI (Directly Responsible Individual). "You go to a meeting at Apple, there will be a list of items on the agenda. Next to the action item is a name. The name is the DRI, the one person who is responsible for getting that done—not the several people, not the two in a box executive management that other companies have. The one person."[85]

Getting back to hiring people who are a "decent fit"—the plan to manage cultural homogeneity starts in the interview process. Organizations try to keep disruptive individuals from joining by filtering them at various stages. Even before a job interview, prospective employees will be filtered out from a glance at their resume and a peek at their online profile. If the candidate makes it to the interview stage, they will be asked carefully engineered questions to weed out potential troublemakers. They may even have to sit for a psych test designed by I-O (industrial and organizational) psychologists. Previous employers will be called, searching for any reason why this person may not be a "fit" for the corporate culture. Anyone who has even a whiff of a reputation for not toeing the line will likely end up on the discard pile. Even attempts over the last twenty years to encourage more significant gender and racial diversity inside organizations haven't stopped them from filtering candidates based on their "cultural fit."

According to one 2012 research paper that looks at the attitudes of job interviewers,[86] half of those surveyed ranked "culturally fit" as *the* most important criterion at the interview stage. The same study claims that "employers really want people who they will bond with, who they will feel good around, who will be their friend and maybe even their romantic partner." And, no doubt, people who will support the organization's values, which, of course, are likely also to be the hiring manager's values. If you're hiring someone into the military, you're unlikely to want to be friends or get romantic with someone who attends peace rallies every weekend—and vice versa. Like attracts like. A toxic culture will attract and hire people who fit right in.

So, it's highly unlikely that many organizations are going to hire people with the complete opposite worldview to the interviewer or hiring manager.

At some companies, however, the hiring process deliberately *seeks* diversity. For example, according to Apple's CEO Tim Cook: "You're trying to pick people that fit into the culture of a company. You want a very diverse group with very diverse life experiences looking at every problem. But you also want people to buy into the philosophy, not just buy in, but to deeply believe in it."[87]

Apple's culture famously includes extreme levels of secrecy, often compared to working for the NSA, and a deep conviction that you are there to change the world. It works for them, too. When Steve Jobs returned as CEO in 1997, the company was near bankruptcy and famously got a $150 million investment from Microsoft to stay afloat (the Macworld audience booed during the announcement anyway[88]). By the time Jobs died in 2011, a mere fourteen years later, Apple was the most highly valued company on the planet.

As of September 2019, GM's market capitalization was around $55 billion. Apple's market cap was about $960 billion. Selling cars is obviously different to selling laptops and phones, but does culture —attitudes toward customer service and taking responsibility— have a role to play in the success of Apple?

I don't want to suggest that Apple is perfect. Many people have suggested that Steve Jobs may have been a psychopath. But something about the corporate culture of Apple seems to be set up to treat customers with care.

Unfortunately, most corporate cultures don't work that well.

WHISTLEBLOWIN' IN THE WIND

When someone makes it through the hiring filters but later discovers that their values and ethics don't align with their employer's, she has a handful of options:

1. She can resign, walk away, and look for a place to work where she feels her values aren't going to be challenged.
2. She can stay and try to change the organization from within.
3. She can stay and agree to do things that aren't in accordance with her values to keep her job.
4. She can resign, become a whistleblower, and try to change the organization from the outside.

I have much admiration for whistleblowers. It takes a ton of guts to put your life and career on the line to speak out publicly about wrongdoing, particularly in your industry. They often provide revelations of how psychopathic cultures work. Both by the content of the whistleblower's revelations but also by the way the organization involved responds to them and treats the whistleblower.

Unfortunately, most organizations don't appreciate the honesty and courage that it takes to speak up. They don't see it as an opportunity to make genuine change. They often go on the attack. If you threaten a psychopath's power, expect them to retaliate.

All four of those options are going to place emotional and psychological demands on the person. Changing jobs is usually stressful and requires learning a new culture, developing new relationships, leaving old ones behind, and sometimes moving location. Agreeing to perform tasks that aren't acceptable to your personal moral code also involves a certain amount of personal turmoil, from finding ways to justify it to yourself so you can sleep at night or hiding it from your loved ones and friends to avoid their judgment, right up to legal and professional consequences if you are found out. You basically agree to join Team Psychopath.

Option two, staying inside the organization and trying to change it from within, requires an enormous amount of mental and emotional energy. It would add significantly to our cognitive load and occupational stress. How much energy we want to put into trying to change an organization from within is perhaps determined by the amount of investment (psychological, emotional, or financial) we have in the work the organization is doing. Option two can take the form of working within the four walls of the organization or become a whistleblower while still employed there. Both can lead to substantial personal consequences.

Let's look at some examples where employees have spoken out against their organization's culture—and what happened to them.

THE SPY WHO SPIED ON THE SPIES

Edward Snowden is a former CIA "computer wizard" (his words), who left the agency to contract to Dell as a technologist, cyberstrategist, and "expert in cyber counterintelligence" on their National Security Agency and CIA accounts.

According to Snowden, one of his jobs there was to look for new ways to break into internet and telephone traffic around the world. He became concerned with the legality and morality of what the agencies were doing and, in early 2013, he experienced what he called his "breaking point," after seeing NSA Director

James Clapper blatantly lie about their monitoring activities on television.

On March 12, 2013, during a United States Senate Select Committee on Intelligence hearing, Senator Ron Wyden asked Clapper the following question:[89]

"Does the NSA collect any type of data at all on millions or hundreds of millions of Americans?"

Clapper: "No, sir."

Wyden seemed shocked by Clapper's response because he already knew the truth. With a look of disbelief on his face, perhaps wondering how many laws Clapper was breaking, he tried to give the NSA director another chance.

Wyden: "It does not?"

Clapper: "Not wittingly. There are cases where they could inadvertently perhaps collect, but not wittingly."

Snowden was appalled at the outright deception and decided he had a personal responsibility to let the people know they were being lied to by their government. Just imagine for a moment what must have been going through his mind at the time. He must have known what the consequences of his actions were likely to be. At best, he'd likely spend the rest of his life as a fugitive. Alternatively, he could spend it in prison—or worse. How disturbed about his country's actions must he have been to trigger a course of action that would involve such a massive personal sacrifice?

After Clapper's testimony, Snowden resigned from Dell and took a job at the consulting firm Booz Allen Hamilton, which contracted to the NSA, to gather data and then release details of the NSA's worldwide surveillance activity. A few months later, he took a leave of absence from work and flew to Hong Kong where he met with respected journalist Glenn Greenwald and documentary filmmaker Laura Poitras (who later won the 2015 Academy Award for Best Documentary Feature for *Citizenfour*, about Edward Snowden), to whom he released an unknown number of NSA documents. While at the time of writing it seems that the contents of only a small percentage of those documents have been released, they have contributed significantly to our understanding of how the NSA and its "Five Eyes" partners (Australia, Canada, New Zealand, and the United Kingdom) have been secretly and illegally collecting incredible amounts of private information about global citizens. As Snowden has said, "The biggest change has been in awareness. Before 2013, if you said the NSA was making records of everybody's phone calls and the GCHQ (the Government Communications Headquarters, a British intelligence and security organization) was monitoring lawyers and journalists, people raised eyebrows and called you a conspiracy theorist. Those days are over."

Did Snowden get a commendation from the American government for revealing how the NSA Director had lied to the American people? Did he get a reward? A parade?

Yeah, you know the answer.

He was charged by the U.S. government (and this, remember, is during the Obama years, not Trump, not Bush) with theft of government property and two counts of violating the Espionage Act—despite the fact that the United States Court of Appeals for the Second Circuit said in 2015 that Section 215 of the Patriot Act *did not* authorize the NSA to collect Americans' calling records in bulk, proving that Snowden was absolutely correct in having concerns about the legality of the program.

His personal life has been completely turned upside down. Deliberately attaching his name to the leaks, so his former colleagues wouldn't be accused and interrogated, he tried to seek asylum in Latin America but ended up stranded in Russia after the United States canceled his passport.

When Obama later signed the USA Freedom Act, which restricted the kind of bulk information American intelligence agencies could collect on U.S. citizens, Snowden's disclosures were a significant factor.

Whether or not Snowden is a hero, a coward, or a traitor (the stated view of former U.S. Secretary of State John Kerry)[90] is not a discussion for this book. I merely use his story to illustrate an example. When he witnessed activities that were against his ethics, Snowden not only refused to go along with them; he decided to work to undermine them—at enormous personal cost.

By the way, nothing happened to NSA Director Clapper. After the Snowden dump went public, Clapper admitted that the NSA did indeed collect metadata on millions of American's telephone calls, which directly contradicts his statement to the Senate in the previous year. Wyden accused Clapper of not giving a "straight answer" during the hearings. Congressman Justin Amash openly accused Clapper of criminal perjury and called for his resignation. Senator Rand Paul said, "The director of national intelligence, in March, did directly lie to Congress, which is against the law." Clapper just apologized, saying his response was "erroneous." Then-President Obama said he had "full faith in Director Clapper's leadership." And that was that. Clapper resigned in 2016 and ended up working at the Australian National University in Canberra.

During his eight years in office President Barack Obama hunted down whistleblowers and journalists using the draconian Espionage Act of 1917, with more prosecutions than all previous U.S. administrations combined.

According to Norman Solomon, executive director of the Institute for Public Accuracy and co-founder of RootsAction.org:

> *The absolute twisted passion with which the administration under Obama's leadership has pursued whistleblowers is just appalling. There's just no other administration that comes close.*

For his "war on whistleblowers," former *New York Times* reporter James Risen called Obama "the greatest enemy to press freedom in a generation." [91]

How a society treats its truth-tellers is, I think, a good indication of how psychopathic it has become.

HOW TO END A WAR

One of Snowden's most prominent supporters is also one of his inspirations: Daniel Ellsberg.

Ellsberg is someone whose conscience lead him to anonymously release classified documents, but, unlike Snowden, he did it while still employed.

After getting a Ph.D. in economics from Harvard, Ellsberg worked for the Pentagon in the 1960s and spent two years in South Vietnam. In 1971, he was working for RAND Corporation, an American nonprofit global policy think tank originally formed in 1948 by the Douglas Aircraft Company and Major General Curtis LeMay (who previously commanded the U.S. firebombing of Japan during World War II, which is estimated to have killed more than 500,000 Japanese civilians and left five million homeless) to offer research and analysis to the United States Armed Forces. During his time at RAND, he contributed to a top-secret study of classified documents on the conduct of the Vietnam War that had been commissioned by U.S. Defense Secretary Robert McNamara. These documents, completed in 1968, and which later became known collectively as the Pentagon Papers, revealed that the U.S. government had knowledge that the war could not be won and that, according to the *New York Times*, "demonstrated, among other things, that the Johnson Administration had systematically lied, not only to the public but also to Congress, about a subject of transcendent national interest and significance."

Disillusioned about the Vietnam War, Ellsberg decided to secretly photocopy the Pentagon Papers, eventually passing them to the *New York Times*, *The Washington Post*, and seventeen other newspapers, which revealed to the general public the deception. Ellsberg surrendered himself to the authorities and was charged under the Espionage Act of 1917 and other charges, including theft and conspiracy, carrying a total maximum sentence of 115 years.

In an attempt to destroy his credibility, G. Gordon Liddy, a former FBI agent, and E. Howard Hunt, a former CIA officer (the same guys who were later responsible for the break-in behind the Watergate scandal when they worked for the unbelievably named Committee to Re-Elect the President, or CREEP), broke into Ellsberg's psychiatrist's office to steal his patient file, hoping to find damaging personal information. They found the record, but it didn't give them the ammunition they hoped for. When the court found out about the break-in, which had been sanctioned by John Ehrlichman, President Richard Nixon's counsel and assistant to the president for domestic affairs, as well as further evidence of illegal wiretapping against Ellsberg by the FBI, the judge dismissed all of the charges.

By the way, if you want to read perhaps the craziest autobiography ever written, pick up a copy of Liddy's book *Will* and be amazed as he talks about how he toughened himself up by holding his bare palm over a naked flame until the skin bubbled. Decide for yourself whether or not you think he fits the description of a psychopath.

Today Ellsberg is a vocal and public supporter of fellow transparency activists, such as Snowden, Chelsea Manning (sentenced to 35 years in prison in the United States for leaking military secrets to Wikileaks including the infamous Baghdad airstrike video "Collateral Murder"), and Julian Assange (the founder of WikiLeaks, who, at the time of writing, is currently in jail in the United Kingdom and then facing extradition to the United States).

HOLDING OUT FOR A HERO

One former Goldman executive, Greg Smith, found out the cost of being a whistleblower. Previously the head of Goldman Sachs U.S. equity derivatives sales divisions, Smith did resign and go public with his concerns about the company in 2012, in a letter published in the *New York Times*.[92]

Among other things, he called the company culture "toxic and destructive" where they referred to clients as "muppets" and put the company's profits ahead of clients. After quitting, Smith signed a book deal with a reported $1.5 million advance (which sounds like a lot but was only three times his annual salary at Goldman). Then Goldman's PR forces set out to discredit him, leaking his year-end reviews (where he supposedly asked for a $1 million bonus and was cranky when he didn't get it), and giving off-the-record briefings to various media outlets about Smith's lackluster performance at the bank.[93]

They also provided a "Briefing Toolkit" to all employees to equip them for awkward conversations about Greg Smith, suggesting, for example, that they should imply that he was too low on the totem pole to know anything about anything inside the company and to call him a hypocrite for taking the firm's money for over a decade. When it came out, his book was largely criticized by reviewers[94]—and yet customer reviews on Amazon give it an average of four out of five stars.[95]

How would you feel if you had the PR forces of a massive corporation turned against you, trying to destroy your reputation? It might be enough to make you think twice. The fear of that happening to them might be one reason why decent people don't blow the whistle on a toxic organization.

And why would an organization feel the need to destroy the credibility of a guy like Smith? It seems to me that they could have said: "We thank Greg for making his concerns known and will address them very seriously because we want to run an organization that is completely ethical."

Of course, that's not how psychopaths would handle the situation. They must protect their power at all costs.

When an organization gets into trouble and loses its way, many decent people jump ship and find a place to work where they can feel better about what they are doing. Not all of them go public with their concerns.

The people who don't jump ship tend to be those who either don't mind what the company is doing (i.e., their values are aligned with those of the organization) or who don't think they are competent enough to land another job as good as the one they have. Better the devil you know and that sort of thing.

There might also be a few who think they can change the organization from within. That's a brave move, and I applaud those people, but I'm skeptical that it ever works.

The result is that most of the people who remain to run the toxic organization are themselves toxic. If a company is already toxic, with psychopaths in positions of power, the board might also struggle to hire decent people to run it from outside. If you're a seasoned senior executive with a strong moral code, why would you choose to join a toxic organization and work with psychopaths when you can join one that is healthy? Unless, of course, you're a psychopath yourself. Or you think you have what it takes to right the ship.

THE INFORMANT

Psychopaths who work inside a toxic organization will often prosper. They will happily go along with unethical or criminal activities if it means promotion or personal power. Sometimes they too become whistleblowers, but often for the wrong reason. Let me tell you the story of Mark Whitacre, the man who single-handedly brought about one of America's largest and most famous antitrust cases.

On paper, Whitacre looked perfect. He was a scientist with a Ph.D. in nutritional biochemistry from Cornell University who, within six years of graduating, was the president of the BioProducts Division at the Archer Daniels Midland Company (ADM). ADM is an American food production company founded in 1902, a billion-dollar behemoth selling everything from soybeans to high fructose corn syrup sweeteners. It pretty much dominates the cornerstone ingredients of the American diet and was ranked No. 48 in the 2018 Fortune 500 list of the largest United States corporations by total revenue.

In 1992, Whitacre was promoted to corporate vice president of ADM. That was also the year he started working with the FBI. As it turned out, several of ADM's senior executives, including Whitacre, were involved in illegal price-fixing of the lysine market with several of their global competitors. Lysine is an amino acid that plays a significant role in, among other things, building muscle protein.

Whitacre approached the FBI to bring their attention to the lysine cartel. He agreed to secretly wear a wire to work to record his fellow executives and global cartel partners to gather evidence against them. He also agreed to get his colleagues to confess to their crimes on film, using secretly placed cameras planted by the FBI inside meeting rooms.

Why, you might ask, would a corporate vice president of one of the world's largest food manufacturing companies, who was earning hundreds of thousands of dollars a year, agree to conspire to bring down his colleagues? Was it out of a sense of ethical concern? Was he trying to do the right thing by American consumers who were paying far more than they might have under a free market for their lysine?

Unfortunately, it was none of these concerns.

As it turns out, much to the horror of the FBI agents, who like their confidential informants to be squeaky clean, Whitacre had embezzled $9 million from ADM during his time there and hoped that by drawing the FBI's attention to the lysine price-fixing, they wouldn't discover his other crime. And they probably wouldn't have—if he hadn't directly brought their attention to it with a confession.

Whitacre spent nine years in prison for embezzlement, wire fraud, and price-fixing. Today he is working as the chief science officer and president of operations for Cypress Systems Inc., a Fresno-based biotechnology company. Matt Damon played him in the 2009 film *The Informant*.

For the price-fixing, ADM paid a fine of $100 million. At the time it was the most significant antitrust fine in U.S. history.

ADM vice chairman Michael Andreas, son of the CEO Dwayne Andreas, was sentenced to twenty-four months in prison and a $350,000 fine. Why did he get off so lightly? I don't know—but it can't hurt that his father is "America's champion all-time campaign contributor."[98]

By the way, this wasn't the first (or last) time ADM was accused of price-fixing. In 1920, the company was subject to a suit for fixing the price of linseed oil brought by the U.S. Department of Justice. ADM was also subject to a class-action lawsuit in 2004 for allegedly fixing the prices of high-fructose corn syrup. They settled the case before it went to court for $400 million. They have also pleaded guilty to corruption, charged with several major federal lawsuits related to air pollution, and accused of tax dodging.

Strangely, I can't find any of these stories mentioned on the company's website. On the contrary, it claims that it "conducts business fairly and ethically at all times."[97]

ADM was named the world's most-admired food-production company by *Fortune* magazine for three consecutive years: 2009, 2010, and 2011. Go figure. What does that tell you about how our society rewards psychopathic behavior?

HOLLYWOOD NIGHTS

The 2017 sexual abuse allegations against American film producer Harvey Weinstein are another example of broken, toxic cultures that can extend to an entire industry. Although rumors of Weinstein's "casting couch" practices were apparently rife throughout Hollywood for many years, he got away with it, partly, it seems, because he had built up around himself a "wall of invulnerability," in part through his support of leading Democratic politicians. He boasted of being friends with the Clintons and Barack Obama, providing cash for their campaigns and lending celebrity support to their initiatives and personal brands.[98] Directors, producers, journalists, investors, and agents all ignored or downplayed Weinstein's alleged behavior because of his influence in the industry. Rich movie stars valued their future income higher than protecting their female colleagues. An entire city later claimed they had no idea what was going on, despite movie stars like Uma Thurman having tried to get her agents and director Quentin Tarantino to protect her when Weinstein allegedly shoved himself on her in the mid-1990s.

But come on—did we really expect anything different from Hollywood?

AUSTRALIAN STORIES

We have whistleblowers in Australia, too. In 2012, an employee working for Australian mining services company Thiess (today known as CIMIC) reported to management that "the firm or its agents may have broken Australian or Indian corruption laws when it sought to win a $6.8 billion coal mining contract in India in 2010." Two years later, when nothing had been done about the incident, the employee took the allegations to the CEO and the company's ethics committee. Instead of doing what I'd expect from a healthy company—commending the employee and making the relevant Australian authorities aware of the allegations—the management reportedly fired the employee instead.[99]

A former senior executive of another CIMIC division later testified that "a blind eye was turned to corruption and whistleblowers (were) forced out."[100]

On top of that, the chief financial officer of the company was later found guilty of falsifying the company books.[101]

What would you surmise about the culture of that company?

In 2016 it was revealed that another significant Australian company, the Commonwealth Bank (CBA), fired one of their senior IT managers a couple of months after he refused to sign an IT contract that he thought smelled funny. He later reported that before he was fired, he took his concerns directly to the CEO and CIO, but they both ignored him. His claims eventually resulted in a major bribery investigation and jail time for one of the bank's executives.[102]

Sometimes a whistleblower's courage can lead to the exposure of psychopathic behavior across an entire industry.

CBA employee Jeff Morris was hired as a financial planner in 2008 and was quickly shocked at how corrupt the bank was. He turned whistleblower and claimed the bank was "absolutely rife" with corruption, which went "all the way to the top."[103]

His revelations that "there were crooked plans stitching up literally widows and orphans, and there was a crooked management team covering it up" and that the bank's "remuneration system that was designed to encourage people to do whatever they had to do to make their bonuses" ultimately lead to an Australian Royal Commission into the entire banking industry. The Australian government tried to prevent the inquiry from happening and assured the country that it wasn't necessary, and everything was just fine. Maybe not surprising, considering the Prime Minister of Australia at the time, Malcolm Turnbull, was a former Goldman Sachs CEO.

Despite the government's assurances, the inquiry found the Australian financial services industry was *indeed* rife with widespread fraud and corruption—and, as Jeff Morris had claimed, that it went all the way to the top. According to the commission's final report, "there can be no doubt that the primary responsibility for misconduct in the financial services industry lies with the entities concerned and those who managed and controlled those entities: their boards and senior management."[104]

Remember, in an earlier chapter, I mentioned that some psychologists believe the rate of psychopaths in the financial services industry is even higher than 10 percent?[105]

Gordon Gekko was influential here, too.

Another significant Australian bank, the National Australia

Bank (NAB), *didn't* fire employee Dennis Gentilin when he informed management about fraudulent trading in 2004. Instead, there was an internal investigation that finally lead to the jailing of four of his colleagues and the resignations of NAB CEO Frank Cicutto and chairman Charles Allen.[106] Although he wasn't fired, Gentilin says he found the experience of being a whistleblower "grueling and harrowing" and went on to write an excellent book about his experience, *The Origins of Ethical Failures.*[107]

In the Royal Commission's view, fifteen years later, the NAB's new chief executive Andrew Thorburn, and new chairman Ken Henry, hadn't learnt the lessons of the bank's past misconduct and held them out for "special criticism" in the final report.[108]

Both men—following in the steps of their predecessors—also fell on their swords.[109]

The Royal Commission revealed that an entire industry can be psychopathic. If that's true of industries like Hollywood and banking, why not an entire economy?

Of course, it isn't just large organizations that engage in these kinds of retaliatory practices. Small businesses often get rid of outspoken staff by laying them off, reducing their pay, cutting back their hours, or moving them to another job that is, in effect, a demotion.

With the declining power of unions, it makes it difficult for an employee to act against their employer if they feel they have been mistreated. Lawsuits are costly and time-consuming, especially when you are going up against a company with deeper pockets. People often decide to just move on with their lives.

The Australian government doesn't like whistleblowers in their ranks, either. In 2017, Australian Tax Office employee Richard

Doyle went public about the ATO's allegedly overly aggressive debt collection practices against small businesses and individuals. Did he get a medal for exposing something in the public interest? A bonus? A free dinner voucher for two? No. As of September 2019, he's facing a 161-year prison sentence.[110]

There have also been some pretty scary crackdowns on journalism in Australia recently. We've seen several raids by the Federal Police on journalists and publishers because of stories that were critical of the government and its policies. Rebecca Ananian-Welsh, senior lecturer, TC Beirne School of Law, The University of Queensland, called the raids "a clear threat to democracy." Even the right-wing Institute of Public Affairs called the raids "disgraceful," and Australia's former Human Rights Commissioner has called Australia the most repressive of the Western democracies.

On Tuesday, June 4, 2019, "Australia Federal Police raided the home of News Corp Australia journalist Annika Smethurst investigating the publication of a leaked plan to allow government spying on Australians."[111]

A lot of journalists in Australia, who have been happy to throw Wikileaks and Julian Assange under the bus, are now complaining loudly about their own situation. Under Australian law, it's not just the sources that leaked the classified information that face jail—it's also the journalists. They can face up to 15 years.

On the same day Smethurst's house was raided, another journalist, Ben Fordham, who works for both Sydney radio 2GB and Sky News (a Murdoch TV station), said he was contacted by the Home Affairs department about a story he published the day before about asylum-seeker boats arriving from Sri Lanka.

Fordham said the ministry was looking for the source which he refused to provide and was told he could be subject to an investigation.[112]

Then the very next day, the AFP also raided the ABC, the Australian Broadcasting Corporation, the government-funded media company. This raid was over articles written in 2017 about alleged misconduct by Australian forces in Afghanistan.

These journalists and their sources should not only be protected by the law; they should be *rewarded* for keeping the public abreast of vital information. They should not be worried about going to jail for doing their job.

Do you get the sense that an entire government can be psychopathic?

THE POPE'S BUTLER DID IT

In 2012, Italian journalist Gianluigi Nuzzi published a book entitled *His Holiness: The Secret Papers of Benedict XVI*. It included confidential memos and letters written to the pope and other senior Vatican officials. One of the letters was written by Archbishop Carlo Maria Viganò, the papal ambassador in the United States. He had complained to the pope about corruption in Vatican finances and said that his transfer to the U.S. had been an effort to shut him up. Viganò, who had previously been the secretary-general of the Governorate of Vatican City State, also wrote about an internal Vatican investigation, which uncovered the blackmailing of gay clergy by individuals outside the Church. Nuzzi had received the memos and letters from the pope's personal butler Paolo Gabriele, who was later arrested. Gabriele claimed to have stolen the documents to fight "evil and corruption" and put the Vatican "back on track."[113] His ethics forced him to act.

Was he congratulated by the pope for his strong moral code? After all, isn't Christianity all about morals?

Of course he wasn't. He was found guilty of theft and forced to serve a prison sentence of eighteen months—in the Vatican, instead of in an ordinary Italian prison, as would typically happen. Why? They were concerned he would reveal more Vatican secrets.

Leaked notes from a private meeting between Pope Francis and Catholic officials in Latin America allegedly had the new pope confirming that the rumors of a "stream of corruption" and a "gay lobby" inside in the Vatican were all true.[114]

How does an institution like the Catholic Church end up with so many sexual predators in its senior ranks? Coincidence? Percentages? Or do predators, like psychopaths, attract and promote people of the same mind-set so they can protect each other?

In 2018, the Pennsylvania Supreme Court released a report[115] that claimed over one thousand children in that state were systematically abused by over three hundred clergy over the course of 70 years.

> *"All of them were brushed aside by church leaders who preferred to protect the abusers and their institution above all," the report reads.*[116]

The report claimed the church had "a playbook for concealing the truth." Protecting the institution instead of child victims sounds to me like the behavior I'd expect from a psychopath.

In recent years there have been many international child sex abuse investigations targeting high profile individuals and organizations ranging from American universities (e.g., Penn State) to Britain's entertainment and political establishment (Jimmy Saville, Rolf Harris, Elm Guest House, etc.).

Jeffrey Epstein, the American financier who was friends with Donald Trump, Bill Clinton, and Prince Andrew, committed suicide in prison under mysterious circumstances. Until 2019, he had managed to avoid much time in jail despite multiple charges of sex trafficking of underage girls going back to 2005 and even a guilty plea in 2008. U.S. attorney Alexander Acosta approved a lenient plea deal for Epstein regarding a case involving prostitution with a fourteen-year-old girl. A decade later, when Acosta was interviewing with Donald Trump's transition team, he allegedly said he had been told to "back off" Epstein because he "belonged to intelligence."[117] Acosta went on to become Trump's Labor Secretary—but resigned when the story about his 2008 deal with Epstein became public.

Many of these cases involve a similar pattern of decade-long cover-ups by people—including politicians of various parties, the media, and police—who knew or suspected what was going on but decided not to say or do anything about it. There were probably a variety of reasons why none of them spoke up, one of them being that their values and the values of the organizations they were protecting intersected.

Politicians who are religious, and who need the support of Christian voters to maintain power, are understandably reluctant to be seen launching investigations or making accusations about churches. Religious police officers also sometimes turn a blind eye to religious criminal activity because they don't want to besmirch the reputation of the church to which they belong. In many cases, religious politicians and police are on close, friendly terms with their local priests, bishops, and pastors. They have been golfing buddies for years and have supported each other's careers.

For example, in 2018, it was revealed that police in the Australian state of Victoria forced one of their detectives to drop an investigation into one of Australia's worst Catholic pedophile priests.[118] We can only begin to imagine how many similar incidents must have taken place over the last fifty years, pressure being placed on police to drop investigations into all sorts of sensitive topics.

When politicians are the subject of an investigation, senior police commanders who rely on them for career advancement might find it opportunistic to ignore evidence and to lose files, while politicians from all parties are worried about protecting the system. In 1983, the British government minister Geoffrey Dickens assembled a dossier on influential and notable child abusers. He told his family it was "explosive" and would "blow the lid" on the abuse. But after he handed the dossier over to the Home Secretary, it was conveniently lost. According to *The Observer*, the Dickens dossier was only one of 114 potentially relevant files on child abuse by the British elite that were found to be missing. One British minister has said that files had been lost "on an industrial scale." A former cabinet minister, Lord Tebbit, has revealed the culture at the time was to protect "the establishment."[119]

Very few of us possess the courage to turn whistleblower like Snowden, Gabriele, Manning, Boyle, and Ellsberg—but some people *will* quit working for organizations, voluntarily or not, if they don't feel comfortable with the tasks they are being asked to do.

The question, though, is why *more* people don't quit under such circumstances? Indeed, as I mentioned earlier, there is a certain degree of stress involved in changing jobs. And we all know that the grass isn't always greener on the other side, better the devil you know, and so forth. Maybe, we conclude, all organizations do corrupt or distasteful things, and we need to hold our noses and push on, sticking our heads in the sand.

Could another reason perhaps be that we assume that the people at the top of the organization know more than we do and, therefore, can make better decisions? Even though their choices may seem unethical to us, we assume they are privy to better information and as a consequence are making the right decisions?

This idea that the people in charge have more information and more experience is sometimes correct but not always—and even when it is true, it doesn't mean that their decisions are necessarily ethical.

For example, many people in the West probably decided, in the lead up to the 2003 Iraq invasion, that our political and military leaders had better information than we did, and therefore their decision to invade was justified, even though the UN General Secretary declared it illegal.[120] Of course, as we later learned, the information they claimed to have (e.g., that Iraq was getting ready to use weapons of mass destruction [WMD] on the West and that Saddam Hussein had given material support to the 9/11 hijackers) was complete nonsense. Even though quite a few experts on Iraq came out *before* the invasion,[121] telling the world Saddam didn't have WMD, it was easier for most of us to think that our political leaders knew what they were doing. Perhaps it would have been better for all considered if we had all been more skeptical of our leadership and demanded they present more evidence to support their claims before they started a new war, which has since led to nearly two hundred thousand civilian deaths,[122] and, according to former U.S. President Barack Obama,[123] created the power vacuum that allowed ISIS to erupt onto the world stage.

So, it's a mistake to convince ourselves that the people at the top always have sufficient and accurate information and are making rational, logical, and unemotional decisions. We cannot evade responsibility for the actions of our governments by recusing ourselves from having to make our judgments. Instead, we must always be questioning our business, political, civic, and religious leaders, demanding evidence and challenging their positions until we are convinced that they are on the right track. If we do that regarding our country's politics, we might be branded a conspiracy whacko or a commie (depending on what era you are living in). If you do it inside of an organization where you work, you'll probably find yourself in the unemployment office. So, taking it upon yourself to be the Skeptic-In-Chief is an unrewarding and challenging path to follow, however noble. But if you don't do it, who will? If you're not the person who is going to stand up and say, "Not on my watch," then who?

Once we start to view our leaders as potential psychopaths, it makes it easier to question their decisions.

BREAKING A FEW EGGS

When we work for an organization where our bosses and colleagues don't seem to have a problem with the ethics of the tasks they are being asked to do, it's easy for us to "go along to get along." Most of us don't like conflict and don't want to put our jobs at risk. We turn a blind eye here and there, and before you know it, we have reconciled to ourselves that what we're doing can't be that terrible because everyone else is doing it, too. Of course, what we fail to realize is that the people who *did* have a problem with it have left the company, and the only people left are those who could stomach it—or who agreed with it wholeheartedly.

However, I don't want to suggest that every single one of the people working at senior levels inside toxic organizations are cold, calculating, mustache-twirling connivers. In many cases, they might think that what they are doing is benign or positive in the long run. Perhaps they genuinely believe that sometimes you have to do distasteful tasks to achieve a beneficial outcome. In philosophy, this is known as *consequentialism*—but in more common parlance, it's called "the ends justify the means" or "you can't make an omelet without breaking a few eggs."

While I don't want to spend too long on consequentialism—that could be another entire book—I do want to look at a few different examples of it.

Soviet leader Josef Stalin's "Great Purge" and his collectivization of the Soviet agricultural sector might be examples of consequentialism. His desire to force the Soviet Union into a more productive economy and to rid her of internal counter-revolutionaries (real or imagined) may have, in his mind, justified breaking a few—or a million—eggs. He might have concluded that it was better that a million people should go to the gulags than have two hundred million people starve or murdered during the next invasion. As it turned out, when the Germans invaded the Soviet Union a few years later, only twenty-seven million Soviet people died, thanks partly to Stalin's push for rapid industrialization in the previous few years.

The dropping of atomic bombs on Japan during World War II, resulting in the death of hundreds of thousands of civilians, is often rationalized by people in the United States as being necessary to prevent a land invasion of Japan, which would have potentially led to even more deaths.

Earlier in WWII, the RAF and USAF dropped hundreds of thousands of phosphorus bombs on civilian centers in Germany —650,000 on Dresden alone. Tens of thousands of innocent people died, mostly women and children noncombatants, "simply for the sake of increasing the terror," according to British Prime Minister Winston Churchill.[124]

Of course, this was justified as a means of helping the Allies win the war.

From 1990 until 2003, the United Nations imposed debilitating economic sanctions on Iraq, resulting in the deaths of between 500,000 and 1 million people (depending on which source you believe)—half of them children. Denis Halliday, the appointed United Nations Humanitarian Coordinator in Baghdad, resigned in 1998 after a thirty-four-year career with the UN, saying, "I don't want to administer a program that satisfies the definition of genocide." Halliday's successor also resigned in protest, calling the effects of the sanctions a "true human tragedy." The stated aim of the sanctions was to eliminate Iraq's weapons of mass destruction.

When asked by Lesley Stahl of CBS News if the price of 500,000 dead children was worth it, former U.S. Secretary of State Madeleine Albright, who at the time was Bill Clinton's UN Ambassador, replied, "I think this is a very hard choice, but the price—we think the price is worth it."[125] Although the total number of dead children is now debated, Albright's response, to a number she apparently accepted at the time, is the point.

Consequentialism is used every day by people working inside a variety of organizations—*and* by us as consumers.

Let's consider the use of Third World labor to build our high-tech electronics.

By most reports, the working conditions at Chinese factories, such as Foxconn, are deplorable.[126] Workers live in crowded dorms, are forced to work long hours, and are punished with hard physical labor and the withholding of wages if they don't do what they are told. In January 2012, about 150 Foxconn employees threatened to commit mass suicide in protest at their working conditions. Few people in Western countries would find these conditions acceptable, yet we all own the products they manufacture—the BlackBerry, iPad, iPhone, Kindle, PlayStation 4, Xbox One, Nokia, and Wii U. If we think about it at all, we justify it to ourselves by saying that there isn't anything we can do about it, or perhaps we tell ourselves that at least they are getting a wage and it would be worse if Foxconn stopped employing them. Or we tell ourselves that even if *we* stop buying their products, others will continue to buy them, and so there isn't much point. And, likely, people working for Apple, Dell, Acer, Google, Blackberry, Cisco, Hewlett-Packard, Nintendo, Amazon, Sony, and Microsoft tell themselves something similar so that they can sleep at night, too.

And we've already seen how consequentialism even makes its way into organizations that are supposed to be the founders and protectors of our moral codes—religions. How many high-ranking popes, cardinals, and bishops in the Catholic Church were involved in moving child-raping priests around from diocese to diocese, or knew about the practice but did nothing about it except buy the silence of the victims, to protect the reputation and funds of the Church and their careers? When even religious leaders are guilty

of sacrificing their ethics because "the ends justify the means,"
how much hope can we have for corporate CEOs?

Intelligence organizations are excellent at using consequentialism to justify their actions. From the 1950s until the 1970s, the
CIA secretly and illegally performed a range of experiments on
human subjects called Project MKUltra,[127] intended to identify and
develop drugs and procedures to be used in interrogations and
torture, to weaken the individual to force confessions through
mind control. The research was conducted at eighty institutions,
including forty-four colleges and universities, as well as hospitals,
prisons, and pharmaceutical companies, via a series of CIA front
organizations. A 1957 CIA report stated:

> *Precautions must be taken not only to protect operations from
> exposure to enemy forces but also to conceal these activities from
> the American public in general. The knowledge that the agency
> is engaging in unethical and illicit activities would have serious
> repercussions in political and diplomatic circles.*

How many people must have been privy to the nature of these
experiments? Hundreds? Thousands? Did they justify it to themselves by thinking, "If it helps us defeat the Communists, it's all
worthwhile"?

The use of torture (or "enhanced interrogation," to use the
popular euphemism), physical and sexual abuse, rape, sodomy,
and murder by the United States military at Abu Ghraib is yet
another example. How many military personnel were able to
rationalize these practices? Only one, Sergeant Joseph M. Darby,
was horrified enough to become a whistleblower and make publicly available the Abu Ghraib photos. As a reward, he and his
wife were shunned by friends and neighbors, their property

vandalized, and they now reside in protective military custody at an undisclosed location. His wife, Bernadette, reported, "We did not receive the response I thought we would. People were, they were mean, saying he was a walking dead man, he was walking around with a bull's-eye on his head. It was scary."[128]

"People aren't pissed because I turned someone in for abuse," Darby told *Mother Jones*. "People are pissed because I turned in an American soldier for abusing an Iraqi. They don't care about right and wrong."[129]

With stories like Darby's, it's no wonder many people decide to turn a blind eye and keep their heads down, doing what's asked of them, and taking a Xanax to help them sleep at night.

It's easy to understand why many of us will prioritize keeping our jobs, our income, and our lifestyle intact, even if it means allowing something ethically dubious to happen on our watch—especially if those affected are people we don't know personally, so we don't have to see the results on a daily basis.

Maybe consequentialism has even been hard-wired into us by evolutionary biology. As long as our immediate tribe benefits from an action, who cares what happens to that other tribe over the hill? They don't even speak the same dialect as us, and they worship strange gods. If our ancestors cared more about the over-the-hill tribe than they did about their own, or even if they cared about the two equally, they might find themselves kicked out of the tribe, thereby impairing their opportunity to pass on their over-the-hill-tribe-caring genes to the next generation. This seems to be the evolutionary basis for attitudes like xenophobia. Primate studies show that chimps and bonobos, our closest evolutionary relatives, also exhibit an inherent fear of outsiders.[130]

Is it somehow cognitively and emotionally more comfortable for us to visualize and internalize the "ends"—that is, some reward—than it is to internalize the consequences of our actions on others—how our actions might affect someone else's happiness?

It doesn't take a psychopath to turn a blind eye, but by doing so, we make the psychopath's jobs easier.

Let's go back to what it takes to change the system from the inside. There are also issues of expediency and the perceived effort required to buck the system. Doing what's expected of you by your boss and colleagues is much easier than challenging the culture of an organization. People who try to significantly change a psychopathic culture are likely to face immense pressure to desist.

PROTECT AND SERVE

Of course, we also can end up with psychopaths in the police force driving toxic law enforcement cultures.

In the excellent '70s film *Serpico*, based on a true story, Al Pacino plays the role of Frank Serpico, a New York cop who discovers a hidden world of corruption and graft inside the NYPD. After witnessing police violence and payoffs, he decides to go on the record to his bosses. For his trouble, he is harassed and threatened by his NYPD colleagues, leading to him being shot in the face during a drug bust when his colleagues don't provide backup.

When Pacino was making the film, he asked the real Frank Serpico why he had stepped forward. Serpico replied, "Well, Al, I don't know. I guess I would have to say it would be because…if I didn't, who would I be when I listened to a piece of music?"

I love this quote. It speaks about his character and integrity.

Why didn't the other cops in the NYPD at the time do or say anything? Is it possible that every cop was just naturally comfortable with graft and corruption? Or did they go along to get along?

The NYPD doesn't seem to have fixed its culture since Serpico's days. Adrian Schoolcraft joined the NYPD after the attacks on New York City on September 11, 2001. In 2008, he became concerned about arrest quotas and investigations, believing an overemphasis on arrests lead to wrongful arrests and terrible police work. After raising his concerns inside his precinct, he says he was harassed, receiving a terrible evaluation (despite having previously won the Meritorious Police Duty Medal in 2006, and in 2008 being cited for his dedication to the New York City Police Department and the City of New York).

At one point, he found a paper in his locker reading: "If you don't like your job, maybe you should get another job." He claimed that he was sent by the department to psychological counseling and reassigned to a desk job. When he brought up his concerns to NYPD investigators, he was placed under "forced monitoring." Not long after that, twelve high-ranking police officers, including the Deputy Chief Michael Marino, entered his apartment while he was at home, getting a key from the landlord by telling him that they believed Schoolcraft was suicidal. They then had him involuntarily committed to a psychiatric ward, handcuffed to a bed and prevented from using a telephone.

When his father finally tracked him down six days later and had him released, Schoolcraft was suspended from the force and stopped receiving a paycheck. In the following weeks, NYPD officers continued to regularly visit his house, knocking on his door and sitting outside.

Schoolcraft was finally motivated to hand over a series of recordings he had secretly made of his conversations with his superiors, including during the home invasion, to alternative newspaper *The Village Voice*. They became known as "The NYPD Tapes."

In March 2012, the paper published an article that revealed that a secret NYPD investigation had vindicated Schoolcraft, finding evidence of quotas and underreporting of crimes. *The New York Times* said the report concluded there was "a concerted effort to deliberately underreport crime in the 81st Precinct."

Schoolcraft filed a lawsuit against the NYPD, eventually receiving a mere $600,000 in compensation. Deputy Chief Michael Marino retired on a disability pension in 2014, which means he will receive $135,000 a year, most of it tax-free.[131]

Does the NYPD's handling of the Schoolcraft incident suggest that it has a healthy organizational culture? Who are they protecting and serving?

CHAPTER FOUR

MY COLD DEAD HANDS

*"If a lie is only printed often enough,
it becomes a quasi-truth, and if such a truth is
repeated often enough, it becomes an article of belief,
a dogma, and men will die for it."*

—*The Crown of a Life,* Isa Blagden (1869)

In his book *Political Parties* (1911), Robert Michels, a German sociologist, wrote that all complex organizations, regardless of how democratic they start out, eventually develop into oligarchies (where a small group of people has control). It's known as the "Iron Law of Oligarchy."[132]

If an individual has risen to the top of their particular field, whether it's in the business world, politics, or religion, we should naturally expect them to do everything in their power to stay on top, as they will have little motivation to change the system that got them there in the first place, unless, of course, those changes are designed to increase their power. As we saw in the last chapter, this desire to maintain the status quo inside their organizations can lead to a lack of reform and brutal attacks on criticism.

But what if the attacks come from outside the organization?

In this chapter, I want to explore the different kinds of tools the elite, some of whom are psychopaths, use to maintain their power and stage their war on the minds of the masses. The tools include religion, lobby groups, front groups, the corporate media, the education system, and the broader use of outright lies and propaganda.

It seems reasonable to assume that the elite will want to protect their organizations, and therefore themselves, from external criticism and reform, as much as they do from internal changes. This explains why such people are usually politically conservative—they want to conserve the status quo. Even if they vote for the less conservative of the major political parties in their country (for example, the Democratic Party in the USA, the Labor Party in the UK or the Australian Labor Party in Australia, etc.), you can bet they will still be relatively conservative on most issues that affect their wealth and power. They might be pro-gay marriage or support doing something about climate change or gun control—but what is their position on increasing taxes on the top 1 percent of income earners or increasing corporate tax rates? What is their view on increasing government regulations and oversight in their particular industry? What is their position on capping executive pay and bonuses or jail time for white-collar crime?

Take, for example, Qantas' openly gay CEO Alan Joyce (Qantas is Australia's largest airline). While very outspoken on issues like same-sex marriage, calling it "the morally right thing to do," he also defends his $24 million salary,[133] something others find morally unjustifiable.

You would expect them to be against policies that might have an impact on the continued success of their organization, which, in turn, would also affect their power. Things have been working out pretty well for them the way they are, so, naturally, they don't want to shake the apple cart. I get it; I really do. But what's best for their power isn't necessarily what's best for the rest of society. And you would expect them to use their control to fight for keeping the system stacked in their favor.

Let's say that there is a political party that wants to pass legislation that might weaken an organization's financial success—maybe deregulation of their industry, perhaps the introduction of new carbon emission regulations, possibly increasing the power of labor unions, and so on. What would you expect the CEO of an organization in that industry to do? I would expect her to try to use whatever power she has to prevent the political party from passing that legislation. And what tools does she potentially have at her disposal, as the CEO of a significant and financially successful corporation?

For a start, she probably has access to:

- Lots of money.
- Lots of lawyers.
- Lots of political influence.
- Lots of media influence.
- Lots of friends in high places—significant shareholders of her company who are also substantial shareholders of other significant corporations that also have lots of money, lawyers, and political and media influence.

And if her organization's financial success is being threatened, would you expect her to use each of these tools to her advantage? I would. It just stands to reason. It doesn't make her a terrible person—it just makes her human. She doesn't have to be a psychopath to want to protect her lifestyle. The lengths that she is willing to go to protect it will determine whether or not she is a psychopath, but not the initial desire to preserve her lifestyle.

The desire of the people in the top ranks of our organizations to protect their power, and the loads of cash and influence they have at their disposal to do so, is the flaw that lies deep in the heart of capitalism.

As Einstein pointed out, large organizations usually control immense power and the means to influence democracy well beyond the reach of any individual or even most groups of concerned citizens—and even more power than most political parties. The only thing that can get in their way is usually another equally influential organization with interests that are not precisely aligned. In these situations, we see a struggle for domination between organizational interests. The people sit on the sidelines and watch—or don't watch. How often is the general public aware of the backroom meetings between lobbyists and politicians where they discuss the text of upcoming legislation? Rarely. These meetings are rarely made public and seldom covered by the media. Sometimes, like the negotiations for the Trans-Pacific Partnership, they are kept secret by corporations and politicians.[134]

Businesses, in particular, have a lot of influence on which stories are given coverage in the corporate media. This influence takes many forms. In some cases, it may be a direct influence.

For example, the business or its principal shareholders or executives may also be significant shareholders in the media company (especially when a small number of companies control most of the media)[135] and can exercise their seat on the board or their friendship with members of the board or a threat to dump stock (i.e., sell it cheaply) and drive down the share price (which can cause a range of problems for management and shareholders) to influence the stories that get covered and to what extent.

Alternately, a business may use an indirect form of influence via their advertising budget. As the primary source of revenue for most media corporations comes from advertising—selling access to customer attention—a business that threatens to withhold its advertising spend from a media organization can often get them to pay attention to whatever agenda they have. The CEO calls the publisher and threatens, "If you run that story, then we'll pull all of our advertising and give it to your competitor paper/TV station/website."

A DIFFERENT KIND OF TRUTH

Some people think propaganda only happens in third-world dictatorships, with a cult of personality built up around the "glorious leader" and dramatic posters depicting how the population is genetically or morally superior to others. But that's only one kind of propaganda. In the West, we have just as much, if not more, propaganda in our daily lives, but because we've grown up knowing nothing different, we don't even notice it.

According to French philosopher and sociologist Jacques Ellul, most people are easy prey for propaganda,

> *"because of their firm but entirely erroneous conviction that it is composed only of lies and 'tall stories' and that, conversely, what is true cannot be propaganda. But modern propaganda has long disdained the ridiculous lies of past and outmoded forms of propaganda. It operates instead with many different kinds of truth—half truth, limited truth, truth out of context."*[136]

We need to understand that modern propaganda is far more sophisticated and insidious than the kind Big Brother uses in the novel *Nineteen Eighty-Four*.

We get the word propaganda from the Vatican. The Congregatio de Propaganda Fide or "congregation for propagating the faith" is a committee of cardinals established 1622 by Gregory XV to supervise foreign missions. Propaganda means "to propagate."

Propaganda is defined today as any form of indoctrination in which one group systematically uses manipulative methods to persuade others to conform to a particular way of thinking, any movement to propagate some practice or ideology. Another word for it is simply brainwashing. And we are all brainwashed from the day we are born, by our governments, media, and corporate and religious leaders—the very people we are told we should trust, the very people we are told are looking out for us, the very people who have control of our money, our politics, our education, our information, our spiritual path, and our military.

And they have to do it. The elite, the psychopaths, know that if we wanted to, the public could start a revolution and cripple the economic system that keeps them on top at any time. To prevent that, we need to be kept ignorant of the relevant facts, overworked, poor, heavily in debt, and distracted. And all of that takes systematic brainwashing. To keep the public from organizing and revolting, it's imperative to brainwash them into believing what the elite are doing is right, ethical, and just and that we are poor because we just didn't work hard enough—but we might get there one day if we just keep on believing.

It reminds me of Joe Bageant's description of his "dittohead friend Buck" in his book *Deer Hunting with Jesus*:

> *He believes in the American Dream as he perceives it, which is entirely in terms of money. He wants that Jaguar, the big house, and the blonde bimbo with basketball-size tits. At age thirty-nine and divorced, he still believes that's what life is about and is convinced he can nail it if he works hard enough. The sports car, the Rolex, McMansion, the works.*[137]

It's like some form of Stockholm Syndrome, where hostages develop sympathetic sentiments toward their captors and end up sharing their opinions and acquiring romantic feelings for them as a survival strategy during captivity.

David Hume, the eighteenth-century Scottish philosopher, was fascinated with "the easiness with which the many are governed by the few, the implicit submission with which men resign." In his book *Of the Original Contract*, he said that in all societies throughout the world, the real power is in the hands of the governed. So why don't they overthrow their governments and take control of the power? He concluded that the people are governed by either force or by control of opinion. Control their attitudes, their beliefs, and you can control the power. According to Hume, this "extends to the most despotic and most military governments, as well as to the freest and most popular."

Those of us fortunate to live in a democracy are taught that our governments are "for the people, by the people," and we naturally assume this means we aren't being lied to or manipulated. Whether you live in the United States, Australia, the United Kingdom, Canada, New Zealand, France, Germany, or any other developed, democratic, capitalist country, there is a reasonable chance that you are being lied to, day in and day out. Of course, not everything you hear is a lie. And perhaps "lie" is too strong a word. Let's call it being "finessed"—after all, Orwellian newspeak is part and parcel of how the system works!

The idea that we all live in a free democracy, where everyone has equal rights, and an equal say in how society works, is an illusion that has been engineered and perpetuated by the largest of our organizations for as long as our countries have existed. Understanding why these illusions have been created and why they will remain until we re-engineer society is part of the journey to understanding the modern world.

If you asked most astronomers in the early sixteenth century what astronomy was all about, they probably would have told you that it was the study of how the stars and planets revolved around the Earth. The very definition of what they did prevented them from realizing the truth—that the Earth revolved around the Sun with the rest of the planets in our solar system. Sometimes our illusions about how things work can be so influential that they prevent us from seeing the truth—even when it is right there in front of our eyes.

Noam Chomsky, institute professor emeritus at the Massachusetts Institute of Technology, author, political activist, and considered the world's leading intellectual,[138] stated in a 2013 interview that the United States is "no longer a functioning democracy, we're really a plutocracy." [139] And that was several years before Trump won the White House!

Plutocracy is government by the wealthy. Of course, this has been the most common form of government throughout history. Whether we call them kings, emperors, or presidents, the people with political power are usually either wealthy themselves or are financially supported by the wealthy. Recognizing that this is how our so-called democratic governments work today helps us to develop a model that explains a lot of how our propaganda system works.

Unfortunately, the models most of us have been given for understanding how our societies work are broken.

Those of us fortunate enough to have been born in the developed world after World War II have been indoctrinated relentlessly by our governments, by the corporate media, and by corporate advertising. We have been sold a story about how wonderful our societies are and how we fit into that picture. It's not that much different from the kinds of propaganda we would expect in the Soviet Union or under Kim Jong-il.

We have been sold that story for so long and so persuasively that we believe it to be true. Billions of dollars are spent every year reinforcing these ideas in our brains. The indoctrination is so pervasive that it is tough for people to pull themselves out of it.

One of the most prominent ways that we are brainwashed is through corporate media. It's essential to remember that they are for-profit corporations and that they exist for the same reason all for-profit corporations do—to make money for their stakeholders.

Like drug dealers in a depressed urban environment, corporations, especially if they are run by psychopathic cultures, don't care about the health of their customers. They probably don't want their customers to die as that will interfere with the source of the money. However, if a few die here and there—or if the people dying weren't going to contribute to profits in the first place—then that's okay. That's collateral damage. There are always going to be more customers out there to replace them.

PROPAGENDA

The propaganda in Western countries has become so ubiquitous, sophisticated, and disciplined during the late twentieth and early twenty-first centuries that someone coined a new term for it—*propagenda*. Propagenda is the act of creating an environment in which only a specific range of topics are allowed for discussion. Discussions about issues that don't fit the decreed agenda are prevented from getting coverage by the media, the politicians, or the organizations that enable them. They are ignored, obfuscated, shut down, or covered up. You have been conditioned, not just to believe the lies, but not even to notice them.

In their book, *Manufacturing Consent* (1988), Edward S. Herman and Noam Chomsky proposed a theory called "The Propaganda Model" for explaining how the populations of Western democratic countries are kept calm and obedient by the "power elite." Herman and Chomsky demonstrate that there are systemic biases, supported by a series of "filters," in the mass media that have fundamental economic causes. These filters ensure that only the people who have the right biases, which essentially agree with the worldviews of the elite, can get employed and to build a career in the media and academia. Everyone else is either filtered out—fired or prevented from rising through the ranks—or filter themselves out by resigning.

The Australian social psychologist Alex Carey, the first person to provide a dedicated analysis of modern propaganda in democracies, wrote that

> *The twentieth century has been characterized by three developments of great political importance: the growth of democracy, the growth of corporate power, and the growth of corporate propaganda as a means of protecting corporate power against democracy.*[140]

According to Carey, the extension of the right to vote and the rise of the union movement in the first half of the twentieth century were perceived as threats to corporate power. This threat was met by learning to use propaganda "as an effective weapon for managing governments and public opinion."

> *Corporate propaganda has two main objectives: to identify the free-enterprise system in popular consciousness with every cherished value, and to identify interventionist governments and strong unions (the only agencies capable of checking the complete domination of society by the corporations) with tyranny, oppression and even subversion.*

One thing that many people don't realize is that, in the first half of the twentieth century, there were robust newspapers that not only took a strong stance against capitalism and imperialism but also had a very significant readership.

For example, in 1933, the *Daily Herald*, a British newspaper that had opposed British involvement in World War I, supported British industrial strikes, supported the Russian Revolution but later condemned the Nazi-Soviet Pact and the Soviet invasion of Finland, became the world's best-selling daily newspaper and even into the 1960s had almost double the readership of *The Times*, the *Financial Times* and the *Guardian* combined.

According to James Curran, professor of communications at Goldsmiths University of London and author of *Media and Power*, the *Herald* was a "freewheeling vehicle of the left, an important channel for the dissemination of syndicalist and socialist ideas." Even though it achieved 8.1 percent of national daily circulation, the paper only received 3.5 percent of net advertising revenue, significantly impacting its ability to survive.

Corporate advertisers aren't likely to support a newspaper that actively speaks out against capitalism. As British journalist Andrew Marr wrote in his memoir, *My Trade*: "It's hard to make the sums add up when you are kicking the people who write the checks."

The paper staggered on until 1969 when it was bought by a then little-known Australian newspaper owner called Rupert Murdoch who turned it into the sexist, celebrity-obsessed, news-lite *The Sun*. The first headline under Murdoch was "HORSE DOPE SENSATION."

It still has one of the highest circulations of all British newspapers, but of course, it has dispensed with supporting the political issues for which it was initially known.

As U.S. media analyst Robert McChesney succinctly put it, "So long as the media are in corporate hands, the task of social change will be vastly more difficult, if not impossible."[141]

"Propaganda is to democracy what
violence is to a dictatorship."

—Noam Chomsky

Every news editor or radio or television news producer knows that they have a limited number of inches or minutes to fill with content every day. And there are countless stories to fill them with. How do they decide which stories they are going to cover? They take into consideration a combination of factors.

- Is it going to generate attention from our readers, listeners, or viewers? Keep in mind that all corporate media exists to make a profit, typically by selling access to the brains of their audiences to other businesses in the form of advertising. The more attention they can create with their news, the more advertising revenue they can generate from it.

- Does it fit with the existing narrative that we, as a media organization, are promoting? Media companies spend a lot of time trying to work out who their target audience is. Example: Fox News's target audience is older, conservative, religious, white people. The same is true for most of News Corporation's global media properties (except maybe their movies and some of their spin-off cable channels like FXX) and their interests in China. So, if your target audience is older, conservative, religious, white people, and that's who you are trying to sell to advertisers, you are going to choose the news that you show them carefully. It has to map to the narrative to which you've previously held. If you've spent years reinforcing a particular narrative, and you suddenly choose news stories that conflict with it (e.g., if you started saying the insane size of the military budget and not illegal immigrants are the primary cause of America's economic problems), at best you're going to confuse your audience—at worst, you'll piss them and your advertisers off. It's crucial to select stories that reinforce your narrative.

- Does it fit with our overall corporate goals? If a media company is owned by a parent company that also makes billions of dollars from manufacturing and selling weapons, which are sold to Saudi Arabia (for example NBC when GE owned it), then you are unlikely to take a hard stance in your news coverage about how U.S. arms sales to the Saudis often end up in the hands of terrorist organizations.

Here's an example of the last scenario.

In 2010, it was widely covered in the global news that President Obama had agreed to sell a record $60 billion of arms to Saudi Arabia. A quick Google search for "$60bn Saudi arms sale" returns nearly 10,000 entries. It was reported by *The Guardian*, Al Jazeera, BBC, *Financial Times*, *The Independent*, *Wall Street Journal*, and so forth.

But when I tried the same search on NBC's website, I couldn't find a single story covering the sale.

Another example: in 2010, it was widely reported that the United States also reached a separate $25.6 billion deal to sell the Saudis military helicopters, some manufactured by General Electric.

Again, that news was covered by many major news agencies—but not NBC.

THE FOURTH ESTATE

The media used to be called the "Fourth Estate," which comes from the days in England when there were three primary centers of power—the clergy, the nobility, and the commoners. The press was called the fourth estate, the fourth center of power.

Oscar Wilde once wrote:

> In old days men had the rack. Now they have the Press. That is an improvement certainly. But still it is very bad, and wrong, and demoralizing. Somebody—was it Burke?—called journalism the fourth estate. That was true at the time no doubt. But at the present moment it is the only estate. It has eaten up the other three. The Lords Temporal say nothing, the Lords Spiritual have nothing to say, and the House of Commons has nothing to say and says it. We are dominated by Journalism.[142]

The original role of the Fourth Estate was to keep the others honest.

When for-profit corporations run the news media, it makes sense that the news they choose to cover will mostly, if not always, fit neatly within the model of society that the corporations wish to promote. It would not serve for a corporation to run many news stories that might have the long-term effect of reducing their profits. Remember—corporations are, above all else, survival machines. They exist to maintain power. And if psychopaths rise to the top of the media organizations, how do you think they will use them?

Stories that question the values of our society will struggle to see the light of day. For example, how many stories have you seen in the mainstream media that argue against capitalism or the corporatocracy? It's certainly not the case that those arguments can't be made. They *do* get made, in alternative media and in books. But you won't often see them in the mainstream media because they run counter to the values of the corporation.

In the same way, you wouldn't expect a media organization to give fair coverage to scandals involving their own company.

During the 2012 Levenson inquiry into the culture, practices, and ethics of the British press following the *News International* phone-hacking scandal, evidence emerged that Rupert Murdoch and his papers wield enormous influence over both the Labour and Conservative parties in the UK. The conclusion reached by a committee of UK ministers was that "Rupert Murdoch is 'not a fit person' to exercise stewardship of a major international company."[143]

The committee concluded that the culture of the company's newspapers "permeated from the top" and "speaks volumes about the lack of effective corporate governance at News Corporation and News International."

And they didn't just point the finger at Rupert. They pointed it at the entire leadership of News Corp.:

> *The committee concluded that Les Hinton, the former executive chairman of News International, was "complicit" in a cover-up at the newspaper group, and that Colin Myler, former editor of the News of the World, and the paper's ex-head of legal, Tom Crone, deliberately withheld crucial information and answered questions falsely. All three were accused of misleading parliament by the culture select committee.*[144]

A very telling example of how media companies manipulate

the news they choose to cover is too look at News Corporation's coverage of the phone-hacking scandal.

The Australian Centre for Independent Journalism at the University of Technology Sydney (which, unfortunately, closed down in 2017) once analyzed News Corp's handling of its own terrible press.[145] They looked at one week of coverage of the inquiry in a range of Australian papers, including those owned by News Corp (which make up 70 percent of Australian print media). They found that while News Corp's newspapers *did* mention the inquiry, they ran far fewer stories than non-newspapers, and what they did run was buried deep in the paper, and relied mostly on commentary and editorial, much of which was critical of the inquiry.

Not one editorial supported the idea that there should be a similar inquiry into Australia's media.

> *In the week under review, no News Ltd paper acknowledged any problems for News Corporation's power or practices other than phone hacking. And phone hacking was only denounced in editorials once a statement was issued by News CEO John Hartigan describing phone hacking as "a terrible slur on our craft."*

We can see from this small example that corporate media will usually strive to protect its interests and the interests of its industry—logical behavior, to be sure, but it helps us understand the inherent bias that exists at the heart of our news media.

And what do we know about the quality of the news media? A separate study run by the ACIJ found that across ten hard-copy Australia newspapers, "nearly 55 percent of stories analyzed were driven by some form of public relations—a sad indictment on the state of Australian reporting."[146]

People working in the news media, for example, journalists, editors, and so forth, will often argue that there is no bias and that they are faithfully reporting the news as best they can. However, as Chomsky and Herman pointed out in *Manufacturing Consent*, this is what you would expect. Organizations, being survival machines, tend to hire and promote people who "buy into" the mission and purpose of the survival of the institution.

And yet sometimes the curtain is briefly drawn aside, and we get a short glimpse of the wizard revealed in his true colors.

According to an interview on ABC Radio on June 2012, one of Australia's most prominent businesspeople argued that the board of a newspaper *should* have the right to influence the editorial direction of the company's media outlets, especially if the actions were designed to increase the company's profits. Channel Ten (a leading Australian TV network) board member and Hungry Jacks (Australia's version of Burger King) founder, Jack Cowin, told ABC Radio that newspapers are a business, not a public service and that the board has the right to decide what kinds of stories that business should cover.[147]

Cowin also happens to be one of the closest advisers to Gina Rinehart, the mining magnate who tried to buy control of one of Australia's leading newspapers. When Australian Prime Minister Scott Morrison had a state dinner with Donald Trump in September 2019, guess who he took as his honored guest? Gina.

As we can see, "editorial independence" isn't a clear-cut issue.

Any student of the history of newspapers already understands that papers have always been used for political and commercial influence.

According to Michael Wolff's 2008 book, *The Man Who Owns*

The News, Rupert Murdoch entirely altered the political landscape in New York within his first year of owning the *New York
Post* in the mid-1970s:

> *He decides to use the Post as an instrument to elect some-
> body—he understands that it doesn't really matter whom, just that
> the Post be responsible. After interviewing each of the prospective
> candidates for New York City mayor, he settles on the perhaps least
> likely guy—that is, the one who needs him the most. It's Ed Koch, a
> congressman from Greenwich Village... The entire paper is put in
> service to the Koch election. The Post is transformed into an ebul-
> lient narrative of Koch's presence, charm, and inevitability. The
> least charismatic man in the city becomes the most charismatic.[148]*

When Koch was elected mayor of New York in 1977, Murdoch
became one of the most influential people in the city. And this is
only a few years after he arrived in New York and had been seen by
the "old money" as easy picking. Koch was Murdoch's first American political coup. Of course, nearly forty years later, another
Murdoch media entity, Fox News, would play an enormous role
in getting Donald Trump elected president of the United States.

Going back to the late nineteenth century, the term *yellow
journalism* was coined by Erwin Wardman, the editor of the *New
York Press,* to reflect the first "media war"—Pulitzer versus Hearst.
Circulation battles between Joseph Pulitzer's *New York World* and
William Randolph Hearst's *New York Journal* culminated in both
of the papers using scandal-mongering, outlandish headlines, and
rampant sensationalism to try to outsell each other.

One of the turning points in the history of propaganda was the
Spanish-American War (April–August 1898). Hearst and Pulitzer

both fabricated stories and embellished others to increase circulation and justify American intervention, which led to a war and even greater circulation. This strategy was immortalized in fiction in Orson Welles' masterpiece *Citizen Kane*. Kane, the young, ambitious newspaper proprietor, receives a telegram from his reporter in Cuba, who says there isn't any war to report on, so he's spending his time writing poems. Kane issues the smug reply:

> *"You provide the prose poems—*
> *I'll provide the war."*[149]

In Britain during the early twentieth century, Murdoch's predecessors, press barons like Max Aitken (aka Lord Beaverbrook) owner of the *Daily Express*, and Alfred Harmsworth (Lord Northcliffe), owner of the *Daily Mail* and *The Times*, were both heavily involved in anti-German propaganda that promoted Britain's involvement in World War I. One of their competitors claimed that "next to the Kaiser, Lord Northcliffe has done more than any living man to bring about the war."[150]

Northcliffe, who controlled 40 percent of the morning newspaper circulation in Britain, 45 percent of the evening, and 15 percent of the Sunday circulation, actually played a huge role in getting Lloyd George elected prime minister in 1916. For his efforts, he was offered a position in the cabinet. He turned that down—and was officially made "director of propaganda" instead. Imagine Rupert Murdoch being given the same title and you get how ludicrous this was. A media baron, who thought of himself as Napoleon reborn, being given a role in the government.

In return for supporting Lloyd George's coalition government in the 1918 general election, Northcliffe demanded the government accept a list of the names of people who should be given roles in his government. To his credit, Lloyd George refused. That's just one example of how the "free press" works in the West.

In more recent times, we have seen the role of Judith Miller at the *New York Times* in publishing propaganda that helped lead the U.S. into its invasion of Iraq in 2003.

As Salon.com noted:[151]

> *Since her early days at the Times, when she inserted CIA misinformation into a piece on Libya, she's always been a tool of power. She was the voice of the Defense Department, embedded at the Times. She was hyping bullshit stories about Iraq's WMD capabilities as far back as 1998, and in the run-up to the war, her front-page scoops were cited by the Bush administration as evidence that Saddam needed to be taken out, right away...Lying exile grifter Ahmed Chalabi fed her the worst of the nonsense designed to push America into toppling Saddam Hussein (and giving Iraq to him), and she pushed that nonsense into the newspaper of record. She got everything wrong.*

Miller used Chalabi as an anonymous source for her reporting about Saddam's efforts to build a nuclear weapon. Chalabi was born into one of Iraq's wealthiest and most influential families. He left the country after the military coup in 1958 and lived most of his life in the United States. In the intervening years, Chalabi became a banker (the family business) and, after a bank he founded in Jordan collapsed, was convicted and sentenced in absentia to twenty-two years in prison for bank fraud. In 1992, he created an Iraqi opposition group, the INC, that was mainly funded by the United States. Chalabi used some of the funding to hire U.S. lobbying group BKSH & Associates to help him sell the idea of overthrowing Saddam to the American public. Two of the founders of BKSH were Paul Manafort, Donald Trump's former campaign manager, who is currently serving time for five counts of tax fraud and two counts of bank fraud—and Roger Stone, who served as an advisor to the Trump campaign.

Miller didn't mention anything about Chalabi's background of fraud and corruption, his role with the INC, his funding by the U.S. government, or the lobbying firm he hired, when she published her stories in the *New York Times*. And the U.S. government, led by Bush, Cheney, and Rumsfeld, used her stories to back up their argument that Saddam was building weapons of mass destruction and that Iraq needed to be invaded.

So, to put it another way—the U.S. government gave Chalabi tax dollars, which he used to hire a lobbying firm. This firm helped him get anonymous, positive, and unquestioning coverage in the *New York Times*, which the U.S. government then used to justify a considerable military build-up and the invasion of Iraq—also paid for by tax dollars, much of which ended up in the hands of American businesspeople.

Is it any wonder, then, that, according to at least one study,[152] the media is now the least trusted institution in the world? According to Glenn Greenwald of *The Intercept*, "featuring lobbyists and corporate consultants to analyze the news without disclosing their glaring conflicts of interest" is "a scandalous media-wide practice."[153]

In late 2018, he revealed that the Daily Beast, MSNBC, PBS, and CNN all used tainted sources to comment on Saudi Arabia and the murder of journalist Jamal Khashoggi. He had previously disclosed that *The Washington Post*, Khashoggi's employer at the time of his death, simultaneously hired journalists "who maintain among the closest links to the Saudi regime and have the longest and most shameful history of propagandizing on their behalf." If this practice is as widespread as Greenwald suggests, where do we turn for a trusted analysis of events?

THE INTELLIGENT FEW

While propaganda has been around in some form since the dawn of humanity, the origin of modern public relations stems from World War I and perhaps the supreme PR story of all time.

As hard as it may be to believe, in the early twentieth century, the United States' military was outnumbered by Germany's by a factor of twenty. For the first couple of years of WWI, U.S. President Woodrow Wilson had advocated neutrality "in thought and deed" for the United States, and most of the country agreed with him. The war happening in Europe—a ridiculous war that should never have happened—had nothing to do with America.

Then, as now, there were fortunes to be made during a major war. America's neutrality enabled their bankers and manufacturers to finance and supply all sides of the conflict. And they did.

The British, however, with their superior navy, were able to blockade Germany and prevent America from trading with them. In response, the Germans announced that they would use submarines to attack any ships trading with England. This led to some bright spark in the USA deciding to try to ship ammunition to England undetected in the holds of unarmed passenger ships.

Of course, the Germans found out about this cunning and dangerous strategy, and on May 7, 1915, they torpedoed the RMS Lusitania, a passenger ship that was secretly carrying four million rounds of .303 bullets from the USA to England. Both the UK and the USA long denied that the Lusitania was carrying ammunition, but evidence of the cargo was discovered in the wreckage ninety years later. The sinking of the Lusitania, which happened to be carrying 128 Americans among its passengers, began the process of changing American attitudes about entry into the war. (Of course, there was no punishment for the individuals or corporations who were responsible for putting the ammunition in the hold of the ship and endangering the lives of the civilians.) Wilson, though, ran for election again in 1916 (and won) on a neutrality ticket. The sinking of the Lusitania, although long held as the reason America entered the war, really had little to do with it. It wasn't even an American ship. The Germans agreed to halt using torpedoes to sink ships, and Wilson was happy.

Unfortunately, the Germans flip-flopped on the torpedo issue, which upset the Americans. The Germans also tried, unsuccessfully, to get Mexico to attack the U.S., which they found out about and weren't very happy about that either.

Neither of these things, however, were the primary cause of America's entry into the war. As usual, the real reasons were economic. When we want to understand the causes of many political events, we should follow the advice of the Watergate informant Deep Throat and "follow the money." Or, as the ancient Roman statesman Cicero put it "cui bono" (who benefits?).

The U.S. had huge economic investments with the British and French in the lead up to WWI. The Allies (mainly Britain and

France), together with their colonies, had purchased 77 percent of American exports in 1913 —which was all the more significant because the American economy had been struggling at the time. According to banker J. P. Morgan:

> *The war opened during a period of hard time that had continued in America for over a year. Business throughout the country was depressed, farm prices were deflated, unemployment was serious, the heavy industries were working far below capacity, [and] bank clearings were off.*[154]

In the first couple of years after the start of the conflict (before the Americans got directly involved), the Allies purchased a lot of American steel, bolstering the American economy. But the Allies were cash poor, so they had to buy the steel, and other American products, on credit. The Allies took out the biggest loan in financial history from private American banks —brokered of course by Morgan. He also negotiated a deal that positioned his company as the sole munitions and supplies purchaser during World War I for the British and French governments. His cut was a 1 percent commission on $3 billion—about $30 million in 1914 or $753 million in today's dollars.

By the way, Morgan's father, J. P. Morgan Sr., actually created the corporation called U.S. Steel, which, at one point, made 67 percent of all the steel produced in the United States and was known on Wall Street as just "The Corporation" due to its overwhelming size and importance. You have to admire his son's chutzpah—as a banker, he profited by organizing the loans to Britain and France; as the owner of U.S. Steel, he benefited again from the spending of those loans on steel, as well as earning a one percent commission on purchases of cotton, chemicals, and food.

If the Allies were to lose, then they would not be able to pay the banks back (amounting to about $2 billion 1917 dollars), which could cause the U.S. economy to collapse (or so the thinking went at the time). Wilson needed to reverse his position and find a way to convince the American people to get involved in a war he had been saying for two years had nothing to do with them.

To finance the war effort, the government tried to sell "Liberty Bonds." A bond is, simply put, when the government says, "Loan me your money, and we'll pay you back later with interest." But the U.S. public was unenthusiastic, and the government struggled to get the people to hand over their cash.

And that's where the Committee on Public Information came into effect. CPI was charged by President Wilson to "engineer the consent" of the American people for their involvement in World War I. CPI was an independent agency of the government, but it was composed by the Secretary of State, the Secretary of War, and the Secretary of the Navy, so it actually wasn't all that independent. The fourth member of the committee was the civilian Chairman George Creel, an "investigative journalist."

Creel gathered the nation's artists to create thousands of paintings, posters, cartoons, and sculptures promoting the War. He also gathered support from choirs, social clubs, and religious organizations to join "The World's Greatest Adventure in Advertising." He recruited about 75,000 "Four-Minute Men," who spoke about the war at social events for an ideal length of four minutes, considered at that time to be the average human attention span. They covered the draft, rationing, bond drives, victory gardens, and why America was fighting. It was estimated that by the end of the war, they had made more than 7.5 million speeches to 314 million people.

This was, of course, in the years before radio, film, television, and Netflix had any significant penetration. Imagine the same kind of thing happening today—the government organizing tens of thousands of people to travel around the country giving propaganda speeches to convince the people to go to war.

To help sell the Liberty Bonds, Morgan also bought a controlling interest in twenty-five of the top American newspapers. He wanted to make sure he got paid back a $400 million loan to Britain from the first Liberty Bond drive. The "isolationists continued to accuse the House of Morgan of whipping up pro-war sentiment."[155]

After this massive propaganda campaign, the number of Americans ready to go to war rose from roughly 380,000 in 1915 to 4.8 million in all the military branches by the end of World War I.

Of course, none of the reasons why the U.S. had initially stayed out of the war had changed. It still had little chance of spreading to North America. The Mexicans had no intention (or capability) of launching an attack on the U.S. It was justified to the American people using the usual hyperbole, used by autocrats and imperialists since the dawn of time—by resorting to Pavlovian triggers such as "peace," "justice," and "freedom." However, it is quite clear that the U.S. entered WWI largely because of economic reasons.

In the end, World War I cost the American public about $33 billion ($828 trillion when adjusted for inflation), a sum sufficient to have carried on the Revolutionary War continuously for more than 1,000 years at the rate of expenditure that war involved.

About two-thirds were for direct costs; the remainder (over $10 billion) was loaned to America's allies—who never paid it back.

The U.S. was debt-free before the war. After the war, it had a public debt of $25 billion.[156]

Why would the U.S. spend $33 billion to recover $2 billion in loans? That doesn't seem to make much sense. But when you realize that it was the banks who loaned most of the money and the people who funded the war (via their taxes and "Liberty Bonds"), then it starts to become quite clear. It's the same model for Western countries getting involved in foreign wars today. Use public funds to fight the war, while private corporations benefit from the result, through reconstruction contracts and trade agreements with the government of the post-war country. It's another form of the socialization of costs and the privatization of benefits. It's like getting your friends to invest in your business and then keeping all of the profits for yourself and justifying it by saying they are all better off because there is one more successful business in town. I'll go into it in more detail later on in the book.

The Committee on Public Information was the engine behind the reprogramming of the American people. Their success in motivating the U.S. to support a war has been studied, repeated, and refined by successive administrations over the last century. And it expanded to become a global propaganda campaign.

The founder of modern propaganda, Edward Bernays, a nephew of Sigmund Freud, worked for the CPI. Just after WWI, he issued a press release that stated CPI's role after the war was to keep up "a worldwide propaganda to disseminate American accomplishments and ideals."

In the opening of his classic 1928 book *Propaganda*, Bernays explained his view of its role in modern Western societies:

> *The conscious and intelligent manipulation of the organized habits and opinions of the masses is an important element in democratic society. Those who manipulate this unseen mechanism of society constitute an invisible government which is the true ruling power of our country. We are governed, our minds are molded, our tastes formed, our ideas suggested, largely by men we have never heard of. This is a logical result of the way in which our democratic society is organized. Clearly it is the intelligent minorities which need to make use of propaganda continuously and systematically. In the active proselytizing minorities in whom selfish interests and public interests coincide lie the progress and development of America. Only through the active energy of the intelligent few can the public at large become aware of and act upon new ideas.*[157]

Another of my favorite examples of the power of brainwashing by the military-industrial complex is that of the bombings of Hiroshima and Nagasaki by the United States in 1945. Within the first two to four months of the attacks, the acute effects killed 90,000–166,000 people in Hiroshima and 60,000–80,000 in Nagasaki, with roughly half of the deaths in each city occurring on the first day. The vast majority of the casualties were civilians.

In the seventy-three years that have passed since Hiroshima, poll after poll has shown that most Americans think that the bombings were wholly justified. According to a survey in 2015, fifty-six percent of Americans agreed that the attacks were justified, significantly less than the 85 percent who agreed in 1945 but still high considering the facts don't support the conclusion.

The reasons most Americans cite for the justification of the bombings is that they stopped the war with Japan; that Japan started the war with the attack on Pearl Harbor and deserved punishment; and that the attacks prevented the Americans from having to invade Japan causing more deaths on both sides. These "facts" are so deeply ingrained in most American minds that they believe them to be fundamental truths. Unfortunately, they don't stand up to history.

The truth is that the United States started the war with Japan when it froze Japanese assets in the United States and embargoed the sale of oil the country needed. Economic sanctions then, as now, are considered acts of war.[158]

As for using the bombings to end the war, the U.S. was well aware in the middle of 1945 that the Japanese were prepared to surrender and expected it would happen when the USSR entered the war against them in August 1945, as pre-arranged between Truman and Stalin. The primary sticking point for the Japanese was the status of Emperor Hirohito. He was considered a god by his people, and it was impossible for them to hand him over for execution by their enemies. It would be like American Christians handing over Jesus, or Italian Catholics handing over the pope. The Allies refused to clarify what Hirohito's status would be post-surrender. In the end, they left him in place as emperor anyway.

One American who didn't think using the atom bomb was necessary was Dwight Eisenhower, future president and, at the time, the supreme allied commander in Europe. He believed:

> Japan was already defeated and that dropping the bomb
> was completely unnecessary, and…the use of a weapon whose

employment was, I thought, no longer mandatory as a measure to save American lives. It was my belief that Japan was, at that very moment, seeking some way to surrender with a minimum loss of "face."...[159]

Admiral William Leahy, chief of staff to Presidents Franklin Roosevelt and Harry Truman, agreed.

It is my opinion that the use of this barbarous weapon at Hiroshima and Nagasaki was of no material assistance in our war against Japan. The Japanese were already defeated and ready to surrender because of the effective sea blockade and the successful bombing with conventional weapons. My own feeling was that in being the first to use it, we had adopted an ethical standard common to the barbarians of the Dark Ages. I was not taught to make war in that fashion, and wars cannot be won by destroying women and children.[160]

Norman Cousins was a consultant to General MacArthur during the American occupation of Japan. Cousins wrote that

MacArthur...saw no military justification for the dropping of the bomb. The war might have ended weeks earlier, he said, if the United States had agreed, as it later did anyway, to the retention of the institution of the emperor.[161]

If General Dwight Eisenhower, General Douglas MacArthur, and Admiral William Leahy all believed dropping atom bombs on Japan was unnecessary, why do so many American civilians still today think it was?

Probably because they have been told to think that, repeatedly, in a carefully orchestrated propaganda campaign, enforced by the military-industrial complex (that Eisenhower tried to warn us about), that has run continuously since 1945.

As recently as 1995, the fiftieth anniversary of the bombings of Hiroshima and Nagasaki, the Smithsonian Institute was forced to censor its retrospective on the attacks under fierce pressure from Congress and the media because it contained "text that would have raised questions about the morality of the decision to drop the bomb."[162]

On August 15, 1945, about a week after the bombing of Nagasaki, Truman tasked the U.S. Strategic Bombing Survey to conduct a study on the effectiveness of the aerial attacks on Japan, both conventional and atomic. Did they affect the Japanese surrender?

The survey team included hundreds of American officers, civilians, and enlisted men, based in Japan. They interviewed 700 Japanese military, government, and industry officials and had access to hundreds of Japanese wartime documents.

Less than a year later, they published their conclusion—that Japan would likely have surrendered in 1945 without the Soviet declaration of war and without an American invasion: "It cannot be said that the atomic bomb convinced the leaders who effected the peace of the necessity of surrender. The decision to surrender, influenced in part by knowledge of the low state of popular morale, had been taken at least as early as 26 June at a meeting of the Supreme War Guidance Council in the presence of the Emperor."

June 26 was six weeks before the first bomb was dropped on Hiroshima. The emperor wanted to surrender and had been trying to open up discussions with the Soviets, the only country with whom they still had diplomatic relations.

According to many scholars, the final straw would have come on August 15 when the Soviet Union, as agreed months previously with the Truman administration, were planning to declare they were entering the war with Japan.

But instead of waiting, Truman dropped the first atomic bomb on Japan on August 6.

The proposed American invasion of the home islands wasn't scheduled until November.

ONE NATION UNDER GOD

If you're in charge of a significant church, you'll also want to keep your power, which means keeping your church powerful and keeping people religious. You'll use your influence with your congregation, especially those who are business and political leaders, to make sure you do whatever you can to prevent societal changes that could affect your strength.

What kinds of societal changes would make a religion panic?

In his book *One Nation Under God*,[163] Kevin Kruse explains how the idea of America as a Christian nation was promoted in the middle of the twentieth century when the business elite was worried about the direction the U.S. was heading, with the Roosevelt government's New Deal, the rise of union power, and the popularization of the tenets of socialism. So they recruited a vast number of conservative clergymen to preach the connection between faith, freedom, and free enterprise—and paid them handsomely to do it.

Business leaders in the U.S. engineered and funded a long-term campaign to recruit religious leaders to associate any attempt to curb the excesses of big business with the evils of Soviet-style communism. As the Soviet form of communism contained state-mandated atheism, this message also worked in favor of the American religious leaders—the rise of socialist thinking wasn't in their best interests either—and helped brainwash Americans into thinking that any attempt to regulate the free market was anti-Christian and anti-American.

Some preachers thought this connection with capitalism was disgusting and refused to participate. Those that did jump on board, however, were financially rewarded. They got personally wealthy, had large churches funded by grateful business leaders and were given lots of free media coverage.

One preacher who was very happy to lead the clarion call of capitalism was James W. Fifield Jr., the head of the First Congregational Church in Los Angeles. The members of his 100-room cathedral were mostly very wealthy, and Fifield ended up being called "The Apostle to Millionaires." He bought a million-dollar mansion on Wilshire Boulevard and hired a butler, a chauffeur, and a cook. First Congregational paid him $16,000 a year. Adjusted for inflation, that would be roughly a quarter-million dollars today. And this was in the middle of the Great Depression. Praise Jesus! Fifield was a trendsetter for today's obscenely wealthy preachers.

The irony, of course, is that, according to the New Testament, the earliest Christian communities practiced an early form of proto-communism!

Acts 4:32–35 tells us: "All the believers were one in heart and mind. No one claimed that any of their possessions was their own, but they shared everything they had...from time to time those who owned land or houses sold them, brought the money from the sales and put it at the apostles' feet, and it was distributed to anyone who had need."

Fortunately, not many Americans actually read the Bible, so the contradiction wasn't evident.

It was as a result of these efforts that the phrase "In God we trust" became the official motto of the United States. Originally appearing as a verse in "The Star-Spangled Banner," it had appeared on coins intermittently since the Civil War, although Theodore Roosevelt tried to have it removed, believing it was sacrilege. It wasn't until 1955 that Congress decided to put it on paper money, and in 1956, it became the country's first official motto.

And it wasn't until Ronald Reagan that the phrase "God bless America" started being used to close presidential speeches. According to authors David Domke and Kevin Coe, before Reagan, only one president had used that phrase to close out an address— Richard Nixon trying to talk his way out of the Watergate scandal in 1973.[164]

HAVE A LITTLE FAITH IN ME

Political and business leaders have other reasons for promoting religion other than tying it to the prevention of socialism. "Religion is excellent stuff for keeping common people quiet," said Napoleon Bonaparte, and the above stories suggest that business and political leaders in the United States see religion as a useful tool for maintaining social order.

If you can convince the general public that faith is at least as meritorious as reason and evidence-based decision making, perhaps it is a lot easier to get them to support other nonreligious initiatives that cannot be bolstered by evidence—such as Ponzi schemes (named after Charles Ponzi, an Italian swindler and con artist in the U.S. and Canada in the first half of the twentieth century).

For example, the FBI's Utah Securities Fraud Task Force investigated why Mormons often fall victim to typical fraud schemes. It appears that the Latter-Day Saints are highly susceptible to "affinity fraud"—where a con artist preys on a group of people who share a common bond. In 2010, the FBI said its office in Salt Lake City was one of the top five places for Ponzi schemes.[165]

Sixty percent of Utah's population is Mormon, which has made the state a prime target for religious-based affinity fraud, according to Utah's Attorney General Sean Reyes.

Is it possible that the same propensity to fall for affinity fraud makes "people of faith" easier to deceive in other areas as well? Or, conversely, are people who tend to be more skeptical harder to convince of political arguments?

For example, if you had a skeptical population that was used to demanding evidence before they believed anything and their government said, "we need to invade Iraq because Saddam Hussein has weapons of mass destruction," the population might reply "Well, show us some hard evidence, and we might believe you."

However, if you have a population that has been trained to "just have faith," then perhaps it is a lot easier to get their consent without having to worry about annoying little things like proof. It seems quite likely that one reason the Catholic Church was able to get away with hiding child rape for so many decades is that their congregations had too much faith in the clergy.

David Kuo, an evangelical Christian who served as special assistant to President George W. Bush and deputy director of the Office of Faith-Based and Community Initiatives, claimed that the White House used its faith-based initiatives program as a political tool to try to recruit "unconventional" Republican voters—including Christians among America's poor minorities,[166] while privately calling evangelical leaders "nuts," "out of control," and "goofy."[167]

In the United States, polls have found that "78 percent of religious people display the flag on their clothing, in the office or at home, while only 58 percent of nonreligious do likewise. Evangelicals were the most likely to say they displayed the flag; those Americans unaffiliated with religion the least likely."[168] Side note: as an Australian, I find America's obsession with its flag disturbing. That kind of thing doesn't happen here. Or anywhere else I've traveled. It reminds me of the extreme nationalism of Nazi Germany.

Evangelicals also claimed America was the greatest country in the world at a far higher rate than Americans of other or no religious convictions. So at least in America, it seems there is a direct connection between being an evangelical Christian and being a patriotic nationalist.

Of course, having faith is not limited to religion. According to a 2005 Gallup poll, 22 percent of American adults believe in witches, and 36 percent believe in ghosts.[169]

Other Pew surveys have found that 26 percent of Americans believe in spiritual energy located in physical things such as mountains, trees, or crystals; and 25 percent profess belief in astrology (that the location of the stars and planets can affect people's lives).[170]

Why do people still have faith in esoteric ideas in the twenty-first century? Possibly because it's hardwired into us. This kind of thinking serves or used to serve, a fundamental purpose.

There are scientific theories that suggest that there are evolutionary biological reasons for humans, in days gone by, to accept on faith what their elders told them. For example, if a senior person in your tribe told you not to eat a certain kind of berry because it was poisonous, just accepting that theory on faith probably had survival advantages. If you were too skeptical about such pronouncements and ate the berry to see for yourself whether or not it was poisonous, you might not live long enough to pass on your skeptical genetics.

In his book *Thinking, Fast and Slow*, the Nobel Prize winner and the intellectual godfather of behavioral economics, Daniel Kahneman,[171] explains the two different ways the brain forms thoughts. He refers to these ways as "System 1" and "System 2."

System 1 thoughts are fast, automatic, frequent, emotional, stereotypic, and subconscious. These include the thoughts we have that confirm our existing models for how the world works. When we are presented with concepts that appeal to our cognitive biases, they allow us to think quickly and easily. Kahneman's research shows that System 1 thinking makes us feel happy because it requires less effort and energy. However, it can also be easily fooled. Our "gut instinct" can often be wrong.

System 2 thoughts are slow, effortful, infrequent, logical, calculating, and conscious. They require more energy and effort, and, as a result, we tend to avoid them as much as possible.

An example of System 1 thinking is detecting that one object is more distant than another (easy, fast, requires no effort), while an example of System 2 thinking is parking in a narrow space (hard, takes initiative, and concentration).

If we can make decisions via System 1 quickly, easily, without having to engage our thinking muscle, the more mental energy we have to dedicate to other activities, like figuring out how to make more money or get laid (and I have a theory that the former is only useful because it helps the latter). If we have some kind of operating heuristic (rule of thumb) that allows us to make quick decisions about political, religious, and social issues, it saves us time and energy. If we merely accept that God exists, we don't have to think too hard about alternative theories and their implications. This is all the more efficient if our parents and friends have the same heuristic. In days gone by, it meant our ancestors didn't argue with tribal elders and risk being kicked out. When we assume our political party are the good guys and other parties are the bad guys, or when we assume that America always fights for freedom and the Russians are always evil, or that our prime minister is honorable, or that our CEO probably knows what she is doing, we are using System 1 thinking.

Unfortunately, System 1 plays right into the hands of the propagandists. If our brains have been saturated for decades with certain assumptions about how the world works, then it is easy for us to conform to those ideas. It requires much more effort to challenge those fundamental assumptions. It takes serious effort to train ourselves to ask hard, probing questions when watching the daily news. However, the more we force ourselves to think independently, the easier it becomes, especially as we build for ourselves new mental models for understanding how the world works.

Faith, in all its forms, makes life easier. You don't have to think as hard. But does faith make life better?

Religious people might think that modern ills are directly related to a decline in faith, but the evidence suggests the opposite.

It might be a coincidence, but the countries on top of the OECD's Better Life Index[172] usually correspond closely to the world's least religious countries—China and Japan being the major exceptions.[173]

Highly secularized countries also "tend to fare the best in terms of crime rates, prosperity, equality, freedom, democracy, women's rights, human rights, educational attainment, and life expectancy," according to the *LA Times*.[174]

Being skeptical apparently pays off.

WORKER BEES

One of the key pieces of propaganda we must fight against is the idea that a small number of people "deserve" immense wealth and power, because they work so hard, while the rest of society deserves to struggle for a lifetime because they are lazy bums. This concept is becoming pervasive in modern democracies, and its propagation is enormously destructive.

The Ayn Rand (author of *The Fountainhead* and *Atlas Shrugged*) school of thought is that it is the ambitious visionaries who drive society forward and therefore should be allowed to keep the proceeds of their work; otherwise, they won't invent things, and civilization will collapse. There is an element of truth in that. Where would we be without the innovations of Thomas Edison (well, Tesla) and Henry Ford? However, the theory falls apart if you think about it for a few minutes.

Wealth isn't the only reason people accomplish significant innovations. Albert Einstein didn't become particularly wealthy through his work and a great deal of the prosperity we enjoy in the twenty-first century is derived from his breakthroughs. Edison's rival, Nikola Tesla, didn't become wealthy either. His motivation was unraveling the mysteries of science (specifically electricity). The American inventor Buckminster Fuller spent his life designing innovative forms of housing, transport, and engineering without any thought of financial reward (according to his own testimony). So it isn't true to say that all innovation is motivated by wealth. Many inventors simply want to make the world a better place.

The opposite school of thought to Ayn Rand was articulated very succinctly by Elizabeth Warren, Harvard Law School professor, Democratic Senator for Massachusetts and 2019 presidential candidate:

> *There is nobody in this country who got rich on their own. Nobody. You built a factory out there—good for you. But I want to be clear. You moved your goods to market on roads the rest of us paid for. You hired workers the rest of us paid to educate. You were safe in your factory because of police forces and fire forces that the rest of us paid for. You didn't have to worry that marauding bands would come and seize everything at your factory...Now look. You built a factory and it turned into something terrific or a great idea—God bless! Keep a hunk of it. But part of the underlying social contract is you take a hunk of that and pay forward for the next kid who comes along.[175]*

To extend her analogy—could this person have built their business if they had to hunt their own food? Build their own house? Make their own clothes? Teach their own children? I suggest they would have been way too busy trying to survive to pursue their business. On top of that, the customers of their business would also be too busy to be able to buy the business's product or services, so the company would be a failure.

We live in a community, and every person in that community plays a vital role in keeping the community functioning. We might think of it as similar to a bee colony. Is the queen bee more critical than the worker bees? Without the worker bees bringing food into the hive, keeping the hive maintained, sealing honey, building honeycomb, carrying water, and keeping the hive cool, the queen bee would die. She needs the worker bees as much as the colony needs her to continue the species. It's a relationship of mutual benefit, a symbiotic relationship.

The same could be said for human "worker bees" and the entrepreneurs or corporate executives, the "queen bees." We need each other. One cannot survive without the others. Why, then, does one get paid 100 times or 300 times what the other gets paid? Do they work 100 times as hard or as long? Are their IQ scores 100 times higher (and, even if it was, can they take credit for having a high IQ or is it a gift of genetics)?

The queen bees in our society were educated in schools paid for by taxes, taught by teachers who, in turn, survived through being part of an integrated community. "No man is an island" as the English poet John Donne wrote.

Maybe we even need psychopaths? Perhaps many of the great inventors, the ones who didn't care what people said about them, who ignored their families in pursuit of their vision, were psychopaths?[176]

OF THE PEOPLE, BY THE PEOPLE

Political parties, like every other organization, have one over-powering primary instinct—to survive by retaining their power at all costs. They all evolve and morph over time, abandoning, if necessary, their original policies and principles, to survive perceived changes in the realities of the political climate. Like corporations and religious organizations, they obey the laws of "organizational Darwinism." Over time, their values, policies, and platforms evolve to reflect the changing times. In some cases, this has been a great thing—for example, up until the 1970s, both of the major political parties in Australia supported the White Australia Policy (where only white Europeans could lawfully immigrate to Australia), a fact I still find shocking.

There is no reason to think that political organizations would work any differently to the other kinds of organizations we have already explored—people who rise to the top of the party will have a natural incentive to try to preserve their power by main-taining the control that the party has.

In Western democracies, we've been led to believe that our governments are "of the people, by the people, for the people," as Lincoln put it. While this may be a beautiful sentiment and something we should aspire to, the frequency with which people seem to fall for lies told by our governments suggests that might be a naïve view.

Today most Western democracies are dominated by a handful of political parties (themselves controlled by a handful of corporate interests) that have become increasingly difficult to tell apart. The parties on the left have drifted, at least on many economic issues, to the right; in response, the parties on the right have had to move to the extreme right (especially in terms of their rhetoric) to keep a gap between them.[177] The culmination of decades of the U.S. Republican Party's drift to the right was the 2016 presidential win of authoritarian billionaire Donald Trump.

And it's happening around the world. In Australia, according to one analysis:

> *The Australian Labor Party reflects this drift, now occupying a space to the right of the 1980s Liberals. The debate between the two primary parties, however heated, is within narrowing parameters. The two parties are now closer together than at any other time. The clash of economic vision of earlier campaigns is absent. It's no longer about whether the prevailing neoliberal orthodoxy is actually desirable, but merely a question of which party can manage it best.[178]*

Meanwhile, another form of political organization, the union movement, has been systematically weakened worldwide. In the U.S., union membership has fallen to 11.3 percent of all workers. In the private sector, unionization fell to 6.6 percent, down from a peak of 35 percent in the 1950s.[179]

In Australia, the decline is even more severe—from nearly 65 percent in 1948, to around 15 percent today.[180]

As a result of these and other factors, including off-shoring of jobs and automation, growth in real wages in most developed economies (Australia is an exception, thanks mainly to our mining boom) has mostly stagnated since the 1980s. This is seen most clearly in the United States—the world's second-largest economy (after socialist China).[181]

What happened?

One factor was the aforementioned deliberate association of raw, unbridled capitalism with Christianity. There also seems to be a connection between the rise of corporate wealth and influence in the late twentieth century and the decline of progressive politics. According to Julian E. Zelizer, a historian at Princeton University:

> *The Democratic Party in the 1990s ran away from much of the robust economic vision that had defined the party since the progressive and New Deal eras. Many Democrats accepted some of the market-based premises of conservative politics, backing away from central parts of their core domestic agenda like progressive taxation and economic regulation. The growing power of corporate interest groups in Washington, which mobilized huge teams of lobbyists and threw around sizable campaign donations, made both parties less willing to hear demands for redistributive public policy.[182]*

Regulatory mechanisms created after the Great Depression, designed to prevent its recurrence, were systematically dismantled and destroyed by successive governments of all stripes after 1980. Ronald Reagan's attack on America's progressive tax system, which he claimed came "direct from Karl Marx," culminated in his historic reduction in corporate and individual tax rates in 1981, which ultimately benefited wealthier Americans.

This led to today's Taxpayer Protection Pledge, organized by Republican strategist Grover Norquist, "the high priest of Republican tax-cutting," which asks all candidates for federal and state office (in the United States) to commit themselves in writing to the American people to oppose all net tax increases and punishes those who do not.[183]

Consolidation of corporate media ownership and the rise of television as the primary entertainment and news medium led to a population that could be manipulated more efficiently than ever before.

In the United States, the Republicans and the Democrats have swapped ideologies over the last 150 years,[184] with the Republicans becoming more conservative while the Democrats have become more socially liberal than they once were (supporting gay marriage, abortion, etc.), but more economically conservative (the financial industry regulations put into place under FDR in the 1930s were dismantled under Clinton in the 1990s,[185] support for free trade agreements, Obama's continuation of Bush's tax cuts for the rich, etc.). When it comes to foreign policy, it gets harder to tell them apart—both tend to support significant Pentagon budgets, financial and military support for apartheid Israel and Sunni fundamentalists, journalist-executing Saudi Arabia, and trying to clamp down on any nation that doesn't fully accept American domination of global trade. And they both tend to fully support the surveillance state apparatus (the NSA, FBI, and other agencies) while taking a hard stance on government whistleblowers (e.g., Edward Snowden, Chelsea Manning, and Reality Winner).

The late American political theorist Sheldon Wolin, in his book *Democracy Incorporated*,[186] coined the term "inverted totalitarianism" to describe America in the early twenty-first century. Journalist Chris Hedges defines inverted totalitarianism as a system where corporations have corrupted and subverted democracy and where economics trumps politics:

> *Inverted totalitarianism is different from classical forms of totalitarianism. It does not find its expression in a demagogue or charismatic leader but in the faceless anonymity of the corporate state. Our inverted totalitarianism pays outward fealty to the facade of electoral politics, the Constitution, civil liberties, freedom of the press, the independence of the judiciary, and the iconography, traditions and language of American patriotism, but it has effectively seized all of the mechanisms of power to render the citizen impotent.*[187]

As media ownership has been concentrated into the hands of the relative few (something all of the major parties in Western democracies have allowed to happen[188]), and countries have produced more and more billionaires and wealthy corporations with the ability to swing elections, the policies and practices of political parties have had to pander to the pressures placed upon them by the powerful.

This is a natural outcome of capitalism predicted by Karl Marx. He predicted that capital would be accumulated by a small number of people who would achieve economies of scale, which would, in turn, lead to further concentration and centralization of wealth into fewer and fewer hands, with competition leading to the big firms killing or eating the smaller firms, thereby destroying the competition.

Marx explains:

> *It is concentration of capitals already formed, destruction of*
> *their individual independence, expropriation of capitalist by capi-*
> *talist, transformation of many small into few large capitals....Cap-*
> *ital grows in one place to a huge mass in a single hand, because*
> *it has in another place been lost by many....The battle of com-*
> *petition is fought by cheapening of commodities. The cheapness*
> *of commodities demands, ceteris paribus, on the productiveness*
> *of labour, and this again on the scale of production. Therefore,*
> *the larger capitals beat the smaller. It will further be remembered*
> *that, with the development of the capitalist mode of production,*
> *there is an increase in the minimum amount of individual capi-*
> *tal necessary to carry on a business under its normal conditions.*
> *The smaller capitals, therefore, crowd into spheres of production*
> *which Modern Industry has only sporadically or incompletely got*
> *hold of. Here competition rages....It always ends in the ruin of*
> *many small capitalists, whose capitals partly pass into the hands*
> *of their conquerors, partly vanish.*[189]

And this is precisely what happened:

> *Today, mom-and-pop shops have been replaced by monolithic*
> *big-box stores like Walmart, small community banks have been*
> *replaced by global banks like J.P. Morgan Chase, and small farmers*
> *have been replaced by the likes of Archer Daniels Midland.*[190]

And we should ultimately expect that when the wealth of a
nation becomes increasingly concentrated into the hands of a
small group of psychopaths, they will reshape the political landscape to protect their interests as the elite consolidate their control over the media, and their ability to determine the outcome

of elections increases. Political parties, therefore, need to court the media owners and try to win their favor. Those who don't will be relentlessly attacked in the media until their credibility is destroyed. In Australia, successive Labor Prime Ministers Kevin Rudd and Julia Gillard witnessed the ability of the Murdoch media to destabilize their governments with attacks after they announced their intention to impose a carbon tax in 2009.

The incestuous relationship between politicians in Britain and the Murdoch family, exposed during the 2012 Levenson inquiry into the voicemail hacking scandal,[191] perfectly demonstrated how politicians would bend over backward to get on the good side of certain influential media owners. UK Prime Minister David Cameron hired a former News Corp executive, Andy Coulson, as his communications director. Coulson had previously been the editor of the *News of the World* (a Murdoch tabloid paper, which closed in July 2011 amid the phone-hacking scandals) from 2003 until his resignation in 2007, following the conviction of one of the newspaper's reporters concerning the scandal. Coulson himself would later be charged with phone-hacking offenses in July 2012.[192] He was found guilty and sentenced to eighteen months in prison (but served less than five—it's nice to have influential friends).

Also charged in the hacking scandal was Rebekah Brooks, another former editor of *News of the World* and ex-*News International* chief executive. She was cleared of all charges by a jury, which accepted her defense that she had zero knowledge of the illegal acts carried out by the newspaper she was in charge of. In September 2015, Brooks was confirmed as the new CEO of *News UK*, the renamed *News International*.

Another trend in Western democracies is for the political candidates themselves to come from the ranks of the privileged. According to a 2011 report by The Center for Responsive Politics, nearly *half* of the members of the U.S. Congress are millionaires, a status shared by only 1 percent of Americans. These millionaires don't come from just one side of politics either—140 of them were Republicans while the remaining 109 were Democrats.[193]

While millionaires and the rest of us share some interests, we will also naturally differ on many issues. Millionaires from both sides of politics are likely to hold significant financial investments in substantial organizations and businesses; therefore, it would be reasonable to expect them to support policies that protect the wealth and power of those organizations. It would also be wise to expect them to support policies that minimize the taxation of the wealthy. When you end up with a government with interests closely aligned to the elite, it is entirely reasonable to presume that the policies they implement will tend to favor those same interests—even if the policies are clearly based on nonsense.

Therefore when U.S. President George W. Bush (a millionaire) ushered in the Economic Growth and Tax Relief Reconciliation Act of 2001 (aka "Bush's tax cuts for the rich"), nobody should have been surprised.

Bush justified the tax cuts with a rehashed version of President Reagan's favorite justification—supply-side economics—even though economists and scholars have consistently debunked this theory for decades. Developed by an economic adviser to Richard Nixon, supply-side economics claims that lowering marginal tax rates and reducing government regulation will lead to more successful companies, which will then create more jobs and the wealth will "trickle down." It used to be called the horse-and-sparrow theory: If you feed the horse enough oats, some will pass through to the road for the sparrows.

Bush's own father, George H. W. Bush, derided Reagan's supply-side policies as "voodoo economics" during the 1980 election. Economist Paul Krugman wrote in 2007: "Supply-side doctrine, which claimed without evidence that tax cuts would pay for themselves, never got any traction in the world of professional economic research, even among conservatives."[194]

Economist N. Gregory Mankiw, professor and chairman of the economics department at Harvard University, former chairman of the White House Council of Economic Advisers under Bush II's presidency and a conservative economist, once referred to supply-side theories as "fad economics," comparing it to fad diets:

> *People on fad diets put their health at risk but rarely achieve the permanent weight loss they desire. Similarly, when politicians rely on the advice of charlatans and cranks, they rarely get the desirable results they anticipate.* [195]

When Bush's successor Barack Obama (another Harvard-educated millionaire, whose net worth climbed 438 percent during his time in the White House)[196] renewed the tax cuts in 2010,[197] it was predictable. Despite members of his own party calling the bill "an expensive giveaway to the richest Americans at a time when America could not afford it" and his own rhetoric that there were "some elements of this legislation that I don't like," I have to wonder—could a millionaire, educated at an Ivy League university, who relied on millionaires to fund his own election campaigns, do anything different? Admittedly, he eventually did put up the taxes for the rich, but only marginally.

In March 2008, eight months before that year's U.S. election, I wrote a blog post about my skepticism regarding the hope and change hype surrounding Obama. Like a lot of people, I wished that he was the real deal, someone who was really going to clean up Washington. However, I suspected the Harvard-educated poster boy for liberal America might be another puppet of the elite, designed to charm the pants off the Americans disaffected with George W. Bush, but would just be more of the same.[198]

I had a look at who the top contributors to his campaign were in early 2008. The top ten names included Goldman Sachs, JP Morgan Chase & Co., UBS AG, Kirkland & Ellis (the largest law firm in the United States), Exelon Corp., Lehman Brothers, Skadden, Arps (the fourth largest law firm), Sidley Austin (the sixth-largest law firm), and Citigroup Inc.[199]

When Goldman Sachs is at the top of a candidate's list of contributors, it's a decent indication that the candidate isn't perceived as a threat to the interests of the elite.

And these were the days before the Citizens United case removed all obstacles from corporations to donate unlimited amounts of money to political campaigns, so these were donations from political action committees (PACs)—individual contributions from employees or owners but raised through the company. It isn't the company itself writing a giant check—but that's beside the point. People who work at Goldman Sachs, for example, a bunch of investment bankers making million-dollar bonuses, know what they are doing when they invest in a candidate. These people don't *donate* money to a campaign. They *invest* in it. They expect to get something in return for their contribution.

"As a businessman and a very substantial donor to very

important people, when you give, they do whatever the hell you want them to do," Trump told *The Wall Street Journal* in July 2015. "As a businessman, I need that."[200]

Billionaire President Donald Trump continues the trend, despite his promises to "empty the swamp." His appointment of self-described "Reagan supply-sider" Lawrence Kudlow to head up the White House Council of Economic Advisers was an early signal that Trump was planning on making the rich richer.[201]

In the United States, it has become nearly impossible for someone to run for president unless you are either a millionaire or have the backing of many millionaires (or billionaires). As it turns out, there have been very few presidents who were *not* millionaires.[202]

Has the U.S. political system always has been engineered to prevent nonmillionaires running for office?

According to Open Secrets, the cost of the 2016 U.S. elections, including all money spent by presidential candidates, Senate and House candidates, political parties, and independent interest groups trying to influence federal elections, ran to nearly $7 billion.[203] The presidential election itself cost roughly $3 billion.

If billionaires are funding political campaigns for millionaires and billionaires, whose interests do we expect will be given top priority by the incoming government once elected? If elected politicians don't deliver on the interests of their financial supporters, they can be sure that future financial support will be harder to raise. That is to be entirely expected. Where does this leave the rest of the population?

While in Australia the situation may not be as dire, the majority of political donations still come in the form of financial gifts from corporations.[204]

Former Qantas CEO John Menadue warned Australians that "Corporate donations are a major threat to our political and democratic system, whether it be state governments fawning before property developers, the prime minister providing ethanol subsidies to a party donor, or the immigration minister using his visa clientele to tap into ethnic money."[205]

Front organizations in Australia, such as the Cormack Foundation (the largest single donor to the Liberal Party) and John Curtin House (the ALP's single largest donor), provide the major political parties with an anonymous cash flow, as under the Australian Electoral Commission guidelines, they are not bound to disclose how they raised their money.[206]

Sometimes wealthy individuals will buy a significant stake in a media company to have even greater influence over its reporting. In 2012, Australian mining magnate Gina Rinehart, the wealthiest person in Australia and one of the most affluent women in the world, tried to buy Australia's oldest newspaper business, *Fairfax*.[207] She was denied a seat on the board when she refused to sign *Fairfax*'s charter of editorial independence and ended up selling her stake. Her reticence about allowing independence hints at her intentions.

Amazon's CEO Jeff Bezos, the world's richest person, actually *did* buy *The Washington Post*. What his purpose is, we can't say. According to Politico's Jack Shafer: "I assess *Washington Post* coverage of Amazon as pretty even-handed. So does *Fortune*."[208]

But during the 2016 election campaign, *The Washington Post* ran 16 negative stories on Bernie Sanders in 16 hours.[209]

Political candidates who refuse to kiss the ring often find themselves on the outside looking in. U.S. Presidential candidate

Dennis Kucinich has struggled to get media coverage during campaigns, possibly because of his liberal point of view on issues such as American military invasions. During the 2004 presidential campaign, the American ABC network decided not to cover his campaign at all. During the 2008 presidential campaign, Kucinich was "disinvited" from a Democratic presidential debate on MSNBC which was owned by General Electric, one of the largest corporations in the U.S. (GE has since sold NBC to Comcast).

In an interview with *Democracy Now!*, Kucinich expressed his concerns over the role of the media in political campaigns:

> *You know, I think that the attempt by the media to determine who people should vote for and who they shouldn't vote for to determine who the candidates are, and who are not acceptable as candidates is something that raises real questions about the nature of the media's role in our society, and about what right they have to be able to engage in a process of pre-selection. When you understand the corporate nature of the media, it further troubles one who is concerned about the nature of democracy itself.* [210]

Kucinich explained his concerns about significant corporations being able to determine which political candidates the public get to listen to:

> *We're in a conundrum here about what the public's rights are, because this goes far beyond my humble candidacy. It goes right to the question of democratic governance, whether a broadcast network can choose who the candidates will be based on their narrow concerns, because they've contributed—GE, NBC and Raytheon, another one of GE's property, have all contributed substantially*

to Democratic candidates who were in the debate. And the fact of the matter is, with GE building nuclear power plants, they have a vested interest in Yucca Mountain in Nevada being kept open; with GE being involved with Raytheon, another defense contractor, they have an interest in war continuing. So, NBC ends up being their propaganda arm to be able to advance their economic interests. I think we need to have an understanding here, that the larger issue is public financing. All these people who are running for president are good people, but we have a system that—it's a terrible system. It requires people to do the kinds of pirouettes and gymnastics to make it appear that they're pure and chaste while their opponents are not. The truth is that the whole system is rotten…we're going to continue to see our politics in America be as an auction, where policy is sold to the highest bidder. [211]

Awareness of who is funding a candidate's campaign can often give us strong indications about how corporations view that candidate. Would you expect a corporation to support the campaign of a candidate they believed would hurt their interests once elected? Would you expect a media company to cover the campaign of a candidate if they thought her success would damage their business? Of course, there are times when both of those things might happen, for example, if the candidate seems highly likely to win anyway, and the corporation feels like they have a better chance of having at least some influence if they show their support. But all else being equal, you would expect them to do everything in their power to try to prevent a candidate's campaign from having any success if they suspect she is a threat to their interests.

Cui bono? Or, as Detective Lester Freamon put it in one of my favorite TV shows, *The Wire*: "You follow drugs, you get drug addicts and drug dealers. But you start to follow the money, and you don't know where the fuck it's gonna take you."

During the 2016 U.S. Presidential election, 90 percent of the top twenty contributors to Hillary Clinton were corporations or providers of services to corporations. However, 95 percent of the top twenty contributors to Bernie Sanders were unions.[212]

Another sign that made me think Obama was "on board" with the military-industrial complex's agenda back in 2008 was the level of positive press attention he got. If a candidate is terrible news for the military-industrial complex, they don't get media coverage. Conversely, any candidate—including the ones you might think are on the left—that get enough media coverage to make them a viable candidate, have already been vetted and approved by the powers that be in the corporate media. Why would you expect anything different?

The 2016 U.S. presidential election provided further examples of the power of media coverage. According to a Harvard Kennedy School study:

> During the year 2015, major news outlets covered Donald Trump in a way that was unusual given his low initial polling numbers—a high volume of media coverage preceded Trump's rise in the polls. Trump's coverage was positive in tone—he received far more "good press" than "bad press." The volume and tone of the coverage helped propel Trump to the top of Republican polls. Trump's coverage in the eight news outlets in our study was worth roughly $55 million.[213]

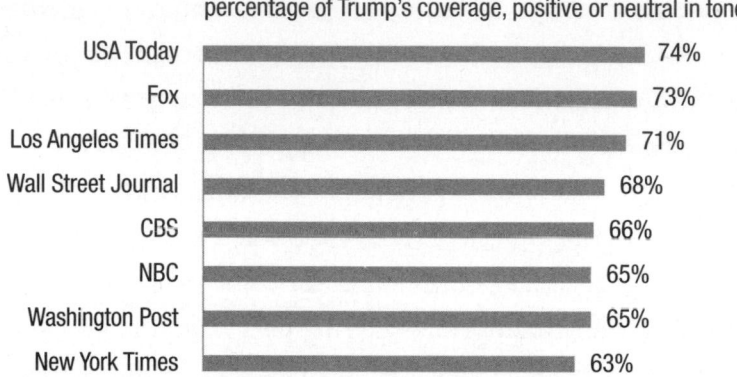

percentage of Trump's coverage, positive or neutral in tone

USA Today	74%
Fox	73%
Los Angeles Times	71%
Wall Street Journal	68%
CBS	66%
NBC	65%
Washington Post	65%
New York Times	63%

Figure 1: Harvard Kennedy School

Note that Trump received this positive free press *despite* his low polling numbers.

By comparison:

Over the course of 2015, the Democratic race got less than half as much news exposure as the Republican race. Less coverage of the Democratic side worked against Bernie Sanders' efforts to make inroads on Clinton's support. Sanders struggled to get badly needed press attention in the early going. With almost no money or national name recognition, he needed news coverage if he was to gain traction. Sanders's initial low poll numbers marked him as less newsworthy than Clinton but, as he gained strength, the news tilted in his favor.

Sanders's low polling numbers were a hindrance to getting press coverage, but Trump's small numbers didn't hinder him at all, probably because of his celebrity and how he built his campaign by saying outrageous things. Trump knew how to play the media better than anyone—possibly better than any candidate in history.

In the UK, a total of £31m (U.S.$49m) was spent by all parties in the 2010 general election, making the 2016 U.S. election spending 120 times greater or 23 times as much per capita, something worth considering. We have to wonder why the U.S. spends so much per capita on elections compared to the rest of the world.

The UK isn't immune to the corrosive influence of political cash. Access to politicians in the UK also comes at a price. Peter Cruddas is an English banker and businessman who has a £10m apartment in Monaco, a £5m house in Hertfordshire, a home in Antibes, a yacht, and a private jet. According to the 2007 *Sunday Times* Rich List, he was named the richest man in the City of London, with an estimated fortune of £860 million. While he was co-treasurer of the ruling Conservative Party, he allegedly told reporters posing as foreign business investors that donors giving £250,000 a year could lobby the prime minister directly and have their views "fed in" to the government. When the story came out, Cruddas resigned his position.[214]

If you have enough wealth, you can buy political influence, effectively buying politicians. Yet most of the people still believe, most of the time, that democracy represents them. They think this for two reasons—it is convenient, as it doesn't require them to try to change anything (System 1); and because they are told to believe it, repeatedly, by the political parties and the corporate media.

If the people are going to take control of the democratic process, it needs significant reform. Voting for the "lesser of two evils," as many people justify their vote for one of the major parties, is never going to result in genuine reform.

My friend Tony Kynaston suggests we should start a new global political party—the "Don't Vote for Me" party. It would

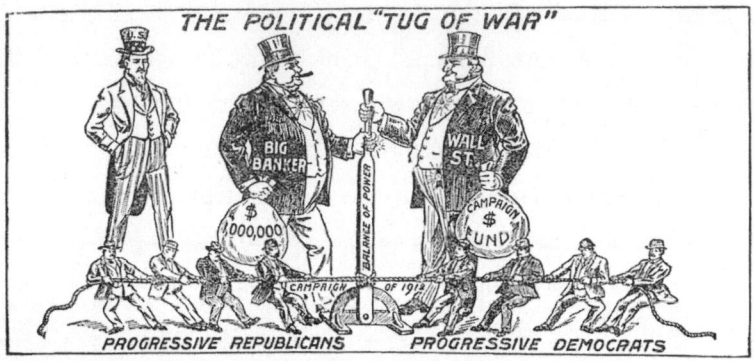

Wall Street—Which way shall we throw the 1912 election, old pal?

Big Banker—As we are "non-partisan reformers" we must elect the candidates of either party who secretly bind themselves to support the private central bank bill, oppose government money and favor corporation currency.

Uncle Sam (to himself)—Why don't them goldarn fool progressives all get hold of the same end of that rope, or flock by themselves and form the National Progressive Party?

purely exist to provide an alternative to the mainstream parties and to send a message. Candidates who get elected would do the bare minimum possible to retain their seat—they wouldn't vote on bills, wouldn't accept bribes or donations, would sit for a volunteer lie-detector test every six months, and would act as the eyes and ears of the population, agreeing to provide regular and honest feedback about what's happening in the halls of power.

Currently, the only other solution I can see to break the back of the system is to vote against the major parties, sending a broad message that we aren't going to take it anymore. I tend to vote for independents or minor parties, even though I know they don't stand a chance in hell of getting into power. If enough of us vote against the major parties, eventually we will send a message—it's time for a change.

In political systems as we have in Australia, this tactic has merit. In the 2010 federal elections, neither of the major parties garnered enough votes to form a government. They were forced to form alliances with minor parties and independents who, in turn, were able to negotiate changes to their policies. Unfortunately, this didn't end well—the party that ended up winning government, the Australian Labor Party, lead at the time by Julia Gillard, was mercilessly attacked by the Murdoch press for trying to introduce a carbon tax—one of the policies they were forced to adopt by the alliance they formed to win government.

In the United States, some people worry that voting for minor parties plays into the hands of the majors. Some claim that Trump was elected, at least in part, because too many people didn't vote for Clinton. But of course, that's precisely what the major parties want you to feel—that you *have* to vote for one or the other major party.

However, what would happen if enough people continually voted away from the major parties at each election? Would this eventually engineer a change to the political landscape?

Another thing we need for genuine political reform is a new media, free of corporate influence. When people are told how to think and how to vote by a handful of corporate-owned media entities, it is nearly impossible for them to think outside the box. When the media belongs to a cozy coalition with corporations and governments, they will continue to fill the minds of the public with propaganda designed to endorse the status quo. And as it's highly unlikely that the corporate media is going to change their tune suddenly, we desperately need a new media, by the people and for the people, to help people to think about the issues in a new light.

Fortunately, in the twenty-first century, we have the tools to make the new media a reality. There was a time in the early 2000s when it seemed like that new media might have a chance. People were blogging, podcasting, tweeting, and crafting a new dialogue as a result. Unfortunately, the corporate dollars soon started flowing in, and these new forms of media were consumed and co-opted to fit the objectives of the wealthy elite.

Here's how it usually works:

As soon as an independent blog or podcast gets enough of an audience to become influential, they are acquired by a big corporation. The Huffington Post is an excellent example. It started as an alternative media source, inviting writers from across the spectrum to provide thoughtful analysis about current issues. However, when it was acquired by AOL (who also purchased Weblogs, Inc. from Jason Calacanis) in 2011 for U.S.$315 million, its content started to change. Today its front page is as likely to have stories about celebrity gossip and breast implants as it is genuine political coverage. In other words, it has become another mainstream corporate media entity. AOL, like any major corporation, was owned by a significant group of wealthy and influential organizations whose officers sat on the board and governed how it was run. Board members of AOL included Fredric Reynolds, formerly of CBS, Hugh Johnston formerly of PepsiCo, and Eve Burton, previously of The Hearst Corporation. You know where their bread is buttered. Today AOL is part of Verizon.

Unfortunately, this kind of tale is all too common.

When my media company, The Podcast Network[215], was still in its infancy, I briefly entertained offers from MSN and News Corporation, who both offered to take a majority stake in the business. I feared that if I accepted the offers, I would end up being gradually forced out of the company, and it would become another mainstream content company—or shut down. Of course, I would have profited from it, and therein lies the rub: if you don't dance with the devil, you can't afford the running costs of a significant media business. And where else will this money come from, if not from the wealthy elite? It's a conundrum that any media entrepreneur has to face. You either sell out or float your business on the stock exchange—where it will also become the plaything of investors whose agenda is likely not to be friendly to anyone trying to change the system.

We desperately need a new funding model for media companies, one that breaks the control of the wealthy elite. Is crowdfunding (e.g., Kickstarter) the way to go? Does this model provide an alternative to building the media companies of the twenty-first century? There are some early signs that this may be the case—at least on a small scale.

These days on The Podcast Network, most of our shows are paid for by listener subscriptions. While that was a risky proposition when I started testing it in 2014, by 2019 it has become more common to find podcasters asking their listeners for a paid subscription, often using services like Patreon to manage the funds.

And in 2017–18, I was able to raise enough funds from my podcast audience (and Tony Kynaston, who I first met after he became a listener) on Kickstarter to help finance my first history documentary, *Marketing the Messiah*.[216]

A group of very lovely people supported this book itself in a crowdfunding campaign on *publishizer.com*.

THE BEWILDERED HERD

One of the main ways the elite fight the war on our minds is by owning or influencing the corporate media. They battle it out, with slightly different agendas, to get the public to do and think how they want them to.

In his 1922 book *Public Opinion*, Walter Lippmann, the American journalist who popularized the terms "Cold War" and "stereotype," referred to the public as "the bewildered herd."

He went on to say:

> *That the manufacture of consent is capable of great refinements no one, I think, denies. The process by which public opinions arise is certainly no less intricate than it has appeared in these pages, and the opportunities for manipulation open to anyone who understands the process are plain enough.*

And so the elite, the psychopaths, invest enormous time, funds, and energy to "manufacture the consent" of the public.

Colossal advertising budgets also give organizations the ability to determine, to a large extent, which media companies survive and which do not. When publishers, television and radio stations, blogs and podcasts rely on advertising to pay the bills, they become very amenable to the demands of the advertisers. As they say, the golden rule is that he who has the gold makes the rules.

When *Mother Jones* magazine launched in 1976, they were approached by cigarette companies offering them a steady stream of advertising revenue. Despite ethical concerns, the *Mother Jones* board decided to accept the advertising, believing they could successfully uphold their editorial integrity.

Their resolve was put to the test a few years later when, in 1979, the magazine published an article called "Why Dick Can't Stop Smoking," which described nicotine as addictive and asserted the tobacco industry used political donations to influence Congress. As punishment for daring to run a story that ran counter the interests of their advertisers, Philip Morris, Brown & Williamson, and other cigarette companies not only pulled their advertising from that particular issue of the magazine, they pulled their entire multi-year advertising commitment to the publication.[217]

Now, you might think, "Well, fair enough, why would Philip Morris pay money to support a publisher that is damaging their business?" And, of course, you're right. They wouldn't. But that's the heart of the issue.

The general public relies on the media to tell us what's going on in society. Publishers rely on advertising, and advertisers don't want them publishing information that, although it might be in the interests of their readers, runs counter to the interests of the advertiser. In this way, the advertisers try to influence public discourse—which is fine. Advertisers have a right to do that. The thing we need to watch out for is that corporations don't use their power to influence the direction of so much of our media that we can no longer find an unbiased or even just both sides of a story.

Publishers, on the other hand, *love* to run controversial stories, because they boost audience numbers, which drives up revenue.

As the saying goes, "If it bleeds, it leads."

When I'm researching an issue for one of my podcasts, I find it often takes a tremendous amount of time and effort to find an alternative version of events than the one that is being pushed by the mainstream media. Take the Trump–Russia collusion story that dominated so much of American media after the 2016 election. It was nearly impossible to find a balanced version of that story in the press. Many articles (and therefore many Americans) assumed that hard evidence of collusion would appear in the Mueller Report. When Mueller declared he didn't find enough evidence of a conspiracy for an indictment, people were shocked and stunned. Had they been led astray for two years by the media? If so, who was responsible?

Was it the Democrats trying to deflect attention from their failure to stop the Russians from interfering in the 2016 election? Was it the DNC trying to divert attention from how they screwed over Bernie Sanders during the primaries and then lost the election? Was it the media just profiting from the chaos? Was it Wall Street who continued to bleed America dry and run their foreign wars while everyone was distracted by a big, sweaty nothingburger? Was it a little of all of those things? I don't know the answer—but I think those are the right questions to be asking about now because that is what is destroying America's democracy. Not the Russians. Not Trump. It's the forces that allowed Trump to get elected in the first place. Trump is just a symptom of the underlying problems.

I'LL SEE YOU IN COURT

Using expensive lawsuits is another classic tactic organizations use to influence the media. While there is nothing wrong with trying to use the legal system to protect your organization from libel and slander, that's not what I'm talking about here. I'm talking about using the *cost* of defending against litigation to try to dissuade the media from publishing reasonable stories about an organization's activities.

The Church of Scientology, for example, which makes millions of dollars from its tax-exempt status, has a long track record of using its considerable wealth to bury the media under thousands of lawsuits if they try to print stories that criticize the church, its current leader, David Miscavige, or its celebrity golden boy, Tom Cruise. Way back in 1991, *Time Magazine* estimated that the church was spending an average of $20 million a year on legal actions.[218] That figure is probably much higher today.

If you're a publisher and you don't want to spend years and millions defending yourself against Scientology lawsuits, you might decide not to write negative stories about them—which, of course, is just what they want.

Perhaps the Scientologists learned how to do it from observing the tobacco industry.

Back in 1976, British filmmaker Martin Smith produced a documentary, *Death in the West*,[219] about six American cowboys who were dying of lung cancer. The film also featured old Marlboro commercials, interviews with Philip Morris executives, and physicians who provided testimony that cigarettes caused the cowboys' cancer.

After the film aired on British TV, Philip Morris sued Thames Television and obtained a court order preventing the movie from being shown again until their case had been resolved. Their primary objective seems to have been to prevent the film from being shown in the U.S., at the time their leading market, and they knew that *60 Minutes* was negotiating with Thames Television to buy it. Philip Morris agreed to settle the case out of court if Thames agreed to destroy all copies of the film. Although Thames believed they had a reasonable chance of winning the suit, they didn't think they could recoup the cost of the legal defense with future sales of the film, so they agreed to the terms.[220]

Anyone who tries to fight the power of a corporation will find that they have nearly unlimited budgets for spending on lawyers and law firms to threaten and harass smaller companies, not-for-profit organizations, and individuals with legal action. They can tie up these more modest, less-funded groups in court for years, eroding their ability to promote their agendas. They can also finance private detectives to dig up dirt on people and politicians they want to threaten with blackmail, like disgraced Hollywood film mogul Harvey Weinstein who hired Israeli firm Black Cube to run an "army of spies" to subvert and intimidate his accusers.[221]

Donald Trump is another infamous user of litigation to silence his critics and crush his enemies, a tactic he learned from Roy Cohn, the notorious lawyer who made his name chasing alleged communists during the McCarthy hearings. Before becoming president, Trump had been a plaintiff in over 1900 lawsuits. Some of those he used "to distance himself from failures and to place responsibility on others."[222] And he has continued to sue people since becoming president, including porn stars, even after his "long-time personal attorney and 'fixer,' the real-estate and taxi-medallion entrepreneur Michael Cohen, received a three-year sentence for his guilty pleas related to tax evasion, bank fraud, lying to Congress, and campaign-finance violations."[223]

In 1990, McDonald's Corporation brought a libel case against environmental activists associated with London Greenpeace who had been distributing fact sheets that were critical of the fast-food company. Two of the activists, Helen Steel and David Morris, decided to fight the case. It's known as the McLibel case (technically called *McDonald's Corporation v. Steel & Morris*).[224] The trial lasted nearly ten years, which made it the longest-running case in English history. McDonald's spent several million pounds on the matter—Steel & Morris spent £30,000. The case was so embarrassing to McDonald's that in 1995, they offered, during a private meeting with the defendants, to drop the case if Steel & Morris agreed to stop criticizing McDonald's in public and kept their criticisms to private conversations with friends. Steel & Morris countered that they would agree to the terms if McDonald's ceased advertising its products and instead only recommended the restaurant privately to friends.

Although a British judge found in favor of McDonald's, he also ruled that many of the outrageous allegations in the pamphlet were mainly true. Steel & Morris took their case to the European Court of Human Rights that found the original case had breached Article 6 (right to a fair trial) and Article 10 (right to freedom of expression) of the European Convention on Human Rights and ordered that the UK government pay Steel and Morris £57,000 in compensation.

Using litigation to block libel and slander is fine. But when organizations or individuals use it to crush any criticism, it's evidence of a psychopath or psychopathic culture.

MEET ME IN THE LOBBY

Another standard tactic organizations use is the "third-party technique." This is where they use seemingly independent third parties to influence the media, the public, and politicians.

Ready-made "experts" on contentious issues, secretly funded and unleashed by industry front organizations and lobby groups, appear in the media and meetings with politicians, well-armed with biased narratives. These experts are useful in influencing the way stories get covered in the media, and therefore the public perception of the issues, as well as how legislation is voted on by politicians.

A front group, according to SourceWatch.org, is "an organization that purports to represent one agenda while in reality it serves some other interest whose sponsorship is hidden or rarely mentioned—typically, a corporate or government sponsor."

Front groups work to saturate the media with the views of their clients, intending to influence the public and how they vote—pushing them toward the politicians that the lobbyists have also engaged in writing the legislation favorable to the client. Sometimes front groups take the form of think tanks, which operate to engage with national media to develop stories that influence public opinion and political decisions.

For example, it's understood that in the last decade, Middle Eastern countries such as Saudi Arabia, Qatar, and the UAE have spent vast sums of money influencing American think tanks in Washington—especially those that provide opinions regarding American's foreign policy in the Middle East.[225] The way this kind of influence works is subtle. The country offers to donate funds to support a think tank—nothing wrong with that on the surface. Middle Eastern countries want American politicians and business leaders to have a better understanding of their culture and history, so they provide funds to enable that kind of research and analysis. However, the hidden, often unspoken, contract is that the think tank receiving the funding will avoid criticizing the provider of the funds. So if, for example, a think tank is getting funds from the Saudis, they might avoid talking about the Saudi history of human rights abuses.

According to the Center for Responsive Politics, in 2013 more than 12,000 registered lobbyists spent over three billion dollars attempting to influence the policies of the U.S. federal government, and similar efforts have been documented in the states, where both the amount and importance of lobbying has increased sharply since the late 1980s.[226]

How many of those conversations make it into public awareness? A tiny percentage. Why don't they get more media coverage? We might assume because (a) people don't care enough and it doesn't sell papers (or online clicks), and (b) it's not in the interests of the media elite to bring greater awareness to the lobbying process, as they actively engage their own lobbyists.

If the public hears anything at all about the lobbying process, we are usually given a heavily edited and sanitized version of events, massaged into shape by public relations professionals for general consumption and propagated by the corporate-owned media who are part of the game.

"This is about giant corporations who figured out that by spending, hey, a few tens of millions of dollars, if they can influence outcomes here in Washington, they can make billions of dollars," according to Senator Elizabeth Warren, Democrat, of Massachusetts.[227]

In 2018, total lobbying spending in the United States rose to $3.46 billion—an increase of one hundred percent over twenty years.[228]

Depending on which source you believe, somewhere between 12,000 and 100,000 lobbyists are working in Washington, DC.[229] The primary objective of these lobbyists? "To protect the company against changes in government policy."[230]

A study found that between 2007 and 2012, 200 of America's most politically active corporations spent a combined $5.8 billion on federal lobbying and campaign contributions. Those years were examined because they fell three years before and three years after the infamous "Citizens United" decision in the U.S. Supreme Court (which removed restrictions on "independent" political spending by corporations and unions).[231]

But the $5.8 billion these 200 corporations spent on lobbying and campaign donations is insignificant compared to what they got back in return: $4.4 trillion (yes, that's trillion with a T) in federal business and support.[232] That's a 760:1 return on investment. According to the report, "the $4.4 trillion total represents two-thirds of the $6.5 trillion that individual taxpayers paid into the federal treasury" over that time. That's a pretty sweet business model.

In their book about front groups, *Merchants of Doubt*, historians Naomi Oreskes and Erik Conway explained how a small group of scientists took money from various organizations for over forty years to write articles that mislead the public about the scientific data on subjects including the ozone hole, climate change, and cigarettes:

> *In case after case, Fred Singer, Fred Seitz, and a handful of other scientists joined forces with think tanks and private corporations to challenge scientific evidence on a host of contemporary issues. In the early years, much of the money for this effort came*

from the tobacco industry; in later years, it came from founda-
tions, think tanks, and the fossil fuel industry.[233]

One of the documents Oreskes & Conway uncovered was *Bad Science: A Resource Book*. They describe it as "a how-to handbook for fact fighters, providing example after example of successful strategies for undermining science, and a list of experts with scientific credentials available to comment on any issue about which a think tank or corporation needed a negative sound bite."[234]

That's what front groups do best. They sufficiently sow the seeds of doubt about a particular issue, so the corporations can avoid being forced to change their behavior as long as possible.

According to SourceWatch.org:

> *[The tobacco industry is] notorious for using front groups to create confusion about the health risks associated with smoking, but other industries use similar tactics as well. The pharmaceutical and healthcare industries use front groups disguised as "patient's rights" advocates to market their products and to lobby against government policies that might affect their profits. Food companies, corporate polluters, politicians—anyone who has a message that they are trying to sell to a skeptical audience is tempted to set up a front group to deliver messages that they know the public will reject if the identity of the sponsor is known.*

In Britain, one of the most notorious tobacco front groups was ARISE (Associates for Research into the Science of Enjoyment). It claimed to be an "apolitical affiliation of independent scientists and academics" who researched how people enjoyed terrific things like chocolate, tea, coffee, alcohol, and tobacco—but was actually run by the PR agency Fishburn Hedges and funded mostly by tobacco companies. Between September 1993 and March 1994, the group generated 195 newspaper articles and radio and television interviews in places such as the *Wall Street Journal*, the *International Herald Tribune*, the *Independent*, the *Evening Standard*, *El País*, *La Repubblica*, *Rai*, and the BBC. Professor David Warburton of the University of Reading, who claimed to run the group, was head of psychopharmacology at the University of Reading and wrote and published several articles, which questioned findings regarding the addictive qualities of nicotine. The University of Reading also received indirect funding, more than $500,000, from the tobacco companies via ARISE, which should give you an idea of how deep the rabbit hole goes. Front groups, run by PR firms, co-opting corruptible scientists and the universities they work for, to spread spin about products that are banned from advertising via cooperative media companies.[235]

So, whenever you read or see an opinion by an "expert," it's always worth suspending your belief in what they are saying until you know more about the interests that expert represents.

The use of front groups might have reached its apex in 2009 with the rise of the American "Tea Party" movement. The Tea Party first rose to prominence when its members started protesting at Congressional "town hall" meetings to discuss healthcare reform. Although the media portrayed the Tea Party as a grassroots movement, it appears to have actually been a front-group funded and coordinated by several wealthy individuals, in particular oil magnate brothers David and Charles Koch, via their other front groups Americans for Prosperity and FreedomWorks, to fight against taxes on carbon use and the activation of a cap and trade program.[236]

David Axelrod, the chief strategist for Barack Obama's presidential campaigns, called the Tea Party "a grassroots citizens' movement brought to you by a bunch of oil billionaires."

Is this really different from the established political parties? Don't the Republicans and the Democrats also accept funds from corporate donors? Yes, of course, they do—and it's a shame the media doesn't pay more attention to those donations and what the quid pro quo is.

One difference is that the corporations involved in funding the mainstream parties don't often feel the need to hide behind a front group.

Front groups are incredibly useful when it comes to helping media companies present a "false balance." This is what it's called when the media presents an issue as being more balanced between opposing viewpoints than the evidence actually supports. A classic example of false balance is the media's reporting on science issues, including the topics of human-made versus natural climate change.

Although the vast majority of climate scientists attribute global warming to the effects of human industry, you can always find a tiny number of scientists who will take a contrary position. By giving equivalent television time and column inches to scientists on both sides, the media makes it seem like there is a substantial deviation within the scientific community, when in fact there is an overwhelming consensus amongst climate scientists that humans are causing global warming.

A false balance is also often evident in the way Western media covers international conflicts. For example, after the death of Fidel Castro in 2016, the *New York Times* published a long and extremely biased account of his life and the Cuban revolution,[237] which I dissected at length on my Cold War podcast.[238] As I pointed out in those episodes, one of the other ways the media provides a false balance is via the sin of omission—leaving out pertinent information, which is necessary when developing a balanced view of a subject. In the case of the Castro obituary, the NYT coverage omitted relevant facts regarding the U.S.' financial and military support of Cuba's pre-revolutionary dictatorship, the amount of Cuban industry that was controlled by U.S. corporate interests before the revolution, as well as the valid reasons for a lot of the revolutionary government's actions in the subsequent decades.

As American Cold War journalist I.F. Stone wrote in 1952:

> *Emphasis, omission, and distortion rather than outright lying are the tools of the war propagandists...*[239]

I'd argue that the use of front groups in American politics ramped up when Ronald Reagan was elected president. It's hard to think of a better scenario for corporations than an aging, pliant, charismatic actor with a long history of being a corporate shill becoming a president who is willing to say whatever is written for him.[240]

In 1954, Reagan began hosting the General Electric Theater on television.[241]

GE's public relations department developed the concept. Condensed versions of plays and books would be acted out by leading talent, with Ronnie talking about excellent GE products during commercial breaks. By the time GE eventually fired him in 1962 for complaining about one of their largest customers (Tennessee Valley Authority) as an example of the evils of "big government," he had become both famous and wealthy, due to his part ownership of the series. He had also transitioned from being a Democrat and a self-described "New Dealer to the core" to a political conservative, calling his years with GE his "post-graduate education in political science."[242]

Before his GE years, Reagan had another part-time career—snitching suspected communists inside Hollywood to the FBI as early as 1946, often with very little evidence. Reagan would give the FBI names of actors, directors, and writers that he thought might be a bit too red. During his tenure as president of the Screen Actors Guild in the '40s and '50s, he made personnel files on SAG members available to the FBI. In return, the FBI, with the approval of director J. Edgar Hoover, worked on his behalf, investigating his estranged daughter's life and marriage, with agents secretly gathering information about her and passing it on to her father.

Just before Reagan's campaign to become governor of California, Hoover again personally intervened to prevent his agents from interviewing Reagan about his adopted son's involvement with the son of Mafia boss, Joseph Bonanno, aka Joey Bananas,[243] to spare him embarrassment. It pays to have friends in high places, especially for someone with presidential ambitions.

Knowledge of Reagan's involvement with the FBI was kept a secret from the public until finally revealed via a Freedom of Information request in 2012.

What better candidate for a puppet president than someone who became wealthy as the official spokesman for America's largest corporation and worked part-time as an FBI snitch?

FUD (FEAR, UNCERTAINTY, DOUBT)

Front groups have played an enormous role in media coverage of climate change. For many years now, much of the media coverage has continued to suggest that there is still a high degree of doubt about the cause of climate change, even though the vast majority of climate scientists (over 97 percent) agree that humans cause it.

One 2004 media study, which examined 636 articles from four top U.S. newspapers between 1988 and 2002, found that most reports gave as much time to the small group of climate change doubters as they did to the scientific consensus.

A 2013 study of major Australian newspapers by the Australian Centre for Independent Journalism at the University of Technology in Sydney found that one-third of articles in 2011 and 2012 did not accept the consensus of climate scientists. The study found that Australia's two most prominent newspapers by circulation, the *Daily Telegraph* and the *Herald Sun* (both, unsurprisingly, owned by Rupert Murdoch's News Corporation), published articles that were skeptical about anthropogenic climate change more than 60 percent of the time.

Frank Luntz, a Republican strategist, wrote a memo in 2003 that contained the following advice for Republicans when discussing global warming:

> *You need to be even more active in recruiting experts who are sympathetic to your view, and much more active in making them part of your message. People are willing to trust scientists, engineers, and other leading research professionals, and less willing to trust politicians. If you wish to challenge the prevailing wisdom*

about global warming, it is more effective to have professionals making the case than politicians.[244]

The Luntz report also had some advice on terminology:

It's time for us to start talking about "climate change" instead of global warming and "conservation" instead of preservation. "Climate change" is less frightening than "global warming." As one focus group participant noted, climate change "sounds like you're going from Pittsburgh to Fort Lauderdale." While global warming has catastrophic connotations attached to it, climate change suggests a more controllable and less emotional challenge.[245]

It's getting increasingly difficult these days to read, watch, or listen to the news and know whether or not the "expert" you are listening to is a member of a front group. It's a pretty safe bet that, more often than not, they are.

The Energy and Policy Institute (EPI) in the USA released a report that documents "how and where fossil fuel companies and front groups have attacked renewable energy standards and net metering policies throughout the country in 2013 and 2014." According to the report:

Fossil fuel-funded front groups operate in multiple areas to influence the policy-making process in their attempts to eliminate clean energy policies. First, groups like the Beacon Hill Institute provide flawed reports or analysis claiming clean energy policies have negative impacts. Next, allied front groups or "think tanks" use the flawed data in testimony, opinion columns, and in the media. Then, front groups, like Americans for Prosperity, spread disinformation through their grassroots networks, in postcards mailed to the public, and in television ads attacking the clean energy policy. Finally, lobbyists from front groups, utilities, and other fossil fuel companies use their influence from campaign contributions and meetings with decision makers to push for anti-clean energy efforts. [246]

The general public usually won't take the time or energy required to fact-check the statements they hear in the media. Neither do many of us have the skills to analyze for ourselves the accuracy of such reports. Most of us are busy working to keep the roof over our heads and food in our kids' mouths. When you keep the population so busy they don't have time to think, it's so much easier to pull the wool over their eyes—especially if you have unlimited funds to saturate the media with your version of the truth.

According to The Center for Media and Democracy's PR Watch, the Kochs and other corporations, such as corporate and trade group funders as ExxonMobil, Chevron, the American Petroleum Institute, Syngenta, Bayer CropScience, CropLife America, Procter & Gamble, the Personal Care Products Council, Coca-Cola, Dr. Pepper/Snapple, and McDonald's, have bankrolled the American Council on Science and Health that "poses as an independent science-based organization devoted to outing 'junk science,' but consumer advocates have called it 'a consumer front organization for its business backers' that 'glove[s] the hand that feeds it.' [247]

As just one example of ACSH's work, PR Watch claims they published reports calling fracking "a safe and efficient path to energy independence," despite the hazardous chemical cocktail used in hydraulic fracturing, which spoils millions of gallons of fresh drinking water each year.

And front groups, of course, are a global tactic.

Australia's right-wing front groups have also been busy in recent years creating a "disturbance in the Force" over subjects from climate change to the plain packaging of tobacco.

One of the most notorious front groups is the benign-sounding Institute of Public Affairs (IPA)—which is, in fact, a right-wing, corporate-funded think tank based in Melbourne. It was established in 1943 by G. J. Coles, founder of one of Australia's largest retailing behemoths, during an era in Australia when the conservative movement was struggling. In 1944, the IPA participated in the formation of the Liberal Party (despite the progressive-sounding name, the Liberal Party is Australia's conservative party, akin to the Republicans in the U.S. or the Tories in the UK). Today it is one of the two major political parties in Australia and the current government.

> The IPA key policy positions include: advocacy for privatization and deregulation; attacks on the positions of unions and non-government organizations; support of assimilationist indigenous policy; and refutation of the science involved with environmental issues, such as climate change.[248]

According to John Roskam, executive director of IPA, "of all the serious (climate) skeptics in Australia, we have helped and supported just about all of them in their work one way or another."[249] One of Roskam's previous jobs was—wait for it—manager of government and corporate affairs for mining giant Rio Tinto Group. Who would have thought that the leader of a significant climate change–denialist group used to hold an executive role at a mining company? I am shocked, I tell you, shocked!

The IPA made headlines in early 2012 for sending out hundreds of free copies of a new book on climate change by one of their pet denialists to targeted schools around the country. Roskam claimed that "school kids are being indoctrinated by teachers every day. There should be two sides to the story, and the science is far from settled."[250]

If 97 percent of climate experts agree humans are causing global warming,[251] I wonder what level of consensus he would need? 98 percent? 99 percent? Just give us a number, John.

Finding one or two fringe scientists willing to accept money to support ideas that deny the current state of scientific consensus, but which suit the destructive policies of a few significant corporations, is turning into a new corporate blood sport. Just like a mafia don trying to fix the next boxing fight, if your bribery fund is significant enough, and you look long enough, you'll always be able to find a scientist who is in a tight spot, whose career isn't going too well, and who is willing to take a fall in the third round if you make some of his problems go away in return for a one-way ticket to Palookaville. "I coulda been a contender!"

It's like trying to find a general in a Latin American country who has been passed over for a promotion and wants a shot at being president. There's always at least one.

We wonder if Roskam would also like schools to teach that the world rests on the back of a giant turtle and that it's turtles all the way down? Surely, he can find someone out there to endorse that view if paid enough money.

As Carl Sagan once said:

> *They laughed at Columbus, they laughed at Fulton, they laughed at the Wright Brothers. But they also laughed at Bozo*

the Clown. The fact that some geniuses were laughed at does not imply that all who are laughed at are geniuses.

One thing these front groups specialize in is the deterioration of the public understanding of science and the scientific process. They create FUD (fear, uncertainty, and doubt, a tactic I learned about in my Microsoft days) about science, which is then merrily distributed by the corporate media as if it is valid. The consequence is that we have a population of people who say inane things such as "science doesn't know anything" or "science has made mistakes before," instead of appreciating that the scientific process involves the finest minds in a field performing the best experiments possible with the most accurate instruments available and then debating the results until they come to a consensus on the best interpretation. Even when they come to this consensus, they leave the subject open to future improvements in experimental methodology and tools, which allows current scientific opinion on subjects to change over time.

The list of fringe science groups is growing. They typically have very sensible-sounding names, like the "Discovery Institute" (funded by evangelical Christian groups to promote the idea of intelligent design), the "Global Energy Balance Network" (funded by Coca-Cola to promote the notion that obesity is due to lifestyle alone and not excessive calorie consumption) and the "Association of American Physicians and Surgeons" (which promotes AIDS denialism and links between abortion and breast cancer).

Front groups work hard behind the scenes to use money from mining companies to individuals and organizations who are willing to challenge scientific consensus—for a buck. Just one such mining company, Peabody Energy, the world's biggest private-sector publicly traded coal company, "has funded at least two dozen groups that cast doubt on manmade climate change and oppose environment regulations."[252]

The U.S.-based Science and Public Policy Institute (SPPI), where Lord Christopher Monckton, the infamous climate change denialist, is the chief policy advisor, emerged from another think tank, the Center for Science and Public Policy (CSPP), which was launched with a grant from oil giant Exxon.[253]

The corporate media happily plays their role by allowing the denialists equal or better airtime or column inches in the name of "media balance," creating debate and confusion where none is deserved. This, of course, creates ferocious public debates that help drive the sale of papers or get people to watch television shows. Higher sales and ratings help sell more advertising. And so the world turns.

These are just a few examples to remind you that you absolutely cannot take for granted anything you read, watch, or listen to. They are just some of the ways that the elite use their money and influence to protect their future from progress —and keep themselves in power.

With psychopaths in control of front organizations and lobby groups, we can never be sure of what is real and what is not.

LAWS AND SAUSAGES

According to Eric Schmidt, the former executive chairman of Google, "The average American doesn't realize how much of the laws are written by lobbyists. It's shocking how the system actually works."[254]

While it's reasonable that corporate lobbyists should have as much of a say about the shaping of new legislation as anyone else in a democracy, it appears that they often have significantly more influence than we might imagine. In some cases, the actual laws that are eventually passed end up with significant sections that are word-for-word written by lobbyists. A case in point is a 2013 amendment to the Dodd-Frank Act, designed originally to protect the U.S. from another Wall Street collapse like they had in 2008.

Out of a total of eighty-five lines in the amendment, seventy of them were written by lobbyists representing Citigroup.

The amendment, which of course reduced the level of protection the original Act provided, was passed in the House by a vast majority of both Republicans *and* Democrats—even though it was opposed by the Obama administration and was unlikely to pass the Senate (who, in fact, referred the bill to the United States Senate Committee on Banking, Housing, and Urban Affairs, where it died). When asked why the House Democrats would pass it under these circumstances, people close to the situation gave this answer: "Republicans have enough votes to pass it themselves, so vulnerable House Democrats might as well join them, and collect industry money for their campaigns."[255]

Some people suggest that lobbyist input into legislation isn't always a terrible thing. They help out, like harmless little Oompa Loompas, when the budgets of legislators have been cut because people make a big fuss out of "big government."[256]

But I'd suggest that's partly *why* you hear a lot of fuss about government budgets in the first place. The idea is to keep governments broke and underfunded. Why?

The smaller the budgets government departments have, the fewer the resources they can hire, the lower the salaries they can pay, which makes them less competitive with significant corporations in hiring smart young grads or experienced executives. The result is that government departments have less know-how or the resources to stop the corporate lobbyists from pushing through their preferred legislation.

It also means governments will have another excuse to privatize important public assets that provide essential services, creating profits dispersed as bonuses to business leaders and dividends to shareholders, instead of those profits being spent on additional public services.

WAR IS A RACKET

Lobbyists and front groups are also used to keep countries at war. War is not only *big* business; it's also one of the *easiest* ways for a company to fill its coffers.

As Major General Smedley Butler, one of the most decorated U.S. Marines in history, wrote in his classic book, *War Is a Racket*:

> *I spent 33 years and four months in active military service and during that period I spent most of my time as a high-class muscle man for Big Business, for Wall Street and the bankers. In short, I was a racketeer, a gangster for capitalism. I helped make Mexico and especially Tampico safe for American oil interests in 1914. I helped make Haiti and Cuba a decent place for the National City Bank boys to collect revenues in. I helped in the raping of half a dozen Central American republics for the benefit of Wall Street.*

I helped purify Nicaragua for the International Banking House of Brown Brothers in 1902–1912. I brought light to the Dominican Republic for the American sugar interests in 1916. I helped make Honduras right for the American fruit companies in 1903. In China in 1927 I helped see to it that Standard Oil went on its way unmolested. Looking back on it, I might have given Al Capone a few hints. The best he could do was to operate his racket in three districts. I operated on three continents.

War is a sure-fire way to quickly siphon money out of the public treasury, as I've explained in detail on the economics episodes of the Cold War podcast.[257] This is a lesson American business leaders learned during World War II when they discovered that war was an excellent way to pull the country out of continual economic depressions.

From the late decades of the nineteenth century, starting with the "Panic of 1873," which was the original "Great Depression," the U.S. economy suffered from severe and regular recessions, leading up to the more famous depression of the 1930s.[258]

While there were many factors involved, a consensus emerged among the American political and business elite that the solution was to expand the export of American manufactured products to foreign markets. The country's manufacturers and farmers were getting *too* good at their jobs—they were overproducing for domestic consumption and needed to find new sources of revenue. In other words, they were making too much stuff, more than they could sell at home, so they needed to either make less, which means downsizing (not great for the economy) or find new markets—overseas markets. The problem with this solution was that the foreign markets in the early twentieth century were locked up by various colonial powers, trading blocs, groups of countries within a geographical region that protected themselves from imports from non-members. The British Empire's trade bloc contained roughly 25 percent of the world's population. The French had their own, while Germany and Japan sought to build their own, first through trade, then through conquest (as the British, French, and Americans had done before them). The desire of the UK and the U.S. to prevent Germany and Japan from building their economies through territorial acquisition lead to World War II.

Here's a quote from Leslie M. Shaw, secretary of the United States Treasury under President Theodore Roosevelt, from his lecture to the students and faculty of Chicago University, March 1, 1907:

> *The time is coming when the manufactories will outgrow the country, and men by the hundreds of thousands will be turned out of the factory. The factories are multiplying faster than our trade, and we will shortly have a surplus, with no one abroad to buy and no one at home to absorb because the laborer has not been paid enough to buy back what he has created. The last century was the worst in the world's history for wars. I look to see this century bring out the greatest conflict ever waged in the world. It will be a war for markets and all the nations of the world will be in the fight as they are all after the same markets to dispose of the surplus of their factories.*[259]

A "war for markets" was one of the underlying causes of both World War I and II. This wasn't Marx or Lenin speaking. It was the secretary of the United States Treasury.

Dean Acheson, secretary of state under Truman, and one of the architects of the Marshall Plan and the Cold War, expressed something similar in 1944:

It seems clear that we are in for a very bad time, so far as the economic and social position of the country is concerned. We cannot go through another ten years like the ten years at the end of the twenties and the beginning of the thirties, without having the most far-reaching consequences upon our economic and social system. When we look at that problem, we may say it is a problem of markets. You don't have a problem of production. The United States has unlimited creative energy. The important thing is markets. We have got to see that what the country produces is used and is sold under financial arrangements which make its production possible. You must look to foreign markets.[260]

So, selling into international markets was seen as one solution to prevent future recessions. Another was to get the government to spend money from its treasury to revitalize the economy.

The famous British economist John Maynard Keynes wrote a letter to FDR in 1933, amid the Great Depression, suggesting that the answer to economic stagnation was through government spending. He recommended borrowing money to spend on infrastructure and a public works program and mentioned that spending money on war would lead to intense industrial activity. This was eight years before the U.S. would find a justification to join the most enormous war humanity has ever seen.

And it turned out that Keynes was right—during World War II, U.S. corporate profits rose from $6.4 billion in 1940 to $10.8 billion in 1944. That's a 70 percent increase in profits in just four years! American men may have been dying on the Western front, but American businesspeople were prospering back home. After WWII, a lot of business and political leaders decided that Keynes was on to something with this war business—the business of war.

Charles E. Wilson, the president of General Motors and executive vice chairman of the War Production Board, delivered a speech to the Army Ordnance Association in January 1944, where he suggested a continuing alliance between business and the military for "a permanent war economy."

This bastardized version of Keynesianism is known as "*military* Keynesianism." Keynes, I should point out, *hated* this idea.

But here's why businesses love military Keynesianism—if a government tries to spend money on domestic infrastructure, like schools, hospitals, parks, roads, and so forth, people will want to have a say in how it's spent. They will want to get involved—and that slows down the transfer of funds into the hands of big business. However, when it comes to military spending, the people don't get much of a say. The government merely says the magic incantation "Sim Sala Bim, Ala Peanut Butter Sandwiches, national security," and that's the end of it, especially if there's a sense of urgency around the spending, which there always seems to be, whether it's genuine or manufactured.

"Stalin/Mao/Castro/Khrushchev/Khomeini/Gaddafi/Saddam/ bin Laden/ISIS/Kim is going to kill us all! We have to act now!" And so the businesses who win a war-related contract with the Pentagon can just collect their checks without much oversight by the general public or the media. It's a much easier way to get paid than to have to bother with annoying, old-fashioned things like marketing and selling.

After WWII ended, Truman had cut the military budget to the bone and the easy cash for the military-industrial complex dried up.

Fortunately for them, in 1950, the Korean War conveniently provided the impetus for the U.S. to justify a massive U.S. military buildup. Even before the war broke out, individual members of the government were advocating for the U.S. to remain on a permanent war footing, in the top-secret policy paper by the United States National Security Council, known as NSC-68.

Think about how this war racket works for a second.

A country goes to war.

Who pays for that?

The government.

Where do they get the money?

From the federal treasury.

Where does that money come from?

From taxation and borrowing.

Who pays for that?

The people.

And if money is borrowed?

It also gets paid back from the treasury—which comes from taxation.

For example: total U.S. federal revenues in the fiscal year 2015 were about $3.18 trillion.

These revenues came from three primary sources:

$1.48 trillion (47 percent) from income taxes paid by individuals
$1.07 trillion (34 percent) from payroll taxes paid jointly by
    workers and employers

$341.7 billion (11 percent) from corporate income taxes paid by businesses.

So more than two-thirds of federal revenues come from taxes that individuals pay, directly or indirectly. Today the U.S. military spending is about $600 billion per annum. That's about 20 percent of revenue. Since 2001, the U.S. has spent about *$1.7 trillion* on the military.

However—that's just for direct military budgets. According to an analysis by Boston University, the real sum is a *lot* higher. If you also factor in things like *additional* war-related spending, including additions to the Pentagon base budget and Veterans health and medical disability expenses, they alone total just under $1 trillion. Then you have to factor in the cost of Homeland Security, which has been heightened because of the wars. Plus the interest the government takes on from the borrowing to pay for the wars. If you factor in the other indirect costs, the sum is closer to $4.4 trillion.

So where does the money go? One study in 2013 suggested that the Pentagon has dispersed around $385 billion to private companies for work done outside the U.S. since late 2001. By the second Gulf War, contractors represented roughly one half of deployed personnel in Iraq, with the company now known as KBR—we'll talk more about them in a minute—employing more than 50,000 people.

But wait, there's more. It's not just manufacturers of the tools of war or the people who make guns and tanks and bullets or supply mercenaries that benefit from wartime spending. American businesses of all sizes, from Google[261] down to removalists (the U.S. Defense Department spends roughly $8 billion annually moving some 500,000 people to new assignments; about $2 billion is spent transporting household goods, and $6 billion is spent on allowances and indirect costs), get a slice of the military pie.

Way back in the mid-1980s, the Pentagon was critiqued for wasteful spending when the news emerged that they paid $640 apiece for fifty-four toilet seats.[262] That might sound like a lot of money for a toilet seat (especially in 1980 dollars, even allowing for the fact it was for a custom-built toilet enclosure for the P-3C Orion antisubmarine aircraft) but more recent studies have found the Pentagon's wasteful spending of late makes the $640 toilet seat seem minuscule. One recent study found Pentagon wastage added up to over $33 billion—such as $150 million spent on private villas for a handful of Pentagon employees in Afghanistan and $2.7 billion spent on space blimps.[263]

All of those 800 massive U.S. bases in foreign countries have to supply their personnel with food and clothing and computers and cars and pens and Starbucks and Burger King. TomDispatch discovered 1.7 million individual contracts,[264] many of those benefiting from what they refer to as "the growing use of uncompetitive contracts and contracts lacking incentives to control costs, outright fraud, and the repeated awarding of non-competitive sweetheart contracts to companies with histories of fraud and abuse," for services outside the United States since the start of the Afghan war (the fiscal year 2002). Who pays for all of that?

The people. Individual taxpayers.

So war becomes a smooth transfer of wealth out of the public treasury into the hands of private contractors and corporations. If a corporation wants to make money under normal conditions, it needs to work hard to sell its product to a customer. You have to advertise, you have to fight to win contracts with businesses, and you have to deal with constant scrutiny—but if you get a war contract, you don't have to work so hard. The Pentagon employees aren't spending their own money, and if there's the urgency of a war situation, the funds are made available and spent as quickly as possible.

And there is very little oversight on where the money goes.

It's just a fire hose of easy money that flows out of the public treasury into the coffers of the corporation. And the most significant benefactor of U.S. military budgets in the last decade? KBR—Kellogg Brown & Root—who has received over $44 billion in military contracts.[265] That's a lot of cornflakes! No, wait, wrong Kellogg. They were originally called Brown & Root, better known to critics during the Vietnam War as "Burn & Loot," and they made a lot of money in the 1930s from government contracts scored for them by their close friend, local Texan congressman Lyndon Baines Johnson, whose political career they helped finance. As LBJ's career advanced, he helped B&R win government contracts to build airports, pipelines, and military bases, while they, in turn, poured money into his campaign war chest. You might have heard of the company that acquired B&R in 1962—Halliburton. In 1995, Dick Cheney became Halliburton's president and CEO after helping jumpstart the Pentagon's ever-greater reliance on private contractors when he was President George H.W. Bush's secretary of defense.

In 2009, the Pentagon's top auditor testified that KBR accounted for "the vast majority" of wartime fraud. In 2007, after years of terrible publicity, Halliburton spun KBR off as an independent company and moved its headquarters from Houston to

Dubai. The list of controversies surrounding KBR includes allegations of corruption, bribery, negligence, sexual assault, human trafficking, and knowingly exposing their employees to poisonous smoke from "burn pits."[266, 267]

None of that has stopped KBR winning ongoing Pentagon contracts though, according to their investor presentations.[268]

But it's not just the companies that are running the overseas operations and bases that are benefiting. It's also, of course, the arms suppliers.

The world spent $1.69 trillion on the military in 2016.[269]

In 2011, the 100 largest U.S. contractors sold $410 billion in arms and military services to the U.S. military *in one year alone*. These are companies like Lockheed Martin, Boeing, BAE Systems, General Dynamics, Raytheon, and Northrop Grumman. They make missiles, artillery, aircraft, and so forth.

Again, it's easy money that flows from the public treasury into private corporations. It is nothing new to argue that members of the corporate defense industry—famously labeled the military-industrial complex by President Eisenhower—are, in essence, merchants of war.

In his first speech as president in 1953, just after the death of Stalin, Eisenhower said:

> *Every gun that is made, every warship launched, every rocket fired signifies, in the final sense, a theft from those who hunger and are not fed, those who are cold and are not clothed. This world in arms is not spending money alone. It is spending the sweat of its laborers, the genius of its scientists, the hopes of its children. The cost of one modern heavy bomber is this: a modern brick school in*

more than 30 cities. It is two electric power plants, each serving a town of 60,000 population. It is two fine, fully equipped hospitals. It is some fifty miles of concrete pavement. We pay for a single fighter plane with a half million bushels of wheat. We pay for a single destroyer with new homes that could have housed more than 8,000 people. This is, I repeat, the best way of life to be found on the road the world has been taking.

In his last speech as President in 1961, he warned:

In the councils of government, we must guard against the acquisition of unwarranted influence, whether sought or unsought, by the military-industrial complex. The potential for the disastrous rise of misplaced power exists and will persist.

Something you might not know—in the original draft of this speech, Eisenhower referred to it as the military-industrial-*congressional* complex. But the term *congressional* was dropped at the last minute to appease the then-currently elected officials. This is according to Eisenhower biographer Geoffrey Perret and supported by forty-two-year CIA veteran Melvin Goodman, later a senior fellow at the Center for International Policy and adjunct professor of government at Johns Hopkins University, who says he heard it from Eisenhower's brother, Milton.

When Milton asked about the dropped reference to Congress, Eisenhower replied: "It was more than enough to take on the military and private industry. I couldn't take on the Congress as well."[270]

Of course, arms dealers don't only profit from their own country's spending. They also sell to *other* countries.

The U.S. is by far the most significant supplier of arms to the developing world. They sell about 30 percent of the world's weapons. And the biggest buyers? The Middle East, especially the U.S.'s long-standing partner, Saudi Arabia. From 2010 to 2016, the Obama administration authorized a record $60 billion in U.S. military sales to Saudi Arabia—triple the transactions under the George W. Bush administration. Mind you, this is one of the most brutal and corrupt regimes on the planet. Saudi Arabia is consistently ranked among the "worst of the worst" in Freedom House's annual survey of political and civil rights.[271] And there is growing evidence that the Saudi government was directly involved in the 9/11 attacks.[272]

And of course, Trump is going to try to beat Obama's record.[273] This is despite the CIA concluding Saudi Crown Prince Mohammad bin Salman ordered the hacksaw assassination of *Washington Post* journalist Jamal Khashoggi.

The arms trade is pretty brilliant. Here's how it works. U.S. arms dealers sell to developing countries, particularly those controlled by military or religious dictators. But that means that the U.S.'s military superiority declines. So the U.S. needs to buy more arms for itself! And then, of course, one of these dictators inevitably does something to justify a war with the U.S.

OMG, he's got a bomb!

How do you know?

We sold it to him!

And the U.S. then needs to supply the dictator's internal opposition—generously referred to as "rebels" in the Western media, instead of "insurgents," a term reserved for rebels fighting the dictators that we like or our own occupying armies—with more arms so they can resist him. Finally, if these rebels don't succeed, the

Pentagon sends in the U.S. military with even *more* weapons. If the U.S. military defeats the dictator's forces, using the latest American-made weapons versus slightly out-of-date American-made weapons, they will install his opposition (the rebels) into government and make sure they have enough American-made weapons to threaten the people into obedience. And the cycle starts again.

Of course, it isn't just American arms dealers involved here—Russia is the world's second-largest arms supplier. But the U.S. is the most significant—by a long shot.[274]

This is *precisely* what happened with Iraq. During the Iraq–Iran war in the early '80s, the Reagan administration supplied Saddam with billions of dollars of credits. Who did Ronnie send to do the deal? Donald Rumsfeld. What did Saddam do with the U.S. credits? He bought weapons from Jordan, Saudi Arabia, Kuwait, and Egypt. Where did they get them from? The United States. The U.S. was also directly shipping military helicopters and "dual use" hardware to Iraq. That's hardware that can be used for military and nonmilitary purposes. The U.S. also knew that Iraq was using mustard and sarin gas against the Iranians and the Kurds but turned a blind eye to it. How did they know? They sold it to Iraq.

This isn't a conspiracy theory. This is on the record. In May 1986, the U.S. Department of Commerce licensed seventy biological exports to Iraq, including at least twenty-one batches of lethal strains of anthrax, cyanide, and weapons-grade botulin poison.[275]

Richard Murphy, Assistant Secretary of State, said: "The U.S.-Iraqi relationship is…important to our long-term political and economic objectives."[276]

These objectives, no doubt, include selling more weapons in the Middle East.

And ISIS—where do their weapons come from? While a lot of them are old Soviet weapons left over from the '80s, they also have a lot of U.S. weapons. The U.S. sells arms to Iraq, Turkey, and Syria, which then end up in the hands of ISIS.[277]

So remember—*war is big business*. And it's *easy* business. It's the easiest and fastest way to transfer vast sums of wealth out of the public coffers and into the hands of corporations. And it doesn't get talked about nearly enough when considering the factors that lead us into war.

Another important consideration: it's well understood that the U.S. technology industry derives a ton of benefits from military spending.

Here's how it works. The U.S. uses tax dollars to fund technology research and development (R&D) at places likes DARPA—Defense Department's Advanced Research Projects Agency—which is where guys like Vint Cerf invented the internet.[278] And places like MIT were nearly entirely funded by the Pentagon up until the '70s. Transistors, the cornerstone of the computing industry, were developed at Bell Labs, part of AT&T. AT&T, at the time, had a government-mandated monopoly. So they could afford to create new technology. And of course, a lot of technology R&D done by private industry is funded by the Pentagon with an eye to developing new weapons. I'm sure everyone has seen the terrifying videos of the horse-like robots developed at Boston Dynamics (BD).

Who funded BD?

The Pentagon.

Who pays for that?

The taxpayers.

Anyway, that technological R&D then makes its way into the hands of private companies like IBM and Apple and Microsoft, and so on. And they adapt it and sell it back to the people—*the people who funded it in the first place*. And, of course, lots of corporations and their executives become very wealthy out of the process of publicly funded research. And you might think, "Well, those corporations pay it back in taxes on their profits"—but we know how that's working out, don't we? These companies today use very sophisticated loopholes to offshore their profits in countries like Ireland, where they pay minimal taxes. Not much of it makes its way back to the U.S. This we know, thanks to the Panama Papers.

Government contracts, especially those coming out of the Pentagon, are notoriously poorly managed and easily gamed. There is little bottom-line accountability, and nobody is paying enough attention, especially during times where there is a sense of urgency (like during an invasion of a country in the Middle East). If there is an audit and profligate spending is discovered, there might be a few negative news cycles, maybe even a Senate hearing, but it will all disappear relatively quickly.

How many people remember that time in 2004 when the U.S. sent $12 billion in cash to Iraq, where it promptly disappeared, and there were no records kept of whom it was given to? [279]

About a year after the U.S. illegally[280] invaded Iraq in 2003, some bright sparks in Washington decided it would be a solid idea to ship billions of dollars *in cash* to the war-torn country, in theory, to help with the reconstruction after the devastation caused by the invasion.

The money was shipped in secret as 281 million notes, weighing

363 tons, flown from the U.S. Federal Reserve in New York to Baghdad once or twice a month on military aircraft.

What happened to it when it arrived in Iraq? Well—that's the $12 billion question.

The money was to be administered by the Coalition Provisional Authority (CPA), a transitional government set up by the U.S., UK, Australia, and Poland.

The $12 billion came from Iraqi assets seized after the first Gulf War, from the sale of Iraqi oil, and surplus payments from the UN oil-for-food program. It belonged to the people of Iraq and should have been dispersed with some level of accountability. Instead, the CPA, under the leadership of American Paul Bremer, a former managing director at Kissinger and Associates, a worldwide consulting firm founded by Henry Kissinger, put no internal auditing into place, and, as a later report found, allowed nearly $9 billion to disappear, quite possibly as a result of fraud and corruption.[281]

According to investigations carried out by the U.S. government, it was literally handed out as cash to unknown people, with no invoices or receipts required.

One of the handy things about this money was that as it belonged to Iraq, few people in America cared what was done with it. And, of course, the Iraqis were in no state at the time to worry about it either. They might have been better equipped to play a role in the dispersal of the funds once the Iraqi provisional government took control in July 2004, but Bremer made sure the money had already been spent before that happened. And to make sure nobody on the American side of things could be held responsible for the disappearance of the funds, two days before he left Iraq, Bremer signed "Order 17," which gave everyone associated with the CPA and the American government immunity. One of his former top aides is quoted as saying that Bremer "wanted to make sure our military, civilians, and contractors were protected from Iraqi law."[282]

Invade a country, make $9 billion of *their cash* disappear, and make sure no one associated with it can be prosecuted later—all in a matter of months and in broad daylight. Forget about *Ocean's Eleven*. Surely this is one of the greatest heists in history.

Now we can only imagine who ended up with these missing billions. If you knew a friend of yours had $12 billion in untraceable cash sitting in his office and was handing it out willy nilly, how quickly would you be there with your hand out? At least one of Bremer's management team doesn't think it's a problem where the money went.

Rear Admiral David Oliver, who was the director of management and budget under the CPA, when asked by the BBC where the money went, replied:

"I have no idea—I can't tell you whether or not the money went to the right things or didn't—nor do I actually think it's important."

BBC: "Not important?"

Oliver: "No. The coalition—and I think it was between 300 and 600 people, civilians—and you want to bring in 3,000 auditors to make sure money's being spent?"

BBC: "Yes, but the fact is that billions of dollars have disappeared without a trace."

Oliver: "Of their money. Billions of dollars of their money, yeah, I understand. I'm saying what difference does it make?"[283]

Okay, so billions of dollars being squandered is okay when

it's not taxpayer's money, according to David Oliver. What about when it *is* the taxpayer's money?

Someone, somewhere, is benefiting from those government contracts. Cui bono? I'd start by looking at offshore tax havens.

So to summarize, here are some of the ways people profit from war.

1. By selling weapons, both to their own country and other countries, funded by tax dollars.
2. By selling other goods required during and after a war, including everything from food and clothing to reconstruction efforts—also funded by tax dollars.
3. By gaining access to undeveloped markets with new sources of natural resources and cheap labor.
4. By locking up control of export markets that they can sell their goods and services to.
5. By using war to get technological research done that then makes its way into the hands of corporations.

I'm not arguing that economics is the *only* reason we go to war, but it's a significant factor and one that doesn't get talked about nearly enough. And it's another way the elite increase their wealth.

I could go on with examples of wasteful military spending, but I'm sure you get the idea. That's not to say private and public companies don't also waste money—they absolutely do—but it isn't taxpayer money that could have been spent on improving healthcare, education, or infrastructure.

What does war have to do with psychopaths?

It's a quick way to get rich. Who cares if people die as a result?

MONEY CAN'T BUY ME LOVE— BUT IT CAN BUY A GOVERNMENT

We've looked at indirect ways the elite manipulate democracy so they can remain in power.

What about direct ways? Can enough money really buy elections?

Though it isn't always the case, a 2014 study that analyzed 467 congressional races held in the United States in 2012 found that candidates who out-fundraised their opponents were nine times more likely to win elections.[284]

And politicians obviously know this.

Candidates who upset the people with the money can quickly find themselves coming second-place in the campaign funding stake and consequently out of a job.

This is the basis of the NRA playbook.

The National Rifle Association was founded in 1871 as a recreational group designed to "promote and encourage rifle shooting on a scientific basis."

Today we associate the NRA with promoting gun rights in the U.S., but that's a relatively recent development.

After the assassination of John Kennedy in 1963, with a rifle purchased by mail-order from an ad in the NRA magazine *American Rifleman*, NRA Executive Vice-President Franklin Orth supported a ban on mail-order sales, stating, "We do not think that any sane American, who calls himself an American, can object to placing into this bill the instrument which killed the president of the United States."

The culture of the NRA moved to the hard right under new

leadership in the early 1980s, in response to the Black Panthers using the Second Amendment to justify an individual's right to carry a loaded weapon in the 1970s.

In 2016, the NRA reported $433.9 million for total revenue. It spends about $3m per year to influence gun policy. They also spend a good chunk getting politicians who support their position on the Second Amendment elected.

Leading up to the 2016 election, the NRA spent more than $30 million in support of Donald Trump.

Get on their wrong side, however, and they can cause trouble for your election campaign.

Take the story of Debra Maggart, an American politician who served in the Tennessee legislature from 2004 to 2012 with solid conservative credentials—she believes gay couples are unfit to parent and have "numerous emotional dysfunctions and psychological issues." She also had an A+ rating with the NRA and supported allowing guns in bars. But when she decided *not* to support a bill that would have allowed guns in cars on properties where the owners did not want guns, the NRA turned against her. They dropped her rating from A+ to a D and aggressively funded her political opponent, a member of the Tea Party. They created a "Defeat Maggart" website and used billboards, robocalls, radio ads, YouTube videos, and twelve full-page newspaper ads to drive her from office.[285]

Of course, the NRA is just one of the thousands of lobby groups that fund election campaigns and whose backroom dealings with politicians are typically hidden from the public.

In 2007, Australia elected the Australian Labor Party to govern the country, sweeping their then wildly popular leader Kevin

Rudd into power. Rudd and his treasurer, Wayne Swan, were determined to make the mining industry, a significant part of the Australian economy and 83 percent owned by foreign interests, pay higher taxes as a result of the "super profits" they were earning from a resources boom, fueled in significant part by exports to China.

The mining industry went on the offensive, spending nearly $22 million in just six weeks on TV ads attacking the new tax and Kevin Rudd.[286]

The Rudd government was also the victim of a constant stream of negative editorials by Rupert Murdoch's newspapers,[287] possibly because the government had started providing financial assistance to the commercial free-to-air television networks which potentially harmed the market expansion of pay-TV provider Foxtel (50 percent owned by News Corporation).

Quite quickly, the ALP decided Rudd was a liability to the party's chances in the upcoming election, and replaced him with a new leader, Julia Gillard, his former deputy, making her Australia's first female prime minister.

That's all it takes, then, to change the democratically elected leader of Australia—$22 million in television ads and Rupert Murdoch's support. Why bother going to the trouble of having elections in the first place?

Gillard quickly moved to make peace with the mining industry. At her first news conference as prime minister on June 24, 2010, she declared "I am throwing open the government's door to the mining industry."

The mining tax survived in a different form, with a different name, but with the guts ripped out of it, which is what happens when mining companies can make and break governments. When it was finally introduced in 2013, instead of delivering $12 billion in revenue in the first two years, it delivered only $126 million in the first six months after its introduction. Think about that for a second—instead of paying $12 billion in new taxes, the mining companies spent a mere $22 million on advertising. Not a terrible return on investment!

Also in mid-2013, due in part to renewed pressure by the Murdoch press, the ALP flip-flopped, replaced Gillard with Rudd, making him prime minister once again. But he quickly lost the 2013 federal election to the Coalition parties lead by Tony Abbott—who had the support of the Murdoch press and who threw the entire mining super profits tax out of the window as soon as he could.

And just in case you still think the news media doesn't try to influence how people vote, you might be interested to know that according to Rudd's chief political strategist during the 2013 election, Murdoch's senior newspaper editors were instructed that "with Rudd's revival in the opinion polls, they were to go hard against him and the government." He argues that the "storm of negative stories emanating from News Corp blew their campaign off course."[288]

Furthermore, in 2018, after yet another Australian prime minister, Malcolm Turnbull, this time from the other side of the political divide, was also stabbed in the back by his party colleagues and forced to resign while holding office, Kevin Rudd wrote an article pointing the finger at—Rupert Murdoch.[289]

Speaking of Turnbull, it's time to talk about his former employer again, Goldman Sachs, the world's most influential investment bank.

It's everywhere—including inside other governments besides Australia.

George W. Bush's last Treasury secretary was the former Goldman CEO, Henry Paulson. In his earlier years, Paulson worked for the administration of Richard Nixon, serving as an assistant to John Ehrlichman, who was convicted of conspiracy, obstruction of justice, and perjury and served eighteen months in prison for his role in Watergate.

Robert Rubin, Bill Clinton's treasury secretary, spent twenty-six years at Goldman before becoming chairman of Citigroup. As I've already mentioned earlier, Goldman employees were the most significant private group of donors to Barack Obama's 2008 campaign. And his chief of staff, Rahm Emanuel, later the mayor of Chicago, was previously Bill Clinton's 1992 finance director where "he ran the biggest fundraising machine the Democratic Party had ever seen. While doing that job he was also on the Goldman Sachs payroll."[290]

Donald Trump, who continually drew attention to how much money Hillary Clinton had earned in speaking engagements for Goldman, named Steven Mnuchin, a former Goldman Sachs partner and senior manager, as his Treasury Secretary. Trump named the president of Goldman Sachs, Gary Cohn, as his choice for director of the National Economic Council.

Goldman Sachs has been buying influence with the U.S. government since the Great Depression. Sidney Weinberg, who started with Goldman Sachs as a janitor's assistant, where his responsibilities included brushing the firm's partners' hats and wiping the mud from their overshoes, worked his way up to the top job in 1930.

A couple of years later, he raised more money for Franklin Roosevelt's first presidential campaign than any other individual.

FDR rewarded him by asking him to create the President's Business Advisory and Planning Council. Even though he was a registered Democrat, Weinberg was happy to play both sides. He supported Eisenhower in his 1952 presidential bid and Johnson's campaign in 1964. As you might imagine, his influence with these presidents was extraordinary.

Since then, Goldman Sachs employees have gone on to become the minister for finance of Sweden, World Bank president, chairman of the New York Stock Exchange, prime minister of Italy, president of the European Commission, governor of the Reserve Bank of Australia, governor of the Reserve Bank of South Africa, chairman of the U.S. Securities and Exchange Commission, governor of New Hampshire, chairman of the U.S. Commodity Futures Trading Commission, chairman of Japan Airlines, president of the Federal Reserve Bank of New York, mayor of Chicago, president of the European Central Bank, secretary of State of Economy and Finance of Spain, governor of the Bank of Greece, governor of the Bank of England, governor of the Bank of Canada—and chief executive officer of Donald Trump's presidential campaign. As I said—they are everywhere.

Meanwhile, Goldman has also been involved in a list of controversies so long that one might suspect they reflect more than momentary lapses of judgment.[291]

For their key role in causing the 2008 global financial crisis, which played a significant role in the failure of many businesses and declines in consumer wealth estimated in trillions of U.S. dollars, the firm, who according to the SEC deliberately "misled investors," agreed to pay a $550 million fine, "one of the largest penalties ever paid by a Wall Street firm, to settle charges of securities fraud linked to mortgage investments."[292]

But, of course, no one went to jail. Instead, nearly 1000 Goldman bankers and traders were paid million-dollar bonuses,[293] and Goldman CEO Lloyd Blankfein, instead of going to jail, took home $42.9 million in salary and bonuses in 2008.[294]

Too big to fail, indeed.

While on the campaign trail in 2016, Trump said: "Our movement is about replacing a failed and corrupt political establishment with a new government controlled by you, the American people."

But according to *USA Today*, as of June 2017, six months later, "More than 100 former federal lobbyists have found jobs in the Trump administration" and "roughly two-thirds of them—sixty-nine—work in the agencies they have lobbied at some point in their careers," according to research by American Bridge 21st Century. Fifteen of them work in the executive office of the president. Under Trump, the number of lobbyists in Washington is on the rise for the first time in a decade.

Of course, breaking a promise not to hire lobbyists isn't unique to Donald Trump. His predecessor, Barack Obama, made the same promise during his 2008 campaign, pledging to close "the revolving door that lets lobbyists come into government freely and lets them use their time in public service as a way to promote their own interests...when they leave." By 2013, there were sixty-five former lobbyists in his administration.

Hillary Rodham Clinton, the Democratic presidential candidate in 2016, didn't even bother to make the same anti-lobbying pledge as Obama did when they were both running in 2008. And why would she? They were a huge financial support to her 2016 campaign.

THE POISONING OF MINDS

One of the most aggressive battlegrounds for the war on the minds of the masses over the last forty years has been inside the education system. If you can engineer the education system to churn out new generations of obedient capitalists, who have been taught from a young age to conform, and not to question the narrative, and to associate reform with the evils of autocratic regimes, then it's much easier to maintain your power.

Aristotle supposedly said, "Give me a child until he is seven, and I will show you the man." In other words, get 'em while they're young. And he was the tutor of Alexander the Great, so he should know a thing or two about shaping young minds.

If you were a strategic planner for the corporate takeover of education, how would you do it? I'd have a simple four-step plan:

1. Drive up the costs of education, forcing kids to go into deep debt, and therefore needing a high-paying corporate job once they graduate.
2. Lobby the government to cut education funding.
3. Swoop in with my corporate checkbook and offer to pick up the deficit—in return for influencing the subjects taught and the teachers doing the teaching.
4. Push for fewer humanities courses—because they teach kids logic and philosophy—and push for more "practical" subjects, like engineering and economics.

Doesn't that sound close to what's been happening in capitalist countries since the 1980s?

In the early days of the Cold War, American conservatives were worried that the education system might be responsible for rising criticism of capitalism.

William F. Buckley, publisher, television host, CIA agent, and father of the modern conservative movement, complained in his 1951 book, *God and Man at Yale: The Superstitions of "Academic Freedom,"* that universities like his alma mater (where he was a member of the secret Skull and Bones society) "serve as indoctrination camps for liberalism."[295]

This complaint was picked up two decades later by lawyer Lewis Powell. Powell worked for a significant law firm in Richmond, Virginia, focusing on corporate law and representing clients such as the Tobacco Institute. He was later appointed an associate justice of the Supreme Court of the United States by Richard Nixon and is best known for writing his memorandum "Attack on the American Free Enterprise System," aka the "Powell Memorandum."[296]

His memo was motivated, in part, by Ralph Nader's attempts in the 1960s to expose how General Motors was putting profit above safety. Powell had been a director of the board of tobacco giant Philip Morris and didn't like it when people exposed corporate corruption. As his title suggests, he saw it as an attack on the American system by what he perceived to be an infiltration of communists into the education faculty who were guiding the young minds of America.

Composed in 1971 (long after we might have imagined the McCarthyistic fear of "Reds under the bed" had dissipated),

Powell's memo to Eugene Sydnor, the chairman of the Education Committee of the U.S. Chamber of Commerce, pointed out that these American schools and universities were funded and supported by businesses:

> *The campuses from which much of this criticism emanates are supported by tax funds generated mainly from American business, contributions from capital funds controlled or generated by American business. The boards of trustees at universities are overwhelmingly composed of men and women who are leaders in the business system and most of the media, including the national TV systems are owned and theoretically controlled by corporations which depend on profits and the enterprise system on which they survive.*

What should business leaders do about it? According to Powell, they needed to go on the front foot.

> *The day is long past when the chief executive officer of a major corporation discharges his responsibility by maintaining a satisfactory growth of profits, with due regard to the corporation's public and social responsibilities. If our system is to survive, top management must be equally concerned with protecting and preserving the system itself.*

His solution involved corporate America and the chamber of commerce getting more directly involved in the education system, both at the secondary and campus level:

> *Should not the Chamber also request specific courses in such schools dealing with the entire scope of the problem addressed by this memorandum?*

He also advised them to monitor textbooks and television programming for any "insidious type of criticism of the enterprise system" and to counter it by providing "staffs of eminent scholars, writers, and speakers who will do the thinking, the analysis, the writing, and the speaking."

Does that sound familiar? It could be the blueprint for Fox News and a whole host of institutions of the modern right. He is talking about using corporate-funded propaganda to prevent criticism of capitalism.

And how has education in the U.S. changed since Powell's memo? It's definitely become more expensive.

According to *The Economist*, "The cost of university (in the U.S.) per student has risen by almost five times the rate of inflation since 1983."

In Australia, a university education was completely free, paid for by the government, until 1983. Since then the fees have steadily climbed but have avoided several attempts by conservative governments to deregulate them totally.

Meanwhile, while fees have soared, the quality of a college education in the U.S. has declined: "A federal survey showed that the literacy of college-educated citizens declined between 1992 and 2003." [297]

"You have to go into near-permanent debt to get a college degree," according to one source,[298] but then you graduate with unsure employment prospects—one report estimates that 45 percent of college grads worked in a "non-college job," which is defined as a role in which fewer than 50 percent of the workers in that job need a bachelor's degree.[299]

But one thing is for sure—it's a hell of lot harder to be a political activist when you are up to your eyeballs in debt at the beginning of your working life. You'll probably want to knuckle down, work hard, get that debt paid off as soon as possible—which of course makes you an obedient, compliant worker bee. Start your adult life buried in debt, with huge penalties for default, including destroying your credit rating before you even get started.[300] Are you really going to go on strike for higher wages when you might lose your job as a result, which means you'll default on your student debt, which means you'll never be able to buy a car or a house? Probably not.

By increasing the cost of education, the elite can reduce the number of young people willing to protest unfair working conditions.

Decades later, Powell's philosophy was taken on board by the Koch brothers.

In 2011, the details of a 2008 grant agreement between Florida State University and the Charles Koch Foundation were made public. It was revealed that the foundation had given $1.5 million to the university. Part of the deal was that the foundation had an influence on which individual professors would get the funds. During the first round of hiring after the "grant," Koch rejected nearly 60 percent of the faculty's hiring suggestions.[301] And you end up with a conservative foundation determining who gets to teach students.

In his 2015 book, *Schooling Corporate Citizens: How Accountability Reform Has Damaged Civic Education and Undermined Democracy*,[302] Ronald Evans argues that the "accountability movement" in education (i.e., making schools and teachers accountable for, and paid on, student results) is motivated by the desires of corporate interests and their lobbies to educate a compliant, efficient workforce. In describing the tension between corporate interests and educators, he refers to a "tone of confrontation."

In 2007, American conservative writer David Horowitz penned *The Professors: The 101 Most Dangerous Academics in America*,[303] in which he railed against the "shocking and perverse culture of academics who are poisoning the minds of today's college students." This guy is also the author of books with such heart-warming titles as *Hating Whitey and Other Progressive Causes*.

Trump's Education Secretary, Betsy DeVos—wife of billionaire Amway heir Richard DeVos, daughter of billionaire industrialist Edgar Prince and sister of Erik Prince, the founder of the notorious mercenary outfit Blackwater[304]—is a big fan of pushing American education in the direction of "charter schools"—schools that are privately run but publicly funded.[305]

As they are private, these schools can do a lot of things that public schools cannot—like make it harder for minorities to attend.[306] And as they take "charitable donations" from the wealthy elite,[307] you have to wonder how much influence these foundations demand over the direction of the education and the hiring of teachers, as required by Charles Koch.

DON'T ROCK THE BOAT

If someone has risen to the top of their company, party, church, or industry, it would be extremely unnatural to expect them to push through significant revolutionary changes. The system as it stands has worked for them, so why would they want to change it dramatically?

And yet, if you look throughout history, you can find examples of these revolutionary leaders—but unless they have come into power as the result of an actual revolution, for example, Fidel Castro or Joseph Stalin, you'll often find they don't last very long in their jobs. People who try to turn the system upside down usually get turfed out pretty quickly—often by the other members of the elite.

Here's the story of a guy who tried to change too many things too quickly and was punished for it.

Australians remember the government of Gough Whitlam. Elected to government in December 1972, after his party had spent twenty years in the political wilderness, Whitlam, standing six-foot-four with silver hair combed back from his high forehead and bushy attack eyebrows that could take the tops off bottles, didn't want to wait until his cabinet could meet two weeks later before he started implementing some of his campaign promises. So he and his deputy leader Lance Barnard formed a "duumvirate" (an alliance of two) whereby they split between them all of the ministerial and quasi-ministerial roles typically held by a full cabinet. Together they revolutionized Australian society—they moved to establish full relations with China (after the previous Australian government had refused to recognize the Chinese government for twenty-four years), exempted the entire population from conscription, freed those in jail for avoiding conscription, reopened a case pending before a government tribunal into equal pay for women (and appointed the first woman to the tribunal), eliminated sales tax on contraceptive pills, banned racially discriminatory sporting teams from visiting Australia, instructed the Australia delegation at the UN to vote in favor of sanctions against apartheid South Africa and Rhodesia, and ordered home all Australian troops still in Vietnam.

Not a bad start!

And he didn't stop there. Over the next three years, Whitlam's government introduced free university education for all Australians, launched universal health insurance (yes, my American friends, Australia has had universal health since the early 1970s), introduced the Trade Practices Act, introduced land rights for indigenous Australians, passed Australia's first environmental legislation, introduced social welfare reforms including welfare payments for homeless people and a single mother's benefit, abolished the death penalty, introduced non-punitive divorce laws, reduced the voting age to eighteen, replaced "God Save the Queen" with "Advance Australia Fair" as the national anthem, introduced a Racial Discrimination Act, established the National Gallery of Australia, the Australia Council for the Arts, and the Australian Heritage Commission; and gave Papua New Guinea their independence. Whew. I'm exhausted just writing the list.

After he moved Australia toward joining the Non-Aligned Movement (a group of countries who do not want to be officially aligned with or against any major power bloc, created in 1961 by Yugoslavia's president, Josip Broz Tito; India's first prime minister, Jawaharlal Nehru; Egypt's second president, Gamal Abdel Nasser; Ghana's first president, Kwame Nkrumah; and Indonesia's first president, Sukarno), threatened to close the CIA's top-secret Pine Gap spy base in central Australia (the existence of which was unknown to the general public at the time), and some of his ministers publicly condemned the U.S. bombing of Vietnam as "corrupt and barbaric," a CIA station officer in Saigon said, "We were told the Australians might as well be regarded as North Vietnamese collaborators."[308]

Victor Marchetti, a CIA officer who had helped set up Pine Gap, later told journalist John Pilger, "This threat to close Pine Gap caused apoplexy in the White House."[309] Little did Whitlam realize at the time that the CIA (with the assistance of Britain's MI6) was bugging the communications of the Australian political and trade union elite.

Under Australia's constitution, the governor-general, who represents the Queen, has the power to appoint and dismiss the prime minister of Australia under specific circumstances, for example, if he decides the PM has lost the confidence of the Parliament, which is precisely what the governor-general of Australia, Sir John Kerr, decided in 1975, when he dismissed Whitlam's government and installed the opposition party into power. The government was, at the time, embroiled in several controversies, constantly criticized by the opposition and the media, with an economy that was stagnating (Whitlam came into power in the same year the OPEC crisis began, which crippled economies around the globe). Kerr's decision to dismiss the government came after the federal opposition party decided to block a supply bill, effectively shutting down the government's ability to fund itself, described as the greatest political and constitutional crisis in Australian history. Whitlam wanted to hold a snap election to break the deadlock, but Kerr decided to dismiss him instead.

According to one CIA contractor who worked at Pine Gap, the Americans referred to Kerr as "our man Kerr."[310] Kerr was also a member of the Australian Association for Cultural Freedom, described by one source as "an elite, invitation-only group...exposed in Congress as being founded, funded, and generally run by the CIA."

Conspiracy theories have run rampant ever since. Did the CIA conspire with Kerr to remove Whitlam? There's no hard evidence to support that theory. Kerr, of course, always denied it. However, a deputy director of the CIA later told Pilger, "Kerr did what he was told to do."[311]

Did the elite punish Whitlam for trying to do too much, too fast, too soon? Did his anti-American policies just piss off the wrong people? Or, did he just run an irresponsible government that just got itself into an economic crisis and paid the political price?

Plenty of politicians campaign on the promise that they are going to make dramatic changes once they are elected and yet very few live up to those promises like Whitlam.

Politicians like Whitlam are, unfortunately, rather rare. Most don't want to rock the boat. And why would they?

Thomas Jefferson once wrote:

> *Men by their constitutions are naturally divided into two parties:*
>
> 1. *Those who fear and distrust the people and wish to draw all powers from them into the hands of the higher classes.*
> 2. *Those who identify themselves with the people, have confidence in them, cherish and consider them as the most honest and safe, although not the wisest depositary of the public interests.*[312]

Politicians seem to fall into these two camps as well. The first type distrusts the people outright, while the second thinks the people are too erratic to be responsible for affairs of state—they are, to use Lippmann's phrase, "the bewildered herd," and need to be led by the intelligentsia, Bernays' "intelligent few," or the "vanguard of the proletariat" as the Bolsheviks referred to themselves.

I prefer to break Western politicians down into two primary flavors—those who promise to return things to how they were in the good ol' days (e.g., "Make America Great Again") and those who campaign on the promise of progress (e.g., "Hope and Change").

Both have no incentive to rock the boat.

The MAGAs typically have an agenda of trying to concentrate wealth and power into the hands of the elite. They usually want to sell off public infrastructure—assets governments have traditionally invested in, built, and maintained because they were for the public benefit, such as telecommunication providers, hospitals, power, water and gas companies, roads and highways, tunnels, and so on. Selling those assets allows the government to reap the short-term cash from the sale to offset budget deficits and get the future running costs off the government's books (which usually means laying off thousands of government employees). It also allows private individuals and corporations to profit from the assets, which are generally providing things people can't live without—like electricity and roads—in markets where there is limited competition and limited incentive for competition to enter because the start-up costs are phenomenal. The typical justification for selling off public assets (often referred to as "privatization," which sounds less threatening than "selling off public assets" because everyone likes the sound of "private" things) is that it will be more efficient, that private industry can do a much better job of running the business than a government department. This is, of course, complete nonsense. The privatization of public assets has become a major fixation of governments around the world since the 1980s. Privatization belongs to the same bucket of voodoo as "trickle-down economics." Both have failed over and over again, but governments continue to pretend they work.

The Danish institute AKF published a meta-study on the effects of privatization in 2011.[313] They reviewed eighty studies since the year 2000 across sectors, including public transport, healthcare, prisons, employment, water, waste management, social care, and electricity. They concluded that "It is not possible to conclude unambiguously that there is any systematic difference in terms of the economic effects of contracting out technical areas and social services...there is no general evidence here to say that private actors deliver the services cheaper or with a higher quality than the public sector itself does."

While they are busy selling off public assets (to their wealthy friends and campaign funders), the MAGAs will simultaneously be cutting taxes on corporations and the rich, reducing social services, and increasing budgets for the police, military, and prison systems (because you need them on your side if the people get uppity). They also tend to be hawkish, overtly religious—and statistically find themselves embroiled in more sex scandals, especially those associated with prostitutes and underage boys.[314]

The HACs (Hope And Change), if they get elected, will be prepared to spread the wealth around a little bit, by marginally increasing social services, slightly increasing taxation on the wealthy and corporations, while passing some incrementally progressive legislation. But they aren't trying to push through massive changes.

Huey Long was another politician who rocked the boat. The

40th governor of Louisiana, and member of the Senate 1932–35, once argued for a maximum $100 million wealth limit.

This was in 1934. Under his plan, nobody could have more than $100 million, which, adjusted for inflation, would be about $2 billion today. Sounds like enough to me! This was part of his "Share Our Wealth" plan. Where is today's Huey Long? Even Bernie Sanders and Alexandria Ocasio-Cortez look mild compared to him.

They probably remember what happened to Huey. He was assassinated in 1935, shot on the steps of the State Capitol, by the son-in-law of his political opponent.

The HACs exist to give the voters the illusion of a choice. At the end of the day, their campaigns are funded by the rich and the corporations almost to the same tune as the MAGAs.

There's no reason to think that the people who rise to the top of the HAC party in your country is any less a psychopath than the people at the top of the MAGA party.

And here's good evidence to support that idea—both sides get themselves embroiled in corruption scandals at roughly equal rates.

If this list of American politicians convicted of crimes either committed or prosecuted while holding office in the federal government is any guide, then the Republicans and Democrats are about equal when it comes to political corruption (fifty-five Republicans versus forty-nine Democrats).[315]

Although they differ in some of their views and their rhetoric, both types of politicians will more or less want to keep things from changing too dramatically. Neither of them really trusts the public, and neither really wants to change things so much that it destabilizes their hold on power.

Whatever the lines of division might be, we can safely assume that politicians are human (despite David Icke's assurance that they are lizard overlords from another planet) and are driven by Maslowian desires for security and safety. Even the ones that aren't psychopaths want to protect their jobs, their incomes, their future opportunities, and their lifestyles.

Significant changes to the system aren't in their best interests. More than the rest of us, they are familiar with stories of politicians like Whitlam who tried to do too much, too quickly, and burned up like Icarus.

It makes sense that they will want to either support the status quo or, if they can, tweak the system only so much that their party can hold on to power longer than usual. Change brings unknowns, and unknowns bring instability (try saying that in your best Yoda voice). Best to keep things the way they are.

But of course, they can't just come out and say this in public. It's not much of a campaign slogan to say, "If I win, I'm going to keep things just the way they are because I've made it to the top, baby!"

That isn't going to fly with the electorate—except maybe for the elite, who wholeheartedly agree with keeping things the way they are. By the way, it's predominantly the elite of the elite, "the 1 percent of the 1 percent" who are actually financing election campaigns—small donations from the average Joe are just gravy. And who are the elite of the elite? They are "mostly male, tend to be city-dwellers and often work in finance" according to one study.[316] And we've already seen that the rates of psychopaths in the finance industry are extraordinarily high.

So, you've got the elite of the elite, many of whom are possibly psychopaths, who don't want things to change, paying for politicians to run advertising campaigns talking about how much they are going to change things once they get elected. Why would they do that?

Because the elite understand the Three Steps of Democracy:

Step #1: Say whatever you need to say to get elected. It doesn't matter what you say or what you promise.

Step #2: When you get into power, find valid-sounding excuses for why you can't deliver on the promises that don't entrench your power or the power of your key constituents, which is, in effect, the same thing. Traditional excuses include: "We just learned some vital new information not available to us at the time we made that promise," "The situation has changed dramatically since we made that promise, so it is no longer a good idea," "We still plan to deliver on that promise, but we can't do it now for various practical reasons, so it's going to have to wait until after the next election," and "We just can't get it approved by this obstructionist Senate."

Step #3: Wherever possible, distract the public from realizing you have broken your election promises with bread and circuses, political theater, straw man problems, dog-whistle politics, imagined threats to your way of life from the outside, and other forms of political distraction.

Though he by no means invented this model, we have to admit that Donald Trump is the master of it.

THE FIELD OF BROKEN PROMISES

How many election promises actually get broken? A 2009 survey across Europe and the United States found that political parties kept, on average, only 67 percent of their campaign commitments.[317]

This may sound surprisingly high, but we have to remember that not all campaign promises are the same. There are the little promises, which are easier to keep (we're going to fix up a road), and there are the big promises (we're going to build a wall and make Mexico pay for it) that are harder to keep but make for excellent sound bites.

What's more surprising is how cynical people are about political promises.

The authors of the 2009 survey found that if you "ask people around you if they think that political parties keep their electoral promises... you will probably obtain a high rate of negative answers."

Political scholars seem to agree.

American political scientist E. E. Schattschneider long ago argued that "party platforms are fatuities. They persuade no one, deceive no one, and enlighten no one."

British political scientist Anthony King asserted that party manifestos are "empty and meaningless" documents having a "virtually random relationship" with what the party will in fact do in office.

So why do we still pretend democracy works?

Because people have the memory of a goldfish.

And iPhones are just making that... oh look! An update!

...Sorry, where was I? Oh, right.

If people don't truly believe the campaign promises politicians make, why do they vote for them in the first place? Does it have more to do with personality and a sense of tribal connection than we typically acknowledge?

For example, there is substantial evidence to suggest that we gravitate toward tall leaders. Male Fortune 500 chief executive officers tend to be taller than the average American male and the taller of the two presidential candidates wins 58 percent of the time.[318] Donald Trump is, of course, much taller than Hillary Clinton, so maybe that was all that he needed to win? Perhaps height has more to do with how we vote and not what they say or do?

Back to breaking promises. "All politicians lie," people often tell me. "Just accept it and move on."

Of course, they usually only say things like that when defending a politician they support, but that argument goes out the window when they are attacking someone from the other team. But hypocrisy isn't the issue here.

Psychologists tell us that it's our responsibility to set guidelines for how people treat us in a relationship. If you catch your spouse, colleague, manager, or child lying to you multiple times and you do nothing about it, what do you think will happen? Chances are they will keep it up. If they see no disincentive for lying, why would they stop? By allowing them to continue to lie, a psychologist would tell us that we are enabling that person's behavior, like the spouse of an alcoholic enables their continued drinking by not drawing a line in the metaphorical sand and saying, "Get help and quit or I'm leaving."

If we just accept that we're getting lied to by politicians, and don't try to do anything about it, we are also enablers. By accepting their behavior, we're giving them a blank check to continue to lie and break promises. Only by continually calling them on their bullshit and punishing them for it, can we hope to create a world where people in power are forced into being honest about their actions and motivations.

"We do punish them—by voting them out," you might say. But is that really much of a punishment? What happens to politicians after they lose their seat? Most don't end up on the street, living under a bridge. Many of them are very well looked after by the interests they represented while in office. They end up with highly paid executive roles, speaking engagements, consulting offers, and book deals. Of course, not all end up like that, but many do. People just tend not to notice, because once they are out of politics, politicians tend to keep a fairly low public profile.

This isn't a new phenomenon, either.

> *"Politicians have no leisure because they*
> *are always aiming at something beyond political*
> *life itself—power and glory, or happiness."*
>
> —Aristotle

But while they are in power, to prevent us from paying much attention to their broken promises, the elite have perfected the art of distraction.

BRIGHT SHINY OBJECTS

Like every respectable magician in Las Vegas, the elite know how to use misdirection to distract us with one hand while doing something crafty with the other. Magicians understand that the average human mind has limits to how many things it can concentrate on at any one time. An accomplished magician will take advantage of these limits, manipulating the audience's perceptions, drawing them to make false conclusions. They will often first grab their audience's attention with a small shiny object then will use misdirection, through combinations of comedy, sleight of hand or by introducing additional-yet-unimportant objects, to distract the audience while they do the real trick with the original object behind their back.

Every day in the media you will see some new "bright, shiny object," as former presidential candidate and HP CEO Carly Fiorina put it on *Meet the Press*.[319] Fiorina, who probably knows a little bit about the subject, said that in "every election cycle, (politicians) hold up some bright, shiny object" to distract the public from the important issues.

For the record, during her short tenure at HP, Fiorina was paid $100 million, laid off 30,000 U.S. employees, fired three executives during a 5 AM telephone call, and says she later voted to ban same-sex marriage. Make of that what you will.

A BSO (bright, shiny object) is usually designed to titillate, outrage, or scare significant swathes of the public. It forces everyone from politicians, commentators, religious leaders, and the military to weigh in and consumes the media cycle for a day, a week, or longer, until it is replaced with the next BSO.

The list of BSOs include:

Political Theatrics—politicians (and the political ecosystem, including advisers, staffers, consultants, media commentators) playing with hot-button issues, taking a politicized issue that they know will cause an uproar—abortion, immigration, gun regulations, same-sex marriage, climate change, the war on drugs, embryonic stem cell research— and chumming the media with it.

Sensationalism—tabloid-style reporting about generally insignificant matters and events. These days we call it "clickbait" when referring to online stories. The spate of stories trying to connect the Trump administration to Russia in 2016–2019 was a classic example. The stories constantly alluded that something highly illegal had occurred, even though there was scant evidence to support the allegations, as Mueller's report concluded.[320]

Reality TV—low-cost programming that delivers high ratings because people seem to like watching a "real-life" soap opera—which, of course, isn't real and is highly produced, with each moment of emotion carefully planned, shot, edited and, if necessary, re-shot to heighten the emotion.[321] When one of my sisters, Anita, appeared on the early Australian reality TV show *Dog Eat Dog*, she was asked by the producers to play the role of the bitch and on several occasions was asked to repeat a scene and "bitch it up a little." Please note that she has asked me to point out for the record she is not, actually, a bitch. Reality TV is the modern equivalent of Roman gladiator games, with people engrossed each week to see whose entrails end up on the floor of the colosseum and who gets the Emperor's hard-won upward-raised thumb.

Professional Sports—game results, drug scandals, players' salaries, players and their private lives, coach sex scandals, celebrity team owners, owner versus coach tensions, and so forth. Like Reality TV, professional sports is the modern version of gladiator trials.

The Cult of Celebrity—who is dating who, who is getting divorced and why, drug scandals, sex scandals, who is difficult to work with, who has put on weight, who has lost weight, who has had plastic surgery, and so on. Late night shows with celebrity guests are another form of this obsession with actors, musicians, and models.

Hollywood Blockbusters—billions of dollars are poured into making and selling films every year, with an increasing number of films costing $200 million or more, and the hype surrounding upcoming films is the only thing some people can talk about. TV and radio talk shows, breakfast programming, news broadcasts, and even podcasts are saturated with interviews with the stars and directors.

A lot of these BSOs fall under the category of "junk food news"—inconsequential trivia that is designed to titillate, isn't very nourishing, and is cheap to churn out.

Let's be clear—all of these BSOs operate for a number of different reasons—they involve careers for a huge range of people and profits for the businesses that run them. But they are also distractions that help the elite stay in power and are therefore encouraged by the elite in many ways. A population with fewer distractions, or who valued these distractions less, might become more interested, educated, and involved in politics—and this would not be in the interests of the elite.

The "brightest and shiniest of all the bright, shiny objects," according to David Axelrod, a long-time Obama political adviser, is

Donald Trump.[322] During the 2016 election cycle, Trump perfected the art of creating a new BSO every day, sometimes *several* per day, forcing the media and the rest of the candidates to respond to him, focus on him, and pay attention to him. Despite the general consensus that the general public would soon tire of his BSO shenanigans, the tactic worked. His technique of making outrageous statements from the podium and on Twitter, TV, and radio kept the entire political circus on their toes, constantly predicting his imminent political demise, while devoting so much attention to him that it left hardly any room for anyone else. He devoured media minutes like Godzilla attacking Tokyo. He played on our BSO susceptibility.

Trump, of course, was using the BSO technique to get all of the attention while the elite usually use it to distract from things they don't want to get much attention (although he also used them to distract from his previous day's BSO). They know that newspapers only have so many inches to fill—television and radio only so many hours. People only have so much time to read, watch, and listen to the news. So, if you can manipulate the news into covering BSO issues—sex scandals, celebrity gossip, sporting results, fear that our society is being undermined by communists, fascists, Muslims, and "the gays"—they won't be able to focus on the real issues.

And Trump didn't stop with the BSO tactic once he made his home in the Oval Office. If it ain't broke, don't fix it! Since the beginning of his presidency, he has thrown out a new BSO or two on Twitter every single day. A ban on Muslims! We're building a wall! Rolling back Obamacare! Transgenders in the military! Bomb Syria! Threaten the Little Rocket Man! Iran! Biden's corrupt!

Many commentators think that Trump deliberately uses the

BSO strategy to distract media and public attention from his real agenda—signing legislation that pushes the interests of the GOP base. And the media, and the people, continue to fall for the tactic. They are constantly chasing his BSOs around, like kittens chasing a laser light on the floor. Meanwhile, the really important issues, like the military budget, the U.S. support for Israel and Saudi Arabia, unlimited campaign funding, and psychopaths in the system, get mostly ignored.

As Noam Chomsky puts it:

> "At one level, Trump's antics ensure that attention is focused on him, and it makes little difference how. Who even remembers the charge that millions of illegal immigrants voted for Clinton, depriving the pathetic little man of his grand victory? Or the accusation that Obama had wiretapped Trump Tower? The claims themselves don't really matter. It's enough that attention is diverted from what is happening in the background. There, out of the spotlight, the most savage fringe of the Republican Party is carefully advancing policies designed to enrich their true constituency: the constituency of private power and wealth, "the masters of mankind," to borrow Adam Smith's phrase."[323]

It's also critical to understand that the media loves a BSO as much as the politicians. CNN had its most profitable year ever in 2016—the U.S. presidential election helped the network generate over $1 billion in profit. Fox News had an even better election year, with their audience numbers up 11 percent on their previous best and a gross profit of over $1.67 billion.[324]

When you realize that election-based advertising would have been a huge chunk of those profits, it's easy to see how the significant corporate media companies have as much invested in the election circus as the politicians. The crazier BSO things a candidate says, the higher the ratings are, and the more they can charge for advertising.

Using a BSO to distract the public is part of the art of political propaganda.

These are just some of the ways the elite have manipulated the minds of the general public so that we allow them to keep their power. If we are going to address the psychopath problem, we need to understand the conditioning and propaganda we have been subjected to over the course of our lives—and find a way to break free from it.

CHAPTER FIVE

ROCKING
THE VOTE

So the people on the top of the pile, many of them probably psychopaths, don't want to rock the boat, don't want to change things, except in minor ways.

However, most of us in the 99 percent *want* systemic change —dramatically, and as quickly as possible, thanks very much. We want to see dramatic changes that make the system fairer and more equitable. We want to see the effort and the wealth shared more fairly. Not just a *little*—a *lot*. We want politicians to urgently do something about climate change, to fix campaign finance laws, to force the rich to stop hiding their wealth in offshore tax shelters, and to stop psychopaths from fucking everything up.

But what should we do about it? The answer usually given is "vote." Is that really the solution though? We've been *doing* that for one hundred years, and yet we still end up with politicians that people find disappointing and are indeed often shown to be corrupt and venal. Trust in U.S. politicians is at record lows.[325] In Australia, "We are now just four percentage points above Russia, the world's least-trusting nation," according to the annual Edelman Trust Barometer.[326]

The World Values Survey[327] has consistently found that while people around the world tend to think democracy is essential, the majority also feel like the level of democracy is less than it could be, even in the West.

And we're struggling to handle all of the new information being thrust upon us by our iPhones and television sets. According to consumer psychologist Kit Yarrow, PhD.

> *Information overload is one reason we've grown more vulnerable to manipulation. Research suggests that we receive five times more information now than we did 30 years ago.* [328]

Marketers, politicians, and psychologists know that our minds are most comfortable when given easy, black-and-white, binary choices: *These* are the good guys, and *these* are the bad guys. Our brains have limited processing power and the world is increasingly complex. The human brain, which evolved over hundreds of thousands of years when we had to make far fewer daily decisions, doesn't like to work too hard on problems that aren't solving immediate needs like procuring food and shelter. Simplistic, dichotomous thinking is a shortcut for the brain—it gets us through the day and saves our mental energy for more critical things like eating, working, and getting laid (i.e., System 1 and System 2 thinking).

Marketing experts (disclaimer: I run a marketing agency by day[329]) and their clients, like politicians and corporations, totally appreciate the limitations of the human brain. Meanwhile, the 1 percent have near unlimited funds to spend on propaganda and manipulation of the system to their own benefit. They can fund election campaigns, bribe politicians in power, and saturate the media with dog-whistle messaging about politicians who don't take the hint (or the bribe).

This might be one reason why the United States, held up for centuries as the ideal modern democracy, currently ranks only twenty-first in the *Economist*'s "Democracy Index 2017."[330] The magazine has demoted the U.S. from a full democracy to a "flawed democracy." And before you jump to any conclusions (System 1)— this *isn't* because of Trump. "The U.S.'s declining status is primarily due to a significant fall in people's trust in the functioning of public institutions, a trend that was well established before the election of President Donald Trump." In other words, America was a flawed democracy well before the Trump circus.

What's that you say? The United States is a republic, not a democracy? I see that statement promoted proudly a lot on various online forums, and it's simply incorrect. As Eugene Volokh, professor of law at the UCLA School of Law, points[331] out, the United States, as a republic, is a representative democracy, (as are other countries on the index, such as Australia) and a representative democracy is a *form* of democracy. So the U.S. is both a republic *and* a democracy.

We've already seen that trust in politicians is at record lows. How else is democracy failing us?

THE DECLINE OF DEMOCRACY

Have the people in Western democracies made much progress in the last century? Are things dramatically better for the 99 percent than they were one hundred years ago?

Well, yes, in many ways they definitely are. General living standards are much higher, healthcare has massively improved, education and literacy levels are much higher; access to technology and information and transport, and improvements in the quality of food, clean water, life expectancy, etc. Women and minorities have the vote. There's less segregation, and a general increase in tolerance for minorities and people of various sexual preferences.

But those things are also true in China, a single-party socialist country, which has pulled 850 million people out of poverty in the last forty years, without the Western style of democracy.[332] According to American economist Lawrence Summers, currently a professor at Harvard's Kennedy School of Government, at its height, the American economy was doubling living standards roughly every thirty years. China is currently doubling living standards *every decade*.[333] They definitely have less political freedom than other countries,[334] but they have also had less time to work toward it. It wasn't until 1949 that the Chinese finally replaced the Qing dynasty with the People's Republic of China, led by Chairman Mao Zedong. For the previous hundred years, the Chinese had experienced their "century of humiliation," after being forced at gunpoint by the British to allow opium to be freely sold to their people.

Polls suggest that the majority of voters in the United States want campaign finance reform,[335] the federal government to make sure all Americans have health care coverage,[336] and corporations to pay more tax.[337]

But those things don't seem to be a priority for the majority of elected officials.

In Australia, 80 percent of Australians and up to 70 percent of Catholics and Anglicans support the idea of making euthanasia legal.[338] And yet our politicians avoid addressing the issue (with the exception of the State of Victoria, which introduced assisted suicide in mid-2019).

The majority of Australians want politicians to take climate change seriously,[339] but the government is making next-to-zero progress (and some still deny it's a genuine problem). Most Aussies also want marijuana to be decriminalized.[340] Gay marriage was a similar story in Australia—quite popular in the polls for many years before politicians *finally* did something about it, dragging their feet even compared to uber-Catholic countries like Ireland.

If politicians are democratically elected to do what the voters want, what's going on? Perhaps it's because the interests of the politicians are not in alignment with those of the voters?

The unfortunate truth, historically speaking, is that there have been very few occasions in human society where the power of the elite has been reduced through a democratic process. Quite often, the democratic process has either been co-opted by the elite to work in their favor, has utterly failed the economic and justice interests of the people, or has ended in civil wars among the elite.

Going way back in history, the famous democracy of Athens, where only 10–20 percent were allowed to vote, managed to last a couple of hundred years. However, during that time, it was often continually overthrown by a series of tyrants. Eventually the city and its struggling democracy were weakened to the point where they were easily crushed—first by the forces of King Phillip II of Macedon and then by his son, Alexander the Great.

The Roman Republic also had a kind of democracy. The elite still ultimately ran things and, over time, were forced to give the people a little bit of power. That experiment lasted nearly five hundred years before it collapsed after a lengthy series of civil wars, where the elite fought among themselves over power and money. Eventually Julius Caesar's adopted son, Augustus, restored peace and stability by replacing the democratic experiment with a monarchy.

Florence's experiment with democracy in the fourteenth century ended in the quasi-dictatorship of bankers, the Medici family.

France's brief post-revolutionary experiment with democracy in the late eighteenth century ended with Napoleon joining a coup to overthrow the corrupt Directory—and then staging his own coup against the leaders of that coup. He inherited a number of ongoing wars between France and the rest of Europe, whose monarchs weren't too happy about the idea of one of their own being overthrown by the people. Imagine if they allowed that to succeed! The idea might catch on in their own countries. After decades of wars against France, they finally defeated Napoleon and restored the Bourbon monarchy.

Germany's first experiment with democracy in the early twentieth century ended up with the Nazis in power.

And America's model of democracy gave the world President Trump.

As Reinhold Niebuhr, American theologian, ethicist, and the author of the Serenity Prayer, said:

> *The democratic idealists of practically all schools of thought have managed to remain remarkably oblivious to the obvious facts.*

Despite democracy's failings, it is a useful tool for the elite. Giving the public the illusion of choice might have reduced the number of violent revolutions that have taken place in the West during the last 200 years. When people feel like they have zero say in how things are run, they often grab their pitchforks and march on the palaces of the nobility. But if you instill in them the idea that a better alternative is to *vote*, then the potential pitch-fork-bearers might stay at home, crack another cold one, turn the footy back on, and feel like they have done their bit. While there are undoubtedly a long list of politicians, bankers, CEOs, and other leaders who have been sentenced to lengthy jail terms in Western democracies in the last century, the people at the very top seem to avoid it. Like New York's favorite 1980s mafia don,[341] they seem to be covered in Teflon.

As it turns out, when it comes to political outcomes, most people are not making rational decisions based on the real-world impact they will have on their life, partly because they just don't pay much attention to politics and partly because they make political decisions, "on the basis of social identities and partisan loyalties, not an honest examination of reality" in the words of political scientists Christopher Achen and Larry Bartels.[342]

> We believe that abandoning the folk theory of democracy is a prerequisite to both greater intellectual clarity and real political change. Too many democratic reformers have squandered their energy on misguided or quixotic ideas.

Let's look deeper at income and wealth equality in the West.

According to French economist Thomas Piketty, author of the *New York Times* Best Seller *Capital in the Twenty-First Century*,[343] income inequality in the United States has been on the rise since 1980, surpassing even the heights of the "Roaring Twenties."[344]

And the U.S. isn't alone in this trend. Piketty claims that Australia, Canada, and the United Kingdom show a similar rise, although not quite as steep. He goes as far as to say that the level of income inequality in the United States today is "probably higher than in any other society at any time in the past, anywhere in the world." And that's really saying something, when you think about the kings and the peasants in the Middle Ages, or the Senate and the plebeians during the Roman Republic.

This phenomenon of unequal income distribution isn't only happening in the West. Piketty's analysis of six developing countries—Argentina, China, Colombia, India, Indonesia, and South Africa—shows that, while income inequality declined in the first three-quarters of the twentieth century, it has *increased* significantly in five of them in the last forty years, the exception being Columbia.

According to Piketty's analysis, the gap in the distribution of *wealth* (as opposed to income) between the top 1 percent and the 99 percent has also steadily increased in the United States and Europe since 1970.

Basically, the rich are getting richer, taking an increasing share of the wealth and income as time goes on. Although living standards may have dramatically increased around the globe, the living standards of the wealthy have increased at a much higher rate than the rest of us.

This means, of course, that they have more money to spend on manipulating the system to their benefit, which we would expect to result in this trend of unequal wealth and income distribution to continue unabated.

What, then, should the people do? If elections and governments are run by people whose interests aren't in alignment with the will of the people—and if people vote based on what they hear in the media, which is run by corporations whose interests aren't in alignment with the people—what then?

Is it possible that the best years of democracy are behind it?

One course of action is a people's revolution, peaceful or otherwise. Unfortunately, as I touched on earlier, there aren't many strong, historical precedents for how to run a successful revolution.

Even the American Revolution, which is often held up to be the most successful example, wasn't really a win for most segments of society. When the Americans had their revolution in the late eighteenth century (led by a group of tax-dodgers), in many ways they just replaced a small governing group of entitled British elite with a small governing group of entitled American elite. It was unquestionably handy for the wealthy white men, but their revolution didn't provide many benefits in the short term for women, slaves, Native Americans, or the working class.

The incident known as Shay's Rebellion, an armed uprising in Massachusetts during 1786 and 1787, stemmed from the collapse of international trade that followed the revolution. European trading partners, understandably worried about America's reliability, refused to provide them with lines of credit and insisted they pay with hard currency, which wasn't readily available. The consequences of this decision trickled down to American farmers, many who ended up losing their farms due to debt and tax obligations they couldn't meet (oh the irony). Instead of acknowledging the role of the revolution in the creation of the problems and working to resolve it with some kind of tax relief, the Massachusetts government cracked down, and the rebellion intensified.

Things got so terrible that Samuel Adams, one of the Founding Fathers, suspended habeas corpus and passed a law that punished rebellion with execution. A state of martial law was declared, a law was passed to prevent any of the rebels from ever holding elected office, and hundreds of men were indicted. Most were eventually pardoned—only two were executed. It was in regard to Shay's Rebellion that Founding Father Thomas Jefferson wrote:

> *I hold it that a little rebellion now and then is a good thing... It is a medicine necessary for the sound health of government.... God forbid that we should ever be twenty years without such a rebellion.... The tree of liberty must be refreshed from time to time with the blood of patriots and tyrants. It is its natural manure.*

Another Founding Father, Alexander Hamilton, an unsuccessful businessman and tax collector, wrote around this time his personal opinion of democracy:

> *All communities divide themselves into the few and the many. The first are the rich and well-born, the other the mass of the people. The voice of the people has been said to be the voice of God; and however generally this maxim has been quoted and believed, it is not true in fact. The people are turbulent and changing; they seldom judge or determine right. Give therefore to the first class a distinct permanent share in the government... Can a democratic assembly who annually revolve in the mass of the people be supposed steadily to pursue the public good? Nothing but a permanent body can check the imprudence of democracy....*[345]

In the first eighty years after the revolution, Hamilton's "first class," aka the "rich and well-born," did quite well. Inequality in

America grew about as much during those years as it has in the period since 1970, according to authors Peter Lindert and Jeffrey Williamson in their book *Unequal Gains: American Growth and Inequality since 1700*.[346] For example—within the first eighty-five years after the revolution, the top 1 percent of Americans *tripled* their share of property incomes.

During the twentieth century, people's revolutions failed to deliver on their promises for a variety of reasons. They were either co-opted by military oligarchs or immediately attacked by external reactionary forces—and, quite often, both of the above simultaneously.

The various revolutionary movements in India, such as the pacifist one led by Mahatma Gandhi (there were also a number of violent movements), culminated in that country's independence in 1947. However, they were also helped by the collapse of the British Empire after World War II (partly because they couldn't afford to support their colonial possessions and partly because of the Atlantic Charter).

Unfortunately, the independence of India led to its hasty partition, the displacement of 14 million people, and large-scale violence, with estimates of up to 2 million dead just in the Punjab region alone.

Of the people who rose up during the "Arab Spring," revolutions of 2011 in Tunisia, Libya, Egypt, Yemen, Syria, and Bahrain, only the Tunisians managed to create any kind of constitutional democratic government.

Perhaps the best example of a successful revolution we can think of is The Velvet Revolution, a nonviolent transition of power that took place in Czechoslovakia in 1989 and culminated

in the Czech Republic and Slovakia, both of which are now prospering countries.

It's worth noting, however, that this revolution to gain independence from the USSR, like India's escape from Britain's greedy
clutches, coincided with the collapse of communism in Romania,
Bulgaria, Hungary, and Poland, as Mikhail Gorbachev deliberately
transformed the USSR.

Maybe the secret to a successful revolution is simply lucky
timing?

It's also worth noting that, although the Czech Republic today
has one of the lowest levels of income inequality in the EU,[347] the
share of the national income controlled by the 1 percent has
already tripled in the thirty years since the revolution.[348] Give
them time and it's quite possible they will catch up to the levels
of income and wealth disparity in the other "democracies."

So where does that leave us? The people want more freedom,
more control, and more equitable sharing of the wealth. The elite
use their wealth and influence to tip the balance in their favor.
Voting doesn't work. Revolutions don't work. What are we left with?

THE DEPARTMENT OF ETHICS

Before I move on from politics, I want to talk about ethics. I've
argued for many years that Australia should have a Department
of Ethics. We do it for health issues, but surely *all* of our legislation
and economic decisions to be subject to some kind of rigorous and
public ethical review? This department could help work out what
kinds of ethics the people want to see upheld by their politicians,
public servants, business and religious leaders.

When I'm going to vote in an election, the individual or party that I vote for should reflect more than their policies—they should reflect how much I think their ethics match my own. I don't want to vote for a psychopath.

But some people I spoke to about the concept of a Department of Ethics told me there is no place for ethics in government. Having governments involved in philosophy seems to remind people of *Nineteen Eighty-Four* or something.

So I contacted the professionals for advice.

First I rang Dr. Simon Longstaff AO (Order of Australia), who has a PhD in philosophy from Cambridge University and became the inaugural executive director of The Ethics Centre (Australia) in 1991.

Dr. Longstaff reminded me that, once upon a time, ethics did play a bigger role in politics.

What you see in Australia today is that, with rare exceptions, there's often a lack of comfort about advancing ethical arguments in a way that might finally resolve a question. Instead, a typical way to resolve questions is to seek to provide some kind of economic justification for why something should or shouldn't happen.

He compared this with the event, just over 200 years ago, when William Wilberforce stood up in the British parliament and argued the case for the abolition of slavery. He would have been confident that he could advance arguments that were entirely ethical, based on the central claim that no human person should ever have their intrinsic dignity set aside so that they can be traded as if they were just some kind of chattel.

And he would not have ended his speech in the House of Commons by saying "And if everything else fails in my argument, here it is, I have an economics report to say that it costs too much!" It wasn't thinkable that he would do it in those terms; it wasn't necessary.

I suspect that the reasons for ending slavery in the United States had quite a bit to do with economics, but that's a different story. He continued:

But in Australia today, if you look at many, many of the policy discussions, it's as if we can't bring ourselves to resolve them by sound ethical argument, but instead we think that because there are complexities in ethical arguments and differences of opinion as we're a multicultural society, that we'll think "perhaps we can appeal to something that appears to be neutral," namely an economic calculation, so what happens there is that the ethical argument gradually gets edged away from centre of things and towards the sides.

It might be easy for our politicians to avoid discussing ethics because we, the general public, don't have a firm grasp on our own. Maybe it's time to hold them, and ourselves, to a higher standard?

Longstaff also pointed out that the father of liberal economics, Adam Smith, was not an economist; he was the professor of moral philosophy at the University of Glasgow, and that you cannot understand *The Wealth of Nations* unless you also read his other seminal work, *The Theory of Moral Sentiments*, where he explains that the "invisible hand" (a metaphor Smith used to describe the unintended social benefits of individual self-interested actions) only works to spread the benefits if the landlord (that he uses in the example) has a sense of morality:

> By acting according to the dictates of our moral faculties, we necessarily pursue the most effective means for promoting the happiness of mankind.

If the landlord is a psychopath and has no morals, then the benefits of the "invisible hand" end up in offshore tax havens.

Next I spoke with Julian Burnside AO QC (Queen's Counsel, particularly eminent lawyers, mostly barristers, in Australia, appointed by letters patent to be one of Her Majesty's Counsel learned in the law), renowned in Australia for his pro bono legal work in high-profile human rights cases.

When I told Julian that some people I have spoken to declared ethics isn't something governments should get involved in, he strongly disagreed:

> I'm astounded that anyone would suggest that governments don't make ethical decisions—when you consider our country's response to climate change, it plainly involves ethical consider-ations, not the least of which is if you think climate change is real, does this generation of our society hold any obligation to future generations? It's an ethical question.
>
> And every international human rights instrument raises eth-ical considerations, the first of which is, do we share its ethical underpinnings, are we prepared to subscribe to those ethical underpinnings, and will we give effect to them once we've sub-scribed to it. The way human beings are treated by the nation is, at least in part, an ethical question. Even tax questions, I think, may

involve an ethical component. I think it's quite hard, actually, to think of decisions that governments need to make that are wholly outside the domain of ethics.

Many of us, perhaps, do not have a clear enough sense of what is right and wrong for us personally and will go along for the ride, voting for the same party our parents supported, or voting from our hip pocket, or not speaking up at a meeting at work when we hear something we disagree with. This lack of well-developed personal ethics might go a long way to explaining how we allow workplace cultures or entire societies to become toxic.

It's like that old legend about boiling a frog. If you throw a live frog into a pot of boiling water, so the story goes, it will jump straight back out. If, instead, you put it in a pot of cool water and gradually increase the heat, it won't notice the temperature rise until it dies. (Modern biologists point out the legend is nonsense, but let's ignore them and their "fact-based reasoning" for the moment.)

We let one unethical decision slip past us. Then another.

It's like the famous confession of the WWII German Lutheran pastor Martin Niemöller:

First they came for the socialists, and I did not speak out—
Because I was not a socialist.
Then they came for the trade unionists, and I did not speak out—
Because I was not a trade unionist.
Then they came for the Jews, and I did not speak out—
Because I was not a Jew.
Then they came for me—and there was no one left to speak for me.

CHAPTER SIX

CTRL-ALT-DELETE

History teaches us that when people get sick and tired of being lied to by the politicians, by the media, and the rest of the elite, they start to try to change the system through voting, protests, or revolutions. But history also teaches us that when the usual methods of control of the masses stop working, the elite try to protect their interests by ramping up their control mechanisms.

They find excuses to increase the size and militarization of the police force. They find excuses to pass laws that limit traditional civil rights such as free speech and freedom of association. They introduce harsher mandatory sentencing for minor crimes. They increase censorship. They provide less transparency of government legislation. They increase FUD regarding economic or physical security. They promote xenophobia. They target non-compliant journalists and publishers and intellectuals.

These changes are usually sold to the public as being necessary for national security reasons or to fight crime. If there are no genuine security threats, they will be manufactured.

A rather mild example of this response is what happened in the twentieth century with marijuana and the war on drugs.

For a century, the elite manufactured a fear campaign about the dangers of marijuana, which, they claimed, turned people into monsters and drove them mad. Today, of course, such fears have been dismissed, and marijuana has been decriminalized and even legalized in many jurisdictions. What happened? Did medical science finally catch up? No.

Scratch the surface of the twentieth century's marijuana fear campaign, and you'll find it was based not on science or genuine health concerns but on racism, xenophobia, and political machinations.

Cannabis only started to become a public issue in the U.S. after the Spanish American war, when more Mexicans started to emigrate north. The Mexican Revolution, which took place between 1910–20, created a flow of war refugees and political exiles who fled to the United States to escape the violence. Mexicans also left rural areas in search of stability and employment. As a result, Mexican migration to the United States rose sharply. The number of legal migrants grew from around 20,000 per year during the 1910s to about 50,000–100,000 per year during the 1920s. Some of this was also driven by American capitalists looking for cheap labor. The 1924 immigration bill (the purpose of which was "to preserve the ideal of U.S. homogeneity" and to keep out radical elements) lowered the number of immigrants coming in from Europe, so the railroads and sugar beet industry turned to Mexico, who would work for a lot less than Americans. As a response, the labor movement, ultra-patriotic groups, and civic groups in the Southwest organized protests and blamed Mexicans for an increase in crime.

Because Mexicans liked to smoke cannabis, an easy way to target them, without appearing racist, was to criminalize one of their favorite pastimes. And in order to criminalize marijuana, it had to be demonized. The dangers of smoking it had to be blown way out of proportion.

According to Amanda Reiman from the Drug Policy Alliance:

> In 1914, El Paso, Texas, became the first jurisdiction in the U.S. to ban the sale and possession of marijuana. This ban gave police the right to search, detain, and question Mexican immigrants without reason, except the suspicion that they were in possession of marijuana.[349]

This allowed the El Paso authorities to say, "Hey, we aren't persecuting *Mexicans*, we're persecuting *people possessing marijuana.*" Criminalize the behavior and get around the Constitution.

Now you might be thinking that the medical properties of marijuana hadn't been studied and understood in 1915—but that's not the case. The Indian Hemp Drugs Commission Report, completed in 1894, was the result of a massive Indo-British study of cannabis usage in India.

> The report was at least 3,281 pages long, with testimony from almost 1,200 doctors, coolies, yogis, fakirs, heads of lunatic asylums, bhang peasants, tax gatherers, smugglers, army officers, hemp dealers, ganja palace operators and the clergy. They visited asylums all over India to study the prevailing belief that consumption of ganja caused insanity.[350]

Their report stated:

In respect to the alleged mental effects of the drugs, the Commission have come to the conclusion that the moderate use of hemp drugs produces no injurious effects on the mind. In regard to the moral effects of the drugs, the Commission are of opinion that their moderate use produces no moral injury whatever.

This was only the first of many government-commissioned reports that found that marijuana had no significant health effects on the majority of people. Most of these reports ended up in the trash, as they didn't conform to the agenda of the authorities—to demonize the smokers of marijuana.

The New York Times jumped on the hysteria bandwagon, printing headlines like "Kills Six in a Hospital: Mexican, Crazed by Marihuana, Runs Amuck With Butcher Knife"[351] and "Mexican Family Go Insane: Five Said to Have Been Stricken by Eating Marihuana." According to this so-called "newspaper of record":

A widow and her four children have been driven insane by eating the Marihuana plant, according to doctors who say there is no hope of saving the children's lives and that the mother will be insane for the rest of her life.[352]

Does that sound legitimate to you? Do you think a journalist actually spoke with a medical professional who gave that diagnosis? Or was the paper just running anti-drug propaganda as what we would now call "clickbait"?

In the 1930s, Harry Anslinger became America's first "drug czar" and decided to target African Americans who smoked weed —because he apparently didn't like jazz music. Harry once said:

Most marijuana smokers are colored people, jazz musicians, and entertainers. Their satanic music is driven by marijuana, and marijuana smoking by white women makes them want to seek sexual relations with Negroes, entertainers, and others. It is a drug that causes insanity, criminality, and death — the most violence-causing drug in the history of mankind.[353]

The anti-marijuana propaganda continued through successive administrations. During the Cold War, it was positioned as a weapon being used by the Soviets to turn American citizens against their government.

When Richard Nixon won the White House after a law-and-order campaign, he used the War on Drugs to deliberately target African-American voters, political activists, and peace protestors who were against the war in Vietnam. He put together something called the Shafer Commission, formally known as the National Commission on Marihuana and Drug Abuse,[354] to make recommendations about what the government should do about marijuana. Its chairman was former Pennsylvania Governor Raymond P. Shafer. The commission issued a report on its findings in 1972 that called for the decriminalization of marijuana possession in the United States. It concluded that "the criminalization of possession of marihuana for personal use is socially self-defeating."

Considering the range of social concerns in contemporary America, marihuana does not, in our considered judgment, rank very high. We would deemphasize marihuana as a problem.[355]

The report concluded that the health effects are minimal and that the "gateway drug" theory has no basis. If anything, smoking marijuana *inhibits* criminal behavior—they actually found users to be more timid, drowsy, and passive. They decided that the reason people were so worried about drugs wasn't based on any of the usual things people pointed to—health, crime, and so forth. It was because it was associated with kids dropping out, growing their hair long, free love, rock and roll, sex, and questioning authority. "Marihuana becomes more than a drug; it becomes a symbol of the rejection of cherished values." Of course—this report, like the ones that came before it, was ignored by the White House and by the media.

Nixon's assistant for domestic affairs, John Ehrlichman, explained the origin of the War on Drugs this way:

> *The Nixon campaign in 1968, and the Nixon White House after that, had two enemies: the antiwar Left, and black people. You understand what I'm saying? We knew we couldn't make it illegal to be either against the war or black. But by getting the public to associate the hippies with marijuana and blacks with heroin, and then criminalizing both heavily, we could disrupt those communities. We could arrest their leaders, raid their homes, break up their meetings, and vilify them night after night on the evening news. Did we know we were lying about the drugs? Of course we did.*[356]

The War on Drugs was a pretense to disrupt political enemies and has been continued through every American presidential administration as well as in other countries (who were pressured by the United States during the twentieth century to join them in their "war"—but of course all had similar agendas).

Millions of people had their lives destroyed over the fake "War on Drugs." But that's only a mild example of what happens when the elite get threatened by progressives.

FASCISM: THE FINAL TOOL OF CAPITALISTS

Making essentially harmless behaviors illegal in order to disrupt political enemies is also something we see in the early stages of fascism—which some scholars define as a form of extreme capitalism.

It's difficult to talk about fascism without invoking Godwin's Law or sounding like Rik from *The Young Ones,* but with the rise of the extreme right around the world today, it's also impossible to ignore. Fascism is also poorly understood by most people, who think that all fascists need to look identical to the Nazis.

One of the original leaders of the Russian Revolution, Leon Trotsky, writing in 1934, explained fascism this way:

> The historic function of fascism is to smash the working class, destroy its organizations, and stifle political liberties when the capitalists find themselves unable to govern and dominate with the help of democratic machinery.[357]

Despite the overuse of the term *fascist* and the difficulties in defining what genuine fascism looks like, several scholars have attempted to put together a handy guide. Most of them note that fascism in the twenty-first century is unlikely to look precisely as it did in early twentieth-century Italy, Japan, and Germany—and even *those* didn't look precisely the same. So how do we tell when fascism is on the rise? What are the signs to watch out for?

Robert O. Paxton, professor emeritus of the social sciences at Columbia University, defines fascism as:

> ...a form of political behavior marked by obsessive preoccupation with community decline, humiliation, or victimhood and by compensatory cultures of unity, energy, and purity, in which a mass-based party of committed nationalist militants, working in uneasy but effective collaboration with traditional elites, abandons democratic liberties and pursues with redemptive violence and without ethical or legal restraints goals of internal cleansing and external expansion.[358]

The "traditional elites," of course, can and do play upon this genuine discontent to encourage and support fake grassroots movements, known as "astroturfing," as was exposed during the heyday of the Tea Party in the United States, when Big Oil, Big Tobacco, and the wealthy Koch Brothers conspired to take over the GOP.[359]

They stop real grassroots movements from taking hold. Fake ones are better funded, get more media attention (thanks to the connections of their secret backers), and can be used to prevent politicians from listening to the requests of the real grassroots groups.

In his 1995 essay, "Ur Fascism,"[360] Italian novelist and philosopher Umberto Eco came up with fourteen points that he believed represented the general properties of fascist ideology.

1. The cult of tradition
2. The rejection of modernism
3. The cult of action for action's sake

4. Disagreement is treason
5. Fear of difference
6. Appeal to a frustrated middle class
7. Obsession with a plot
8. Cast their enemies as both too strong and too weak
9. Pacifism is trafficking with the enemy
10. Contempt for the weak
11. Everybody is educated to become a hero
12. Machismo
13. Selective populism
14. The use of newspeak

Eco believed that these ideas didn't need to be organized into a coherent political system but that "it is enough that one of them be present to allow fascism to coagulate around it."

Take that list of fascist elements and apply them to the country you live in today. How many of them do you think are present in the media, the pronouncements of elected officials, and in the populace? In Australia, I can tick off at least half of them, maybe more.

So, these are some of the *elements* of fascism. But what are the *stages* of fascism? How does it arise in a nation?

Paxton suggests the following "Five Stages of Fascism":[361]

1. Intellectual exploration, where disillusionment with popular democracy manifests itself in discussions of lost national vigor
2. Rooting, where a fascist movement, aided by political deadlock and polarization, becomes a player on the national stage

3. Arrival to power, where conservatives seeking to control rising leftist opposition invite classical liberals (capitalist, conservative elite) to share power
4. Exercise of power, where the movement and its charismatic leader control the state in balance with state institutions such as the police and traditional elites such as the clergy and business magnates.
5. Radicalization or entropy, where the state either becomes increasingly radical, as did Nazi Germany, or slips into traditional authoritarian rule, as did fascist Italy.

I challenge each of us to apply that list to our own countries and determine which stage we think they are at.

The very nature of fascism appeals to psychopaths and it's hard to deny that the leaders of the major fascist movements in the twentieth century, Mussolini, Hitler, Franco, Himmler, Göring, Hess, etc., didn't fit the bill. Although psychopaths don't tend to have a firm belief system, apart from belief in themselves, they will naturally be attracted to any movement that offers them a shortcut to power and feign belief if that's what it takes—faith in democracy, faith in Jesus, faith in capitalism, or faith in der Führer.

But what about the general Nazi Party membership? What can we say about the regular people who joined the party but didn't hold power? What can we say about people who subscribed to the Nazi point of view that Jewish people were "Untermenschen"—the sub-humans? This kind of extreme hatred of a race of people—and not caring what happens to them—definitely sounds like one of the traits on the PCL-R test.

Did they just "go along" for career advancement, to protect themselves and their loved ones? Or was a large part of the population psychopathic?

Did the party just enable psychopaths to find a place where their psychopathic attitudes were not only acceptable, but encouraged and rewarded?

How does a large percentage of a sophisticated and educated population like 1930s Germany end up supporting something as brutal as fascism? This is a question we better need to understand if we are to prevent it from happening again…assuming it isn't already too late.

I think Germany in the 1930s gives us a terrific example of how entire nations can slide quickly into toxicity when governed by psychopaths.

Speaking of toxic leadership, Donald Trump is about as far right as any American president in recent history. He's even found a way to make people such as my American wife, a registered Democrat, wish that George W. Bush was still in office or that Mitt Romney had run again in 2016. Trump picked up where the Tea Party left off, took their ideas mainstream and used them to take over the GOP. He may not be a fascist, but he does think they are very fine people.[362]

It's interesting to note the bias in the media coverage of the politicians who lean far left versus those who lean far right.

According to an analysis from Media Matters:

> *Cable news channels used variations of the label "far left" or "extreme" in discussions about Democrats, progressives, and their policy ideas over six times more often than they used variations of*

*the label "far right" or "extreme" while talking about their conser-
vative counterparts. Over a four-week period, CNN, MSNBC, and
Fox News discussed extremism on the left or right a total of 547
times; 86% of these instances framed the American political left as
extreme. This trend is in stark contrast to data showing that the
Republican Party is further away from the political center than
the Democratic Party, and it leaves viewers misinformed about
each party's position by lending undue credibility to the right-wing
talking point that Democrats are extreme.*[363]

That should tell us something about the agenda of large media
companies and the people who run them.

Across the globe today parties on the far right of the political
spectrum are taking power.

Australia in recent years has been led by right-wing populists
such as Prime Ministers John Howard, Tony Abbott, and Scott
Morrison—all devout Christians who courted the Christian
Right, openly opposed same-sex marriage, proudly sent asylum
seekers to brutal concentration camps on remote Pacific islands,
reduced human rights protections, increased internet censorship,
clamped down on free speech, denied climate change science, and
kowtowed to successive American administrations, supporting
their illegal war in Iraq and endless "War on Terror" in return for
greater trade opportunities. As of the time of writing, both major
Australian political parties are conspiring to introduce a new law
that will allow them to covertly snoop on encrypted online conversations without a user's knowledge.

In the United Kingdom, the largest right-wing populist party
is the UK Independence Party (UKIP), led by Nigel Farage, one of

the people who pushed for the UK's exit from the European Union (aka Brexit). He's against Muslim immigration and wants to loosen up the country's restrictions on gun ownership. He's supportive of Donald Trump and referred to Steve Bannon as "my sort of chap."

In October 2018 in Brazil, Jair Bolsonaro, a right-wing candidate, advised by Steve Bannon, won their presidential election. According to Bloomberg, "Bolsonaro has said he approves of torture, promises to curtail environmental conservation efforts, and has a history of insulting statements about women, sexual assault, and gay people."[364] *The Economist* referred to him as a "right-wing demagogue" and Glenn Greenwald called Bolsonaro "the most misogynistic, hateful elected official in the democratic world."[365]

In Italy, two populist parties, the Five Star Movement, part of the "New Right," and League, which has been labeled as "xenophobic" and "anti-immigrant," also known as Lega Nord or Northern League, rule in a coalition since their 2018 elections.

In Germany, the far-right Alternative for Germany (AfD) entered the federal parliament for the first time in 2017. AfD leaders have been accused of downplaying Nazi atrocities.

Next door in Austria, the far-right Freedom Party (FPÖ) recently became the junior partner in a coalition with the government of Conservative Chancellor Sebastian Kurz.

The right-wing populist party Sweden Democrats made significant gains in the most recent Swedish elections.

The great democratic powers in the West have a long history of supporting right-wing governments in developing countries and that doesn't seem to have diminished in the 21st century. Trump is a big fan of Bolsonaro.

And in 2009, the Obama administration supported (and perhaps even encouraged) a coup in Honduras led by the military against the elected president, José Manuel Zelaya.[366]

In the first edition of her autobiography, Hillary Clinton admitted that she used her power as secretary of state to deflect criticism of the coup and shift U.S. backing to the new government. For some reason, that section was deleted when it came out in paperback.[367]

The Honduran president since 2014 has been Juan Orlando Hernández, a hotel magnate like Trump, who has faced allegations of corruption and embezzlement and connections to drug traffickers.[368] When people protested apparent corruption in the 2017 election, Hernández rolled out U.S.-trained and supported SWAT teams and unleashed thousands of police, soldiers, and military police to crack down on protesters.[369] At least 40 people were killed and more than 2,000 detained, with many held under a controversial new terrorism law. Meanwhile, Honduras has received nearly $114 million in security support from the United States since 2009.[370]

Where is all this leading? Why are we seeing a rise of right wing authoritarianism in the West?

Does it have anything to do with the rise of the Occupy Movement and the growing awareness about the wealth differential between the 1 percent and the 99 percent?

Or does it have something to do with the growing tensions around climate change?

Or can it be connected to the rise of the internet, with people able to share information outside of the corporate-controlled media?

All of these things threaten the control of the elite over maintaining the status quo.

In the early twentieth century, after the consecutive impacts of World War I, the unequally distributed economic boom times of the 1920s (the last time the 1 percent controlled as big a percentage of the wealth as they do today) and the subsequent crash that lead to the Great Depression, people around the world were agitating for deep systemic change. Knowing they weren't going to get it handed out willingly from the capitalists, they went looking for new ideas. They started to study the theories of Marx and Lenin and to give serious consideration to the ideas contained within socialism—primarily a more equitable distribution of wealth and political power within their countries.

At its core, socialism is the idea that every person inside a society—from the most successful business person to the lowliest toilet cleaner, from the son of a duke to the daughter of a cobbler—has equal value as a human being. Wealth and power should be shared relatively equally, regardless of your intelligence or natural talents or how the market values your particular set of skills.

As Warren Buffett, one of the richest people in the world, points out, if he lived in a society where athletic talent, or fighting on the beaches of Normandy were the only valuable skills, he would be useless, regardless of how hard he worked. He's fortunate that the skills he has are well suited to the time and place he was born.[371]

As I've explained elsewhere, when socialism became more popular in the United States in the early 20th century, and the Roosevelt administration started to marginally redistribute some of the wealth during the New Deal, the elite went into overdrive to discredit and crush the idea of socialism being possible in the U.S.

The FBI, under the leadership of J. Edgar Hoover, covertly and sometimes illegally infiltrated and manipulated fledgling socialist groups under a secret FBI program known as COINTELPRO (from COunter INTELligence PROgram). Hoover ordered his FBI agents to "expose, disrupt, misdirect, discredit, or otherwise neutralize" groups that he deemed "subversive," which simply means not aligned with the existing power structure's ideals. According to Tim Weiner:

> Armed with the intelligence gathered through break-ins, bugs, and taps, COINTELPRO began to attack hundreds, then thousands, of suspected Communists and socialists anonymous hate mail, tax audits by the Internal Revenue Service, and forged documents designed to sow and fertilize seeds of distrust among left-wing factions. The idea was to instill hate, fear, doubt, and self-destruction within the American Left.[372]

The U.S. Senate ran the McCarthy witch-hunts, claiming to be looking for Soviet spies in Hollywood and the government, but they were really just looking to shut down any and all socialist organizations through fear and intimidation. If America believes in freedom of speech, why would they oppress people speaking about socialism? Even if people wanted to vote for a socialist party—isn't the freedom to vote for the leaders they want part of what makes America great? Apparently *not* if the party wants to redistribute the wealth. And America was not alone in the twentieth century in persecuting socialism—the Menzies government in Australia also prosecuted a referendum to outlaw the Communists.

In 1950, Prime Minister Robert Menzies, Australia's longest-serving prime minister, tried to ban the Communist Party of Australia (CPA)—for a *second* time. He'd already banned them in 1940 during his first stint as prime minister, but the ban had been lifted by his successor Prime Minister Curtin in 1942 and then ruled unconstitutional by the High Court. When the CPA organized a strike of coalminers in 1949 during the government of Curtin's successor, Ben Chifley, the army and strike-breakers were used to crush it. Keep in mind that Chifley was the leader of the Australian Labor Party, who supposedly represent Australia's working class.

When Menzies and his party won back the government, he banned the CPA a second time. They appealed to the High Court again, which ruled Menzies' second attempt as still being unconstitutional.[373] So Menzies called a public referendum to try to change the constitution to get around the High Court. The referendum narrowly failed.

For the record, the CPA was just a political party, trying to rally voters around an alternative economic model. They hadn't committed any crimes. Something else of interest: in the same year, Menzies was awarded the Legion of Merit (Chief Commander) by U.S. President Truman for "exceptionally meritorious conduct in the performance of outstanding services 1941–1944 and December 1949–July 1950."

Of course, the ideas of socialism were tied, in the minds of many Americans and Australians, to the brutality of Stalin's autocratic regime in Russia, even though many socialists around the world vehemently disagreed with aspects of that particular implementation, arguing that Stalin's USSR didn't represent the best ideals and values of socialism but merely used socialism as a theoretical front to mask tyrannical behaviors. Even socialists *inside* Russia had disagreed with the Bolsheviks. But instead of endorsing an open and constructive public dialogue about the positive aspects and potential dangers of socialism—as one might expect from a country that values free speech—American leaders just shut it down with brute force because it was a threat to the hegemony of the elite. As a result, today most people living in the West have very little idea about the history of socialism or the ideas behind it. They have been conditioned not to even think about it unless in negative terms.

One last thought on fascism. I often get the impression that people today think that fascism in Germany, Italy, and Japan failed. The West (and Russia) won the war and dismantled the forces of fascism. Hooray for the West (and Russia).

But when you understand that fascism is a tool unleashed by capitalist interests in order to crush the rising forces of dissent and activism—and you realize that, after World War II, the forces of capitalism again took control over those Axis countries—it suggests that fascism did *precisely* what it was supposed to do. The fascists lost—*but capitalism won*, preventing West Germany from becoming a communist country—a genuine possibility in the early 1930s where the Communist Party of Germany was the largest in Europe (East Germany, of course, ended up in the Soviet sphere of control as a result of the Yalta agreement). Italy and Japan also ended up joining the American trading system (as opposed to the Soviet bloc). Especially after the implementation of the cunning Marshall Plan (which was really just a massive transfer of public wealth into the hands of American businesses), American capitalism had most of the European economy stitched up.[374]

Hitler's rise to power in the early years was funded by party members and small business. By the time it looked like he might actually be a serious contender, he started to get more support from the larger German capitalists. According to testimony at the Nuremberg trials, the large capitalists often supported all of the political parties in Germany fairly equally, spreading their bets.

But some of them were pro-Nazi, like the directors of I. G. Farben, Siemens, and Krupp as well as Fritz Thyssen, who ran one of Germany's largest mining and steelmaking companies. Thyssen later wrote a book called *I Paid Hitler*.[375]

What these industrialists wanted, according to one of their agents, was "organized capitalism." They wanted a "strong man" who would be "an alternative to a Communist takeover of the collapsing Weimar regime."

Hitler was also supported, albeit indirectly, by some famous American capitalists. Prescott Bush, father of one future president and grandfather of another, and his father-in-law, George Herbert Walker, were Fritz Thyssen's American bankers and were also connected to the Consolidated Silesian Steel Company, which used slave labor from the concentration camps. Bush was a director of the New York-based Union Banking Corporation, UBC, which was owned by a Thyssen-controlled bank in the Netherlands and was established for him in America by George Herbert Walker. After Hitler came to power, "UBC bought and shipped millions of dollars of gold, fuel, steel, coal, and U.S. treasury bonds to Germany both feeding and financing Hitler's build-up to war." Bush continued to work for the bank even after America entered the war.[376]

Another huge supporter of Hitler in the pre-war years was Fred C. Koch, the father of billionaire right-wing political activists Charles G. and David H. Koch. Koch founded the company Winkler-Koch Engineering, which built a significant oil refinery in Hamburg for the Nazi regime (after building one earlier for the Bolsheviks) to help them get ready for war.

And he was a *huge* admirer of the fascists:

> *Although nobody agrees with me, I am of the opinion that the only sound countries in the world are Germany, Italy, and Japan, simply because they are all working and working hard. The laboring people in those countries are proportionately much better off than they are any place else in the world. When you contrast the state of mind of Germany today with what it was in 1925 you begin to think that perhaps this course of idleness, feeding at the public trough, dependence on government, etc., with which we are afflicted is not permanent and can be overcome.*[377]

In the early 21st century, his billionaire sons were on the front lines of trying to dismantle every element of government oversight of capitalism in the United States—with astonishing success.

Other American companies that were happy to support the Nazis included IBM, Alcoa, Chase Manhattan Bank, J.P. Morgan, Dow Chemical, General Motors, Ford, Standard Oil, and the law firm of Sullivan and Cromwell, in which brothers Allen Dulles (future head of the CIA) and John Foster Dulles (future U.S. secretary of state) were partners.[378]

Not many people know that there was an attempted fascist overthrow of the American government as well in 1934—it's known as "The Business Plot."[379]

According to a witness of the planning of the coup, one of the primary organizers, Gerald MacGuire, said:

We need a fascist government in this country...to save the nation from the communists who want to tear it down and wreck all that we have built in America. The only men who have the patriotism to do it are the soldiers, and Smedley Butler is the ideal leader. He could organize a million men overnight.[380]

Unfortunately for the plotters, Butler, no fan of Wall Street (as we saw earlier), turned them down.

According to the *New York Times*, William E. Dodd, U.S. ambassador to Germany in 1937, was quoted as saying:

A clique of U.S. industrialists is hell-bent to bring a fascist state to supplant our democratic government and is working closely with the fascist regime in Germany and Italy. I have had plenty of opportunity in my post in Berlin to witness how close some of our American ruling families are to the Nazi regime.... Certain American industrialists had a great deal to do with bringing fascist regimes into being in both Germany and Italy. They extend aid to help Fascism occupy the seat of power, and they are helping to keep it there.[381]

Henry Ford, a passionate anti-Semite, was decorated by the Nazis for his services to Nazism. Hitler had a portrait of Henry Ford on his office wall in Munich, directly praised him in *Mein Kampf*, and told a *Detroit News* reporter that he regarded Henry Ford as his inspiration.[382]

Henry Ford once described democracy as "nothing but a 'leveling down of ability' which makes for waste."

As the economist Anthony Sutton put it in his 1976 book, *Wall Street and the Rise of Hitler*:

> *Without the capital supplied by Wall Street, there would have been no I.G. Farben in the first place and almost certainly no Adolf Hitler and World War II.*[383]

The important point to remember is that fascism, historically, has been used when capitalists feel like their power is being threatened. They use fascists to crush socialism—and then crush the fascists in turn, returning back to business as usual.

CHAPTER SEVEN

TAKING CONTROL

O kay, we're at the end of the book so let's summarize what we've talked about.

We've talked about how psychopaths are not all serial killers. They are people with a lack of empathy, a strong desire for personal power, a high appetite for risk, and the ability to turn on the charm. And they are out there, about 1–4 percent of the population. Some of them, I believe, end up in management positions of large organizations.

We've talked about how organizations are survival machines, out to protect their power and the people inside of the organization, as long as they support the organization's objectives of maintaining power.

We've talked about how psychopaths in management levels of organizations will toxify the culture, making the entire organization, industry, or even the nation psychopathic.

We've talked about how psychopaths are aware that there are ninety-nine of us for every one of them, so they need to use all of the tools at their disposal to stop us from taking their power away.

We've talked about how psychopaths in power have no incentives to want to push through any dramatic systemic change in their organization or society, because they are prospering under the status quo.

And we've talked about how capitalism, when it no longer can manufacture the consent of the people, manufactures new extreme excuses to remove civil rights, including fascism as a final solution.

The question I want to finish this book with is—what can we do about all of this?

It's the question I've been pondering for the last twenty years. What can I do? If you're not part of the elite and you don't have the wealth and power to shape society, what can you do?

It's going to take smarter people than me to work out the answers to that question. But I've got a handful of concrete steps I think we, as individuals and as a society, can put into place to protect ourselves from psychopaths and toxic organizational cultures.

IDENTIFY THE PSYCHOPATHIC CULTURES

It seems to me that the most obvious place to start is for us to drive the organizations we work inside of to recognize the real risk of psychopaths ending up in senior management and elected office.

Today this isn't something that is brought up in polite

conversation. It might be water cooler talk, but you won't hear HR talking about it, nor will you see the media asking questions—outside of extreme cases of high-profile business failure or evidence of political crash-and-burn.[384] The only time we hear talk about psychopaths in the boardroom is when they fail massively. What isn't discussed is the damage they also do when they succeed or how to prevent them from causing chaos along the way.

How do we get organizations to take the threat of psychopaths seriously? Especially when some of the management are probably psychopaths? It's going to take some clever engineering.

I would start by looking at the *culture* of the organization and identifying the psychopathic elements. How does the organization treat customers, staff, and the public? How does it treat whistleblowers? How does it treat competitors? Does it have a system of values and an ethics framework that are more than just talking points?

A discussion about potential psychopathic tendencies inside an organization's culture is a good way of broaching the subject of the existence of psychopaths in management.

Psychopathy tests for senior managers and politicians should become a standard policy to ensure that we aren't giving too much power to people who have a higher statistical risk of misusing it for personal gain.

I propose that organizations should be employing psychiatrists to have all staff sit the PCL-R test. In the same way that companies today have drug or breathalyzer tests for employees as a safety measure—one estimate is that about 40 percent of U.S. workers are currently subjected to drug tests during the hiring process.[385]

I don't mean to suggest that psychopaths shouldn't be employed or even given responsibility—on the contrary, they have a unique set of capabilities that organizations will still want to leverage—just that organizations should factor in the risks of giving a psychopath power and engineer safeguards, such as supporting a balanced managerial team where at least half the people have a low PCL-R score and implementing checks and balances in the approvals process for any decisions where psychopaths have a hand in the decision-making to ensure the decision doesn't conflict with the previously agreed-upon ethical guidelines that the company has committed to adhere to.

How we introduce this sort of policy into organizations is where it gets tricky, as we can assume that the psychopaths in senior management won't want to allow any restrictions on their ability to make decisions. Strangely, they probably won't be worried about being revealed as a psychopath—they probably don't really care what other people think about them. They think they are winners. If being a psychopath makes them a winner, they will think, then good for them.

They will only care if they think it might be a threat to their power. And, of course, putting systems into place to prevent their worst impulses *will* limit their power. That's the entire point.

Therefore, it will be up to those of us that aren't psychopaths to force through changes to the corporate culture.

There will be many managers, though, who aren't psychopaths but are suspicious that managers around them are. There will be board members or people who represent major investors in listed companies that will be suspicious of the managers in organizations they are involved in. It's mainly up to these people to engineer the new policies out of a sense of moral obligation.

What can the rest of us do? We have a range of options, from building awareness of the dangers of psychopaths in power, to direct agitation—speaking out about concerns at company meetings, strike action, and so forth.

There are risks involved in all of these activities, so I suggest we create movements inside our organizations, making sure we are not alone in the crusade. It's harder for an organization to eradicate fifty or one hundred people from across the organization than it is to eradicate just one.

MONITOR PSYCHOPATHIC CULTURES

Once we have assessed the organization for a psychopathic culture and know who the psychopaths are, we need to set up systems to monitor their decisions and their actions.

We should push organizations to implement some kind of internal governance body, made up of randomly chosen employees who have passed the PCL-R test and who serve twelve-month terms to monitor executive appointments and decisions for potential psychopathic behavior.

Organizations should issue a public annual report where they rank their company on its ethical health.

Most listed commercial organizations already measure their ongoing activities against a range of metrics in some kind of a "balanced scorecard," which reports on such things as revenue, profit, expenses, sales, market share, customer satisfaction, and so on.

Over the last fifty years, there has been a push by social and environmental activists for a "triple bottom line" (aka TBL or 3BL).

It's an accounting framework that measures three parts of an organization's impact: social, environmental (or ecological), and financial, commonly referred to as "corporate social responsibility."

Organizations measure their impact on "the three P's"—People, Planet, Profit.

Unfortunately, this hasn't been able to get much traction and why would it if psychopaths are running the economy?

I think we can all take it upon ourselves to push our organizations to become a TBL company.

According to my friend Tony Kynaston, a very successful professional investor (and co-host on my QAV Investing Podcast[386]), there are a lot of ethical investment funds out there,[387] but they don't get much media attention outside of investor circles.

And if you don't hear much about the TBL, what about the QBL, the quadruple bottom line (also known as FBL or fourth bottom line)? The QBL adds another P—purpose, sometimes also called spirituality or compassion. It essentially means asking yourself, "Why am I doing this?" Beyond profit, what value am I bringing to the world by running my organization? What is the social impact of our endeavors? And how do we measure that outcome objectively?

One way of monitoring QBL performance are B Corps—a new certification standard that claims a growing community of more than 1,229 certified B Corps from forty-one countries and 121 industries, who are working together toward the goal of redefining success in business. Each B Corp has signed a term sheet that declares that they will consider all stakeholders. It is a rigorous assessment that explores a company's governance, transparency, and environmental and social impact.[388]

Can we push the organizations we work in to become a B Corp?

CLARIFY OUR OWN ETHICS, MORALS, AND VALUES

While it's easy to point fingers at others, it's important we all do an audit on our own personal ethics, morals, and values.

Do I have a clear enough idea of where I stand on these things? Would I immediately know when I am being asked to cross a line? I'm not talking about being asked to murder someone or to burn down a village, I'm talking about more subtle issues that are likely to crop up inside a psychopathic culture, like, as we saw in the sections on the finance industry, rip off customers, or treat customers poorly.

If you were asked to write down a list of your ethical principles and why you chose them, how quickly and confidently would you be able to complete the task?

I tried it myself some years ago and found the task extremely challenging. Especially when I asked myself *why* I believed in certain things. The more I asked myself why I believed in this and not that, the more difficult the process became.

Let's take a recent, brief example such as same-sex marriage.

I supported it.

But then I ask myself, *Why* do I support it? What is my core ethical reason for supporting the issue?

And then it gets tricky.

I might start by saying, "Well, I'm very happily married; in fact, my marriage is the best thing that's ever happened to me, so I want other people to have the same opportunity for happiness, regardless of their sexual preference."

Then I'd have to ask myself how I know that my opinion on the matter is the *right* opinion? How do I know what are the best things for society?

I start to falter at this stage.

It turns out this philosophy business can be quite difficult. Who knew!?

I'm sure there are plenty of books, podcasts, and experts I can consult in the future to help me do a better job of helping me clarify my ethics, morals, and values. The point is to make it a priority, so I don't end up like the boiling frog.

Ethics is the question of right and wrong conduct.

One tool I have found to help with ethical questions is the Moral Foundations Questionnaire, developed by Jesse Graham and Jonathan Haidt at the University of Virginia.[389] Their site also has an Ethical Culture Survey to determine how ethical the organization you work for is. But even these tools will only provide you with a score and compare that score to the general public— they won't help you determine where your values and morals come from.

Values represent the idea that we can't have everything in life. There are only twenty-four hours in a day. Each of us has a limited lifespan and a limit to the things we can focus on. Ideally, we should each live our lives, devoting our time and energy toward the things that we value. This might seem like common sense, but it's amazing how many people are living their lives devoting enormous amounts of time to things they don't really care about.

For example—watching television. According to one 2016 report, Australians spend an average of 101 hours per month watching television on both in-home TV sets and on their screens.[390] That's an average of three to four hours a day! Imagine what else you could do with that time.

I enjoy great television as much as the next person, but I value achieving progress on my own projects more than I do watching the output of someone else's projects. That's why I haven't owned a television set for over a decade. I have too many books to read and projects to finish.

Values make us choose between things that require our time and energy but which are in conflict with each other. Some might appear on a scale of opposites. Others will appear as conflicting outcomes.

Here are some excellent questions I've used to help determine what matters most in life.

1. Imagine you have the opportunity to attend your own funeral. What would you like the people closest to you— your loved ones, your closest friends—to say about you? If the media is going to write an obituary about your life, what would you like it to contain? Go ahead and write your own obituary. That will help you determine what you value.

2. Imagine your life ten years from now. Where are you living (e.g., country, city, suburb, etc.)? Who are you living with (e.g., the person of your dreams, a cat, your best friend, etc.)? How are you spending your days (e.g., what kind of work, what kind of leisure activities, etc.)? What kind of skills do you have that you don't have already (e.g., new languages you can speak, martial arts, cooking, playing guitar, etc.)? What kind of mental and emotional state do you want to be in (e.g., spiritual peace, happiness, etc.)? Map your future self

out on paper. Now this might sound like goal setting, and it is—our goals should be in alignment with our values. Our principal goal in life should be to move ourselves closer to living in tune with our values.

BREAK OUT OF THE MONEY TRAP

One of the ways the majority of us get trapped in a system of living out of tune with our values is that we fall into the money trap.

We allow ourselves to get into a financial situation where we can't afford to say "no" to our employers because our lifestyle requires a reliable income—or two—or three. We saddle ourselves with debts and spend our free cash flow for things we don't really need but are tricked into wanting by constant advertising and peer pressure: that huge-screen TV, that new car, the holiday, the expensive wedding, the expensive gadgets, the new shoes, the latest fashions, dining out at the latest restaurants, etc. The advertising industry works relentlessly to convince us to spend every dollar we have, in fact, to borrow more money and spend that as well, and that we won't be happy until we have everything we could ever want. They tell us we deserve those things because we deserve to be happy.

Even though we all know that things don't make us happy, we still fall for the deception, because we are saturated with the advertising 24/7. Studies suggest that we see, on average, 4500 advertisements every day of our lives on the web, on billboards, on TV, radio, in newspapers and magazines, on the packaging around us, on cars, and on buildings. Our brains get saturated with messages telling us to buy, buy, buy, and that buying will make us happy and fulfilled and successful.

It's ridiculously hard to fight that kind of mental infiltration. And so most of us give in. We buy the new gadget, it makes us happy for a few weeks, and then the feeling wears off and we need to buy something new. Have you ever wondered why that is? It's because the happiness we feel when we buy something new is the result of the neurochemical dopamine, aka "the pleasure molecule." Dopamine is involved in the way our brains have evolved to trick us into doing things that will help us survive, what's referred to as our "reward system." Our brains are literally wired to drive us to achieve rewards, so we get a chemical "hit" of dopamine.

During the twentieth century, marketers worked out how to turn dopamine to their advantage. When we get something we desire, we are administered a hit of dopamine, a chemical reward that gets us high. But it doesn't last, and it isn't designed to last. It's designed to reward you for hunting and killing an antelope, so you can feed your family for the next few days. But then you need to go hunt for another antelope, or your family will starve. Our brains crave those dopamine hits. We get them today, not from hunting for our food, but by shopping for stupid shit we don't need. And by opening up Instagram to see how many likes our latest photo got.[391]

Instead of saving our money and investing it in our future, we live for today's dopamine hits and, in doing so, forfeit our future. When we get ourselves into a situation where we can't afford to quit a job because we don't have enough savings to last the few months it might take to find a better job, it becomes incredibly hard to put your values ahead of immediate needs, like paying the rent or keeping the electricity on. And betraying your values is a slow process. It's boiling the frog. It's a slippery slope. Decision by decision, we give up our values and, as we do, we become part of the system.

While some suggest that modern society has been deliberately engineered to squeeze us into the money trap, it might also just be an evolutionary stable state, or "Nash equilibrium."

In other words, nobody deliberately set out to create society this way—but they encourage it when it suits them.

It's really difficult to go on strike for better working conditions or a greater share of the economic pie when your family will be evicted because you can't pay the rent or the mortgage. People who are working twelve-hour days, taking their work home with them on their laptops, or who work two jobs to pay for their lifestyle, are too tired to organize into political groups or to join labor unions.

Instead they go home, drink a bottle of wine or a few beers or smoke a joint to dull the parts of their brains that nag them about how time is slipping away, then indulge themselves with pure escapism, watching televised sport or reality TV or playing Xbox, and finally fall asleep so they can get up to do it all over again. We find ourselves falling into the money trap and, once you're in it, it's very hard to claw your way back out.

How do we avoid the money trap? There are a number of strategies that have been successfully tested by people I know.

THE SAMMARTINO METHOD

Steve Sammartino has been a mate of mine for ten years and he's a very smart investor. Steve's investment system is foolproof and doesn't require you to know anything about shares or companies or the market. He calls it a "set and forget" system. I call it "The Sammartino Method"[392] and I think everyone should be taught his method when they leave school.

He just lived as frugally as he could, from his early 20s, and put as much money as possible into an "index fund." That's a fund that buys a portfolio containing a parcel of the top 100 stocks on the market. When one stock falls out, it is replaced with another. The great thing about this system, Steve says, is that history shows that the stock market grows, on average, over the long term, by about 11 percent per year, and the index funds tend to keep pace with that. He just kept on sinking his spare cash into a fund until, by age thirty-three, Steve had built up a big-enough share portfolio that he was able to quit his corporate marketing job and live on the dividends. Today he spends his time doing what he loves — he's a futurist, who writes excellent books and gives speeches about the future.

Steve's system is so simple and basic that everyone can do it. All it takes, he says, is discipline.

He recommends that we all read these two books: *The Intelligent Investor*[393] and *A Random Walk Down Wall Street.*[394]

THE QAV SYSTEM

Tony Kynaston, who I have mentioned before, is another good mate of mine. He pushed me to write this book and helped me patiently over the years to refine the ideas inside it. He's also a very smart guy and a very successful investor.

Tony has spent decades developing an investing methodology he calls "QAV," which stands for Quality At Value. It's based on the way people like Warren Buffett have invested for many decades—working out how to buy shares in good quality companies but at the right price. A year ago I would have thought that kind of investing was way too difficult for me, but early in 2019 we started a podcast where he teaches me the system. The great thing about Tony's method is that it doesn't require much in the way of brains. It took a lot of brains to *develop* it, but understanding it is something that even I can do.

He has developed a checklist into which you plug the financial data that companies publish. The checklist results in a score. If it's a positive score, the share is a buy. That's it.

Tony used this method to retire from his job as a corporate executive in his 40s. He calls it a "get rich slowly" method. Unlike the Sammartino Method, Tony's approach requires a bit more work, but his portfolio has grown, on average, at double the rate of the market, so it's worth the effort.

You can check out the podcast with Tony at *qavpodcast.com.au*.

THE OPPOSITE METHOD

I call it the opposite method because it involves doing the opposite of everything you've been told your entire life (and it reminds me of Seinfeld). It requires rejecting "common sense" and making your own path through life.

If we accept that the system we live in pushes us down a certain path that leaves most people broke, stressed, and looking for dopamine hits in Reality TV, Facebook, and shopping, it's a good idea to break out of that system and find a new path.

If you have lots of healthy ways of getting dopamine hits, you won't be as likely to look for unhealthy options. Fill yourself up on the dopamine equivalent of fresh veggies, and you won't be hungry for dopamine pizza.

I try to get a lot of healthy dopamine hits by being engaged in doing things every day that make me feel better about myself, which make me feel like I am making a difference in the world and living by my values. When I left my corporate career and started making podcasts, I noticed that my state of mind improved significantly.

If you are doing things that make you feel better about the direction your life is heading in, you are less likely to go searching for a fake dopamine hit.

I was having breakfast recently with Sammartino, and he was talking about the people we know who have made significant life changes in the last decade. They have all gone from working in high-pressure corporate environments to working for themselves.

Sure, they might earn less money, but they have more freedom—freedom over their schedules, freedom to say no to the kind of work they don't enjoy, freedom to spend more time with their children and spouses during the week, freedom to pursue the activities that are closer to their values and make them feel sincerely joyful about their lives.

Each of us has a limited lifespan. Some of us choose to downscale our lives to trade things for time.

Steve told me that he looked at the things he liked most about his old marketing job, which was presenting ideas to groups of people and said, "What if I could just do that full time?" It was only ten percent of his old job, but it was the ten percent he really enjoyed. So today that's all he does—write books and give talks (which provides an income on top of his investments from the Sammartino Method).

Similarly, I used to enjoy reading books about history, science, and politics (which had nothing to do with my sales job at Microsoft) and then discussing the ideas I found interesting—and now that's what I do for a living. I get paid to read books about subjects I'm interested in and then discuss those ideas on podcasts. I feel like I'm making a difference in the lives of the people who listen to my shows (at least that's what some of them tell me), and that makes me feel more useful. I don't feel the need to go searching for cheap dopamine hits. I get enough feel-good chemicals every day from doing work that I genuinely love and the knowledge that it's making a positive difference in the lives of others.

PROGRAM YOUR BRAIN

When I was growing up in the '70s, there were only two television stations, one radio station, and one newspaper. My media options were pretty limited. We didn't even have a house phone until I was twelve. And of course, there wasn't a computer in the house, let alone internet connectivity or an iPad. At some point, probably in the early '80s, we got a VCR (that's a Video Cassette Recorder for the Millennials reading this), and that dramatically increased our viewing options. Outside of those channels, my reading involved borrowing books from the town or school library.

Today, of course, we suffer not from a scarcity of media options but a barrage of them. Our media cup runneth over. We have so much choice, it's hard to know where to begin. And, as a result, many people decide not to decide. They fall back on the media channels they knew growing up—the masthead newspapers, the local radio station, the big television channels and let them continue to program their media for them.

And so, you end up with significant corporations determining what you watch, read, and listen to. What do you think they are going to fill your head with? Are they going to program your brain with information that might run counter to their corporate agenda? Unlikely.

I work hard to make sure I only read, watch, and listen to sources of information that I think are going to make me smarter, wiser, or more productive.

Over the years of doing that, I've also learned that the world is a complicated place. Psychopaths lie. It pays to be skeptical about what you hear in the news.

But there's a fine line between being a skeptic and a conspiracy theorist. The difference, I think, comes down to evidence. As we've seen in the preceding pages, the people in power in Western democracies—politicians, business leaders, the media, and religious leaders—have lied to the general public regularly over the last century.

Therefore, it is entirely logical to assume we are being lied to today as well. But at the same time, it's problematic just to assume that *everything* is a lie. We need to hold ourselves to a higher standard of evidence before we *believe* something is a lie. It's one thing to be open to alternative theories to the official explanation of events. It's another to *believe* those alternative theories without having substantial evidence.

For example, if a politician urges you to support her call for war and claims the country she wants to go to war with is currently committing atrocities, I think it's entirely reasonable to say, "Prove it." If she says she cannot, due to "national security implications," then I'm sorry, but you don't get my support, at least right now.

If the media tells me that someone committed collusion to win an election, I think it's reasonable to ask for proof before I believe it. Even if I don't like the guy they are accusing of collusion and would love to see him impeached or arrested, I still want to be careful to see facts before I buy into any narrative. It's just as possible that the people trying to sell me on the collusion narrative also have a secret agenda.

The problem with taking an evidence-based mind-set is that it's *hard.* Often the evidence isn't made public. Or, if evidence is provided, we don't have the skillset or training to assess the quality and integrity of it. We, the general public, rely heavily on experts to help us evaluate whether or not the evidence is compelling or not. But where do we find those experts? Often we get them from the media—columnists, opinionists, or talk show hosts who position themselves (and are positioned by their corporate owners) as the people we should listen to. However, as we've seen in earlier chapters, we have to be careful who we listen to, as these people often have hidden alliances and incentives. They are often connected to corporate or political interests, funded by lobbyists, or other interested parties.

Therefore, it's challenging for us to make evidence-based decisions on a range of complicated subjects when we aren't experts—and the experts we are relying on have been corrupted.

The unfortunate reality is that we each need to work hard to find our own trusted sources. We need to take responsibility for our information.

There are still opportunities to find extremely bright, well-informed, and independent individuals who devote vast amounts of their time to assessing what's going on and then publishing their thoughts on podcasts, medium.com, a reddit forum, Facebook, or a blog. I tend to keep a list of my favorite sources of analysis and refer to them when I'm trying to understand a news story.

Unfortunately, you won't find many of them working for corporate media companies for the reasons we've explored in this book. You'll need to go searching.

I keep an updated list of sources I like to read at cameronreilly.com/news-sources. Keep in mind, though, that we should never trust any source one hundred percent because we can never really know what's going on behind the scenes. It's practically impossible to be able to understand what allegiances each particular source might have, who they are accepting hidden payments or gifts from, and so on.

The best we can do is to look for sources that *appear* unbiased. On one of my podcasts, I run contemporary news stories through a checklist of questions designed to help me give each one a score for potential reliability.[395]

Of course, each of us needs to educate ourselves as much as possible on current affairs, developing the best framework we can for reading between the lines of the stories that mean the most to us. None of us are ever going to be experts on everything. But it's not difficult to pick a news story that piques your interest each week and then spend an hour or two researching it instead of watching TV. Read/watch/listen to a handful of stories from different perspectives (left, right, center). Start with the sources you already trust. If they aren't covering the story, find new sources but take their analysis with a grain of salt until you've done some research on the source themselves and ascertained their quality and independence.

I'm also a big fan of reading. Surveys indicated that most people don't read books very often. You're obviously an exception because you're reading this, so you know what I'm talking about.

Whenever I'm talking to smart people I admire, like Sammartino or Kynaston, I like to ask them, "What's the best book you've read recently?"

Find out what smart people are watching and listening to. I've read a bunch of books because Bill Gates recommended them.

When I was eighteen or nineteen, I got one of the best pieces of advice I've ever received. I spent an hour with a millionaire who advised me to invest 10 percent of my income on my brain—for the rest of my life. What did he mean by that? Take ten percent of your earnings and spend it on books or courses that will make you smarter. He said it would be the best investment I would ever make. It may not make you wealthy, but it will make you worldly. Here I am thirty years later, still reading several books a week.

Another way to program your brain is to learn how to think and reason. When I was a young man, I had a quote from Ralph Waldo Emerson pasted on my bookshelf:

What is the hardest task in the world? To think.

I resolved to dedicate myself to becoming better at thinking. I'm still trying to get better at it. Emerson was right. It's hard. Of course, we all think—but do we know *why* we think *what* we think? Can we articulate our ideas and opinions and be confident that they sit on solid foundations? Are we comfortable having a friendly debate with someone with opposing ideas, unafraid to justify our point of view while also being open and willing and excited to be proven wrong by a better argument? I've learned over the years that many people are not comfortable in this situation. If their opinions are challenged, even in a friendly manner, they become tense and even angry. By testing their ideas, you are challenging their very identity. They are firmly rooted in their opinions and have built their lives around them. By examining those opinions, you are threatening everything they know. Or so they think.

A different point of view to take is to consider ourselves tireless searchers for the truth. If I have an opinion about a subject that is incorrect, then I want to know. I don't want to remain ignorant. Ignorance is not bliss in my book. I want to think like a scientist—test my hypotheses and always be willing to throw out an old theory for a better one. To paraphrase Fox Mulder—the truth is out there.

After we develop that mind-set, the next challenge is to learn how to think and reason. Unless we want to become a logician or philosopher, the tools we need to get started are relatively simple.

First, I recommend The Five Whys, developed by Sakichi Toyoda, founder of Toyota Industries (which later spawned the Toyota Motor Corporation). It's a technique I learned while working at Microsoft and is similar to the approach I discussed above for determining our morals and values.

For each opinion you have on any subject, ask yourself, Why? Why is that true? Then, when you have your answer, repeat the process. Why is that true? After you've repeated five iterations of asking "Why?" you'll have a much clearer perspective on the validity of that opinion. And if you ever find yourself in a debate with someone coming from a different perspective, you'll have a much deeper pool of ideas to draw from—and to have the opportunity to improve your thinking, especially if that other person can correct your thinking on the answers you came up with. Remember that the goal is to get to the truth—not to win the argument. There is no long-term or inherent value in winning if you are wrong. Asking "why" is also a useful way of scratching the surface of the thinking of others. "I'm extremely interested in understanding why you believe that to be true?" is a gentle way of having a friendly discussion with someone who you disagree with.

The second tool is to get a handle on some of the most common logical fallacies.[396] A logical fallacy is faulty reasoning, an argument that might sound persuasive but, when scrutinized, contains flaws. They get used with disturbing regularity, often deliberately, from dinner table discussions to political debates and corporate boardrooms. It should be our goal to think as clearly as possible and not fall into the fallacy trap. Falling into a fallacy isn't a sign of low intelligence or a moral failing—it's more about System 1 vs. System 2 thinking. Fallacies appear to us as shortcuts but sometimes they take us in the wrong direction.

Some of the fallacies to be wary of include:

> *The fallacy of the single cause*: this is when we attribute some event or outcome to a single root cause when it might have multiple causes. It's tempting, especially in certain emotional situations, to want to point the finger at a simple cause for some events, like, for example, a tragedy such

as a mass shooting or why Trump was elected. We want fast, emotionally satisfying answers, especially ones that will confirm our existing biases. But there are often many potential causes that may have contributed, and we don't do ourselves or society any benefit by jumping to conclusions.

Post hoc ergo propter hoc: a favorite of fans of the TV show *The West Wing*. The Latin term translates as "after this, therefore because of this." The classic example is "The rooster crows immediately before sunrise; therefore, the rooster causes the sun to rise." The causal relationship between two events might be more complicated than they appear at first glance.

Correlation does not imply causation: Also known as *cum hoc ergo propter hoc* (with this, therefore because of this), similar to the post hoc fallacy but makes a connection between two concurrent events. Just because two events coincide does not mean they are necessarily related. My favorite example is the connection between the rise of global average temperatures and the decline in pirates over the last two hundred years.

Ad hominem: attacking the person instead of the argument. Very common in online debates, this is where a person's character can be quickly maligned in an attempt to negate their argument. For example, I often get called "anti-American" because I point out some of the ways the United States has enforced its economic hegemony, even though I'm married to an American, have an American son, have lots of American friends, and enjoy lots of American culture. It's an ad hominem attack, an attack on my person, rather than debating my facts. Play the ball, not the person.

Appeal to consequences: when someone doesn't want to believe the evidence because they are afraid of the consequences. I come up against this one often in debates about whether or not free will exists. When presented with neuroscientific evidence that free will doesn't exist, people will often complain that if we accept that point of view, our entire legal system will be thrown into chaos. While that may or may not be true, it doesn't change the underlying evidence.

No True Scotsman: when someone says "a true Scotsman would never put ice in his whisky" they are trying to make an appeal to purity. It's a common way of trying to counter an argument against a generalization. When someone says "China can't be a communist country because they allow a measure of free market activity" and I reply with "that's okay, the journey to communism takes different paths for different nations," they might reply "no real communist country would allow a free market," that's an appeal to purity. Things are often more complicated than people want to believe.

HAVE A FRAMEWORK FOR LIFE

I think another central aspect of healthy dopamine is to have a framework by which you navigate life's challenges. By "framework," I mean a philosophy that guides you and helps you interpret life's ups and downs in a healthy fashion.

I often talk to people who don't seem to have spent much time developing their philosophy of life. They may have one they have adopted from their religion or have a mish-mash of things they have picked up from yoga class and motivational Facebook posts, but they don't have a robust set of rules that help them navigate a healthy path through life's long and winding road.

The chances are high that life is going to throw you a series of curveballs. At some point, the odds are that you are going to lose jobs, lose loved ones, lose money, and lose your way. You will also find times when everything seems to be going your way, and you can't do anything wrong. Both of those phases of life present challenges and opportunities. If you don't have a philosophy to guide you through, you can end up patting yourself on the back way too hard, or beating yourself up with way too much ferocity.

Without a philosophy, you might find that bad times rock you more than they otherwise would, and good times can also lead you astray. Anxiety, pride, guilt, resentment, ego, greed, and selfishness will prevent you from having a healthy state of mind, which in turn can drive us toward unhealthy remedies, and go looking for cheap dopamine hits. It's easy in these times to fall for the trap of thinking a promotion, a new lover, or a new car is what we need to make us feel good again. We become easy prey for psychopaths looking to manipulate us into one of their schemes.

I was lucky when I was a young adult to get pointed to a life philosophy that has worked ever since to help me deal with the bad times as well as the good times (if you want to know more, visit threeillusions.com).

It's been my experience that, with a solid philosophy, it is possible to live a life of permanent peace and happiness, regardless of what's going on around you.

As Rudyard Kipling put it:

*…you can meet with Triumph and Disaster
And treat those two impostors just the same.*[397]

I am fortunate to be crazy in love with my wife, to have three wonderful sons whom I'm proud of and love to bits, and to have work that provides fulfillment and stimulation. But the journey to get here took several missteps. I've had jobs I didn't enjoy and found myself in relationships that didn't work. Instead of just putting up with them, I've always tried to be flexible enough to make the changes I needed to make to set things right and live my life according to my values.

If you're unhappy, do something about it. Leave the relationship. Quit your job. See a therapist. Make changes. Sure, it will involve some risks and some unknowns, but change is often its own reward. Life is about the journey.

Make a list of all of the things that are the most important to you in your life. The things that you value most highly. Put them in order of value. Then focus on achieving those. It sounds simple, but how many times do we hear of people on their deathbed saying, "I wish I'd spent less time at the office?" Don't be one of those people.

I often tell people that I have achieved everything on my list except financial success. But I wouldn't trade that for a single one of the other things on the list. It's right at the bottom. And I'm still working on it.

One of the exercises I've often found useful in times of great upheaval is what I call the "reverse timeline." I go back through my life's timeline and think about the earlier situations when I've been going through significant changes.

Think about a time when a relationship or a job ended. It was probably scary and stressful. But what I've found is that when one door closes, another always opens. Those times of great upheaval have always lead to better opportunities and better relationships.

This hindsight helps me to realize, in current times of stress, that there is probably something better for me down the road, I need to pay attention, let life take me forward and be open to new doors that open. I smile and think, "Okay, Universe, what do you have in store for me this time? I'm ready. Bring it on."

I've always taught my kids that when something bad happens in life, most people get angry or miserable or beat themselves up. A better approach, I think, is to ask yourself these two questions:

1. What does this enable me to do that I couldn't do before?
2. How do I turn this situation to my advantage?

Those questions prepare my mind to be open and positive, to stay alert, and to get creative, instead of dwelling in misery.

So if you don't have a philosophy for life, please find one. It doesn't matter right now *what* it is—you can always find a better one later on. Just start looking for one that helps you make sense of life.

CONCLUSION

P sychopaths are a reality, and I think the evidence is pretty strong that they rise to the top of many organizations, toxify the cultures of those organizations, and play a significant role in many of the world's current problems.

We need to do a better job understanding the role they play in society and putting systems into place that help us avoid their most dangerous impulses.

To do that, it's vital that each of us gets our own lives in order, works out our morals, values, and ethics, and lives according to them to the best of our ability. Only then can we do a better job doing our part to guide the world to a better place, leaving it a little better than we found it.

I don't have all of the answers—I'm still trying to work out the right questions. I hope that we can work it out together.

ABOUT THE AUTHOR

Cameron Reilly is an Australian entrepreneur who runs a marketing consulting business and formerly worked for Microsoft, where he developed an interest in psychopaths. In 2004, he became Australia's first podcaster and launched "The Podcast Network," the world's first network of its kind. Since then he has developed a passionate global fan base for his podcasts about historical figures such as Julius and Augustus Caesar, Napoleon Bonaparte, Alexander the Great, Stalin, Churchill, American presidents, the Medici, various popes, kings, and Ho Chi Minh—many of whom were possibly psychopaths. His podcasts have been downloaded millions of times.

With the financial support of his fans, he recently wrote, produced, directed, and hosted a secular documentary about early Christianity, *Marketing The Messiah*.

His first book, *The Three Illusions*, was self-published in 2011.

Over the last fifteen years, Cameron has been featured in many Australian media stories for his role as a pioneer in podcasting and is often invited to speak at industry events. He lives in Brisbane, is married to Chrissy, an American violinist, and has three children.

Learn more at
ThePsychopathEpidemic.com

ENDNOTES

1 Kent A. Kiehl and Morris B. Hoffman, "The Criminal Psychopath: History, Neuroscience, Treatment, And Economics," *US National Library of Medicine*, https://www.ncbi.nlm.nih.gov/pmc/articles/PMC4059069/.

2 Donald W Black, MD, "The Natural History of Antisocial Personality Disorder," *US National Library of Medicine*, https://www.ncbi.nlm.nih.gov/pmc/articles/PMC4500180/.

3 Kent A. Kiehl and Morris B. Hoffman, "The Criminal Psychopath: History, Neuroscience, Treatment, And Economics," *US National Library of Medicine*, https://www.ncbi.nlm.nih.gov/pmc/articles/PMC4059069/.

4 Danielle Egan, "Into the Mind of a Psychopath," *Discover Magazine*, http://discovermagazine.com/2016/june/12-psychopath-and-the-hare.

5 Paul Babiak, M.S., Ph.D.; Jorge Folino, M.D., Ph.D.; Jeffrey Hancock, Ph.D.; Robert D. Hare, Ph.D.; Matthew Logan, Ph.D., M.Ed.; Elizabeth Leon Mayer, Ph.D.; J. Reid Meloy, Ph.D.; Helinä Häkkänen-Nyholm, Ph.D.; Mary Ellen O'Toole, Ph.D.; Anthony Pinizzotto, Ph.D.; Stephen Porter, Ph.D.; Sharon Smith, Ph.D.; and Michael Woodworth, Ph.D., "Psychopathy: An Important Forensic Concept for the 21st Century," *FBI*, https://leb.fbi.gov/articles/featured-articles/psychopathy-an-important-forensic-concept-for-the-21st-century.

6 Martha Stout, *The Sociopath Next Door*, (Broadway Books, New York, 2005).

7 Rob Kall, "Transcript: Psychopaths, Sociopaths and Anti-Social Personalities—interview with Psychiatrist Donald Black," *OpEdNews*, http://bit.ly/2Lw7ecn.

8 Ben Casselman and Andrew Flowers, "Rich Kids Stay Rich, Poor Kids Stay Poor," FiveThirtyEight, https://fivethirtyeight.com/features/rich-kids-stay-rich-poor-kids-stay-poor/.

9 "Prisoners in Australia, 2018," *Australian Bureau Statistics*, https://www.abs.gov.au/ausstats/abs@.nsf/mf/4517.0.

10 Vanessa Desloires, "Oliver Stone says Wall Street culture 'horribly worse' than Gordon Gekko's time," *Sydney Morning Herald*, http://bit.ly/2mhZ5ju.

11 "Gordon Gekko still resonates on Wall Street," *The Age*, http://bit.ly/2mf0AyR.

12 Jon Ronson, *The Psychopath Test*, (Riverhead Books, New York, 2011), 100.

13 Ibid, 99.

14 Sherree DeCovny, "The Financial Psychopath Next Door," *CFA Magazine*, https://cfa.is/2LCoKfn.

15 "We are the 99%," *Wikipedia*, https://en.wikipedia.org/wiki/We_are_the_99%25.

16 Peter H. Lindert and Jeffrey G. Williamson, *Unequal Gains: American Growth and Inequality since 1700*, (New Jersey: Princeton University Press, 2016) https://amzn.to/2NJon1Y.

17 Benjamin Stupples, Alexander Sazonov, and Suzanne Woolley, "UBS Whistleblower Hunts Trillions Hidden in Treasure Isles," *Bloomberg*, https://bloom.bg/2maODKp.

18 Shawn M. Carter, "The 1% in the US makes over $1 million more than everyone else—here's where the gap is largest," *CNBC*, https://cnb.cx/2mdLjOE

19 Albert Einstein, Ideas And Opinions, (Broadway Books, New York, 1995) https://amzn.to/2JYW3Zc.

20 Xanthe Mallett, "Psychopaths versus sociopaths: what is the difference?," *The Conversation* http://bit.ly/2Lw7ic7.

22 John M. Grohol, Psy.D., "Differences Between a Psychopath vs. Sociopath," *PsychCentral*, http://bit.ly/2Lw7nfV.

22 Robert Hare and Paul Babiak, *Snakes In Suits*, (HarperCollins, New York, 2007), 19.

23 Psychopathy Checklist, Wikipedia, http://bit.ly/2LvS1bp.

24 "Neurological basis for lack of empathy in psychopaths," *ScienceDaily*, http://bit.ly/2Ludlsh.

25 Clara Moskowitz, "Criminal Minds Are Different From Yours, Brain Scans Reveal," *LiveScience*, http://bit.ly/2LuJMMO.

26 Nassim Khadem, "CEO bonuses soar as Qantas boss Alan Joyce tops list of highest-paid," *ABC NewsI*, executives https://ab.co/2lyX9Da.

27 Henry Blodget, "Here Are Four Charts That Explain What The Protesters Are Angry About...," *Business Insider*, https://read.bi/2LtWYRU.

28 Glenn Greenwald, "How Covert Agents Infiltrate the Internet to Manipulate, Deceive, and Destroy Reputations," *The Intercept*, http://bit.ly/2JYHrJ6.

29 William Rollo, "Orica fined $430K over Gladstone cyanide release," *ABC News*, https://ab.co/2JYpWsw.

30 "Vatican releases figures on how it disciplined priests accused of sex abuse," *The Guardian*, http://bit.ly/2JZi7CT.

31 "Children Overboard Affair," *Wikipedia*, http://bit.ly/2JYxaga.

32 Richard Dawkins, *The Selfish Gene*, (Oxford University Press, Oxford, 1976).

33 "Darwinism," *Wikipedia*, http://en.wikipedia.org/wiki/Darwinism.

34 "Edison Warning," *The Pittsburgh Press*, 6 Sep 1888, http://bit.ly/32uNRIf.

35 Luke O'Neil, "Hail, Boston: The Uber vs Taxi Livery War Is Changing the Industry," *Boston Magazine*, http://bit.ly/2JYW6US.

36 "Maslow's hierarchy of needs," *Wikipedia*, http://bit.ly/2EGXzzb.

37 "Targeting One Nation," *Sydney Morning Herald*, http://www.smh.com.au/specials/abbottaffair/.

38 "Australian Communist Party v. Commonwealth," *Wikipedia*, http://bit.ly/2KotTwA.

39 "VW worked hand in hand with Brazil's military dictatorship," *Deutsche Welle*, http://bit.ly/32owwjX.

40 David McHugh, "Former Volkswagen CEO charged with fraud in Germany," *Associated Press*, http://bit.ly/32pDe9c.

41 Shaheen Pasha, "Skilling comes out swinging," *CNN*, https://cnn.it/2n0tX8u.

42 Julie Creswell, "Citigroup Agrees to Pay $2 Billion in Enron Scandal," *New York Times*, https://nyti.ms/2BoeVEc.

43 "Goldman Sachs to pay $7 million to Enron creditors," *Chron*, http://bit.ly/2JUZgbW.

44 "Goldman Sachs," *Wikipedia* http://bit.ly/2JZ6ifU.

45 "Goldman Sachs gives top execs bonuses in stock," *USA Today* http://bit.ly/2JYyMq3.

46 Bethany McLean and Peter Elkind, *Smartest Guys in the Room: The Amazing Rise and Scandalous Fall of Enron*, (Portfolio Trade, London, 2003).

47 "Jeffrey Skilling," *Forbes*, http://bit.ly/2Lxqia6.

48 "Pump and Dump," *Wikipedia* https://en.m.wikipedia.org/wiki/Pump_and_dump.

49 "Bitcoin Chart," *MarketWatch*, https://on.mktw.net/2LvRy99.

50 'Michael Koziol & Jennifer Duke, "They hate her': emails show ABC chairman told Michelle Guthrie to fire Emma Alberici," *ABC News*, http://bit.ly/2HGQVZL.

51 Sara Jerving, Katie Jennings, Masako Melissa Hirsch And Susanne Rust, "What Exxon knew about the Earth's melting Arctic," *LA Times*, http://bit.ly/2LxGYyn.

52 Suzanne Goldenberg, "Exxon knew of climate change in 1981," *The Guardian*, http://bit.ly/2JXu8IY.

53 "1969 tobacco industry memo," *UCSF Library*, http://bit.ly/2JYyY8L.

54 "Global Climate Science Communications Plan 1998," *DocumentCloud*, http://bit.ly/2JXPDtf.

55 Peter Ellyard, *Designing 2050*, (TPN Publishing, Melbourne, 2009) https://amzn.to/2B1gdi4.

56 Mahita Gajanan, "President Trump to Reverse Obama's Recognition of Climate Change as a National Security Threat," *Time*, https://ti.me/2JYYEC5.

57 "Earthly concerns," *The Economist*, https://econ.st/2LuVmY3.

58 Stephanie Mencimer, "Do Bishops Run Your Hospital?," *Mother Jones*, http://bit.ly/2LtZ04w.

59 Laurie Goodstein, "Dolan Sought to Protect Church Assets, Files Show," *New York Times* https://nyti.ms/2LtUCCy.

60 Alastair Jamieson, "Inside the Vatican: The $8 billion global institution where nuns answer the phones," *NBC News*, https://nbcnews.to/2LAp91O.

61 Peter Trute, "Sydney church's $1.2b wealth revealed," *Sydney Morning Herald*, http://bit.ly/2nGcDG4.

62 "Sydney Catholic archdiocese controls funds worth $1.2bn," *The Guardian*, http://bit.ly/2nHjUp9.

63 MormonLeaks Compiles Information Connecting Mormon Church to $32 Billion of Investments, *MormonLeaks*, http://bit.ly/2LtBZi4.

64 Peter Henderson, "Mormon Church earns $7 billion a year from tithing, analysis indicates," *NBC News*, https://nbcnews.to/2Lxpxhg.

65 Mormonism and church integrity/City Creek Center Mall in Salt Lake City, *FairMormon*, http://bit.ly/2EBJxho.

66 Caroline Winter, "How the Mormons Make Money," *BusinessWeek*, https://bloom.bg/2IhOWNB.

67 Adam Shand, "Taxpayers support lavish Hillsong lifestyle," The Daily Telegraph, http://bit.ly/2LtZpny.

68 Nicole Chettle, "Hillsong church head Brian Houston accused alleged child abuse victim of 'tempting' father, inquiry told," *ABC News*, https://ab.co/2LxaQuO.

69 Rachel Browne, "Royal Commission sex abuse inquiry censures Hillsong head Brian Houston," *Sydney Morning Herald*, http://bit.ly/2MaOEYh.

70 Dr Jennifer Wilson, "Why is Scott Morrison protecting Hillsong Pastor Brian Houston?," *Independent Australia*, http://bit.ly/2M9FhYu.

71 Fergus Hunter, "Scott Morrison wanted Hillsong pastor Brian Houston at White House dinner: report," *Sydney Morning Herald*, http://bit.ly/2MaxycM.

72 Adam Shand, "Taxpayers support lavish Hillsong lifestyle," *The Daily Telegraph*, http://bit.ly/2LtZpny.

73 "Scathing UN report demands Vatican 'immediately' act against child sexual abuse," *ABC News*, https://ab.co/2LtZM1q.

74 "Royal Commission into Institutional Responses to Child Sexual Abuse," *Wikipedia*, http://bit.ly/2LCnxol.

75 "Royal Commission into Institutional Responses to Child Sexual Abuse Final Report Preface and Executive Summary," *Child Abuse Royal Commission*, http://bit.ly/2ECYuQs.

76 Naaman Zhou, "'He was a witness of truth': why the judges decided Cardinal George Pell was guilty," *The Guardian*, http://bit.ly/2LtBzZI.

77 Jorge Poblete, "Chile's bishops offer to resign en masse over sex-abuse coverup," *LA Times*, https://lat.ms/2LxpHoS

78 Colm O'Gorman, "Sex Crimes and the Vatican," *BBC/Colm O'Gorman*, http://bit.ly/2LxpKky.

79 "Crimen sollicitationis," *Wikipedia*, http://bit.ly/2Lxb1pY.

80 Hans Kung, "Church in worst credibility crisis since Reformation," *The Irish Times* http://bit.ly/2EEjIhu.

81 "John Jay Report: The Nature And Scope Of Sexual Abuse Of Minors By Catholic Priests And Deacons In The United States 1950-2002," *United States Conference Of Catholic Bishops*, http://bit.ly/2ECZeoI.

82 Dennis Mumby, *Communication and Power in Organizations*, (Praeger, New York, 1988).

83 Gretchen Morgenson, "A Vow to End Hollow Nods and Salutes," *New York Times* https://nyti.ms/2Lxbs3A.

84 General Motors website, *Wayback Machine*, http://bit.ly/2Lwf8Tb.

85 Lucy Hattersley, "What it's really like to work for Apple," *Macworld*, http://bit.ly/2LxpO3M.

86 Daniel Fowler, "Employers Often More Interested in Hiring Potential Playmates Than the Very Best Candidates," *American Sociological Review* http://bit.ly/2ECZuUI.

87 Drake Baer, "How Tim Cook implants Apple's culture into new employees," *Business Insider Australia*, http://bit.ly/2EAYrVa.

88 "Macworld Boston 1997 'The Microsoft Deal,'" *YouTube/Apple,*, http://bit.ly/2LuVyqf.

89 "'Does the NSA collect any type of data at all on millions or hundreds of millions of Americans?' -video," *The Guardian/YouTube*, http://bit.ly/2V89Hys.

90 Jonathan Topaz, "Kerry: Snowden a 'coward…Traitor'," *MSNBC*, https://politi.co/2LuchtT.

91 Joanna Walters, "James Risen calls Obama 'greatest enemy of press freedom in a generation,'" *the Guardian*, http://bit.ly/2rTCJnW.

92 Greg Smith, "Why I Am Leaving Goldman Sachs," *New York Times*, https://nyti.ms/2JYiL3v.

93 Kevin Roose, "The Greg Smith vs. Goldman Sachs Death Match Is On," *New York Magazine*, https://nym.ag/2rLX12C.

94 Dominic Rushe, "Why I Left Goldman Sachs author is biggest 'muppet' say reviewers," *The Guardian* http://bit.ly/2LtBTXK.

95 Greg Smith, *Why I Left Goldman Sachs: A Wall Street Story*, (Grand Central Publishing, New York, 2012) https://amzn.to/2LvOYQx.

96 "Dwayne Andreas," *PBS Frontline* https://to.pbs.org/2EzC6HI.

97 "ADM Code of Conduct," *ADM*, https://www.adm.com/our-company/the-adm-way/code-of-conduct.

98 Megan Twohey, Jodi Kantor, Susan Dominus, Jim Rutenberg And Steve Eder, "Weinstein's Complicity Machine," *New York Times*, https://nyti.ms/2LucGMV.

99 Pat McGrath, "Thiess' questionable payments for $6bn mine contract prompt calls for corruption watchdog," *ABC News*, https://ab.co/2ZG8V1n.

100 Conor Duffy, "Whistleblower accuses Leighton International of kickbacks and facilitation payments," *ABC News*, https://ab.co/2If6YoT.

101 Michael Janda and Stephen Letts, "Former Leighton executive Peter Gregg found guilty of cooking the books," *ABC News*, https://ab.co/2VcLQxU.

102 Allie Coyne, "Ex-CBA IT exec sentenced to 3.5 years in jail for bribery," *IT News*, http://bit.ly/2PTQemk.

103 Anne Barker, "Banking royal commission: Speaking out against CBA had 'horrific impact' on whistleblower," *ABC News*, https://ab.co/2PTP6iA.

104 Christian Gergis, "Key findings from the banking Royal Commission final report," *Australian Institute of Company Directors*, http://bit.ly/2PWuSVy.

105 Sherree DeCovny, "The Financial Psychopath Next Door," *CFA Magazine*, https://cfa.is/2LCoKfn.

106 Michael Rowland, "NAB Chairman quits," *ABC*, https://ab.co/2nI2hFP.

107 Dennis Gentilin, *The Origins of Ethical Failures*, (Routledge, Abingdon, 2016).

108 Daniel Ziffer, "NAB bosses come in for special criticism from banking royal commissioner Kenneth Hayne," *ABC News*, https://ab.co/2PVf84S.

109 Martin Farrer, "NAB's bosses Andrew Thorburn and Ken Henry have quit—what took them so long?," *The Guardian*, http://bit.ly/2n2fB7y.

110 Adele Ferguson and Chris Gillett, "ATO whistleblower facing 161-year prison sentence says he 'almost died from the stress'," *ABC News*, https://ab.co/2IjvgqW.

111 Paul Karp, "Federal police raid home of News Corp journalist Annika Smethurst," *The Guardian*, http://bit.ly/2IjFDem.

112 Rebecca Ananian-Welsh, "Why the raids on Australian media present a clear threat to democracy," *ABC News*, https://ab.co/2V7jIw0.

113 Vatican Leaks Scandal, *Wikipedia*, https://en.wikipedia.org/wiki/Vatican_leaks_scandal.

114 Lizzy Davis, "Pope Francis 'admits that gay prelate network exists'," *The Guardian*, http://bit.ly/2m8XKeX.

115 "Pennsylvania priest abuse grand jury report on six dioceses," *The Morning Call*, http://bit.ly/2V9olFF.

116 "Pennsylvania priests 'abused thousands of children'," *BBC*, https://bbc.in/2VaDsPt.

117 Anna North, "Why the Jeffrey Epstein case inspires so many conspiracy theories," *Vox*, http://bit.ly/2IjTMbk.

118 Danny Tran, "Ex-detective Denis Ryan wins compensation," *ABC News* https://ab.co/2LxGisF.

119 Norman Tebbit , "Child abuse 'may well have been' covered up," *BBC*, https://bbc.in/2Luc75L.

120 Legality of the Iraq War, *Wikipedia*, http://bit.ly/2LAjGIo.

121 Catherine McGrath, "Senior intelligence officer, Andrew Wilkie, resigns in protest," *ABC*, https://www.abc.net .au/am/content/s804540.htm.

122 *Iraq Body Count* https://www.iraqbodycount.org/.

123 Shane Smith, "President Barack Obama Speaks With VICE News," *VICE News*, http://bit.ly/2LuJp4S.

124 "Two drafts of a letter from Churchill on area bombing, 28 March 1945 and 1 April 1945," *UK National Archives*, http://bit.ly/2Lu0yvm.

125 Rahul Mahajan, " 'We Think the Price Is Worth It' ," *FAIR*, https://fair.org/extra/we-think-the-price-is-worth-it/.

126 "Apple under fire again for working conditions at Chinese factories," *The Guardian*, http://bit.ly/2LvQtOF.

127 Project MKUltra, *Wikipedia*, https://en.wikipedia.org/wiki/Project_MKUltra.

128 "'Reality Check' ," *ABC Good Morning America / Wayback Machine*, http://bit.ly/2LAkkpi.

129 Justine Sharrock, " 'Am I a Torturer?'," *Mother Jones*, http://bit.ly/2Lu0N9K.

130 Rhitu Chatterjee, "Xenophobia's Evolutionary Roots," *PRI*, http://bit.ly/2LAkwow.

131 Graham Rayman, "NYPD Tapes 4: The Whistleblower, Adrian Schoolcraft," *The Village Voice*, http://bit.ly/2L wfZ6l.

132 "Iron law of oligarchy," *Wikipedia*, http://bit.ly/2LAqlCk.

133 Paul Karp, "Qantas and Virgin bosses reject Morrison government calls to be silent on social issues," *The Guardian*, http://bit.ly/2lgKdlf.

134 Alex Hern and Dominic Rushe, "WikiLeaks publishes secret draft chapter of Trans-Pacific Partnership," *The Guardian* http://bit.ly/2mCPfsn.

135 "The Big Six" *Wikipedia* http://bit.ly/2LudPnH.

136 Jacques Ellul, Propaganda: The Formation of Men's Attitudes, (Vintage Books, New York, 1975).

137 Joe Bageant, *Deer Hunting with Jesus: Dispatches From America's Class War*," (Broadway Books, New York, 2007).

138 Duncan Campbell, "Chomsky is voted world's top public intellectual," The Guardian, http://bit.ly/2otTkQR.

139 Travis Gettys, "Noam Chomsky: We're no longer a functioning democracy, we're really a plutocracy," *Raw Story*, http://bit.ly/2nHNlHy.

140 Alex Carey, *Taking The Risk Out Of Democracy: Corporate Propaganda versus Freedom and Liberty*, (University Of Illinois Press, Illinois, 1995).

141 Robert W. McChesney, *Corporate Media and the Threat to Democracy*, (Seven Stories Press, New York, 1997)

142 "The soul of man under socialism—Oscar Wilde," *libcom*, http://bit.ly/2m0ns5s

143 "Rupert Murdoch 'not a fit person' to lead News Corp–MPs," *BBC*, https://bbc.in/2rQ8uhp

144 Dan Sabbagh and Josh Halliday, "Rupert Murdoch 'not fit' to lead major international company, MPs conclude," *The Guardian*, http://bit.ly/2rP8aQf

145 Wendy Bacon and Jenna Price, "News of the World scandal a litmus test for independent journalism in Australia," *The Conversation*, http://bit.ly/2rS72eE

146 Kieran Adair, "UTS KILLS PRESS: 25 years of independent journalism," *Alt Media*, http://bit.ly/2rS71aA

147 "Just a matter of time before Rinehart on Fairfax board: Jack Cowin," *ABC Radio*, https://ab.co/2rRMjHH

148 Michael Wolff, *The Man Who Owns the News: Inside the Secret World of Rupert Murdoch*, (Broadway Book, New York, 2010)

149 "Citizen Kane—How To Run A Newspaper," *YouTube* http://bit.ly/2EICHaP

150 Adrian Bingham, "Monitoring the popular press: an historical perspective," *H&P*, http://bit.ly/2EFUEWu

151 Alex Pareene, "Judith Miller: From the Times to the nuts," *Salon*, http://bit.ly/2rQ8uOr

152 "2018 Edelman Trust Barometer—Australia Results," *Edelman / Slideshare*, http://bit.ly/2NKZeUu

153 Glenn Greenwald, "MSNBC and Daily Beast Feature UAE Lobbyist David Rothkopf With No Disclosure: a Scandalous Media-Wide Practice," *The Intercept* http://bit.ly/2q7KiGy

154 William Appleman Williams, *The Tragedy Of American Diplomacy*, (W. W. Norton & Company, New York, 1959)

155 Ron Chernow, *The House of Morgan: An American Banking Dynasty and the Rise of Modern Finance*, (Atlantic Monthly Press, Boston, 1990).

156 Kabir Chibber, "Still Paying World War I Debt, 100 Years Later," *The Atlantic*, http://bit.ly/2nzWcLh

157 Edward L Bernays, *Propaganda* (Routledge, Abingdon, 1928)

158 Robert Higgs, *How U.S. Economic Warfare Provoked Japan's Attack on Pearl Harbor*, *Independent Institute*, https://www.independent.org/news/article.asp?id=1930

159 Gar Alperovitz, "The War Was Won Before Hiroshima—And the Generals Who Dropped the Bomb Knew It," *The Nation*, https://www.thenation.com/article/why-the-us-really-bombed-hiroshima/

160 William Leahy, I Was There, (Ayer Co Pub, North Stratford, NH, 1979) 441

161 Norman Cousins, *The Pathology of Power*, (W. W. Norton & Company, New York, 1988) 65, 70-71.

162 Eugene L. Meyer, Jacqueline Trescott, "Smithsonian Scuttles Exhibit," *The Washington Post*, https://wapo.st/2mKoang

163 Kevin Kruse, *One Nation under God: How Corporate America Invented Christian America*, (Basic Books, New York, 2015)

164 David Domke, Kevin Coe, *The God Strategy: How Religion Became a Political Weapon in America*, (Oxford University Press, Oxford, 2010) https://amzn.to/2LvRc2l

165 "Utah Task Force: Fraud Victims' Losses Top $1 Billion New Educational Campaign Warns of Ponzi Schemes and Affinity Fraud," *FBI*, http://bit.ly/2LvRtlT

166 "David Kuo," *Wikipedia* https://en.wikipedia.org/wiki/David_Kuo_(author)

167 "Faith Used for Political Gains," *Christian Broadcasting Network*, http://bit.ly/2LvRyGd

168 Dave Schechter, "Patriotism and the 'God gap'," *CNN*, https://cnn.it/2LvRDcZ

169 Linda Lyons, "Paranormal Beliefs Come (Super)Naturally to Some," *Gallup*, http://bit.ly/2LuHjSs

170 "Many Americans Mix Multiple Faiths," *Pew Research*, https://pewrsr.ch/2LAqvtq

171 Daniel Kahneman, *Thinking, Fast And Slow*, (Farrar, Straus and Giroux, New York, 2013)

172 "OECD's Better Life index," *OECD*, http://www.oecdbetterlifeindex.org/

173 Rick Noack, "These are the world's least religious countries," *The Washington Post* https://wapo.st/2LtDuwI

174 Phil Zuckerman, "Think religion makes society less violent? Think again.," *LA Times*, https://lat.ms/2Lv4rQQ

175 Lucy Madison, "Elizabeth Warren: 'There is nobody in this country who got rich on his own'," *CBS*, https://cbsn.ws/2rS6UMc

176 Eric Barker, "'I treat my wife as an employee whom I cannot fire': How Albert Einstein's family paid the price for his genius," *Business Insider*, http://bit.ly/2n3pMcd

177 Chris hare84, "Political polarization in the United States House of Representatives," *Wikimedia Commons* http://bit.ly/2LuX1Nh

178 "Australian Election 2010," *Political Compass* https://www.politicalcompass.org/aus2010

179 Mike Collins, "The Decline of Unions Is a Middle Class Problem," *Forbes* http://bit.ly/2LuKoUa

180 Sarah Kaine, "The state of the union(s): how a perfect storm weakened the workers' voices," *The Conversation* http://bit.ly/2LwtClT

181 Lawrence Mishel, Elise Gould, and Josh Bivens, "Wage Stagnation in Nine Charts," *Economic Policy Institute*, http://bit.ly/2LyF6VW

182 Julian E. Zelizer, "How America's Vision of Progressive Tax Reform Died," *The Atlantic*, http://bit.ly/2rSCyct

183 "About Grover Norquist," *Americans for Tax Reform*, https://www.atr.org/about-grover

184 Thomas DeMichele, "A Summary of How the Major Parties Switched," *Fact/Myth* http://bit.ly/2LuJd5y

185 Glass-Steagall legislation, *Wikipedia* http://bit.ly/2rSNl6c

186 Sheldon S. Wolin, *Democracy Incorporated: Managed Democracy and the Specter of Inverted Totalitarianism*, (Princeton University Press, New Jersey, 2006)

187 Chris Hedges, "Sheldon Wolin and Inverted Totalitarianism," *TruthDig* http://bit.ly/2rR6gPa

188 "Concentration of media ownership," *Wikipedia* http://bit.ly/2rRL2Ay

189 Karl Marx, *Das Kapital*, (1867) vol 1, ch 25

190 Sean McElwee, "Marx Was Right: Five Surprising Ways Karl Marx Predicted 2014," *Rolling Stone* http://bit.ly/2rSZdp6

191 "News International phone hacking scandal," *Wikipedia* http://bit.ly/2rSm5Fo

192 Lisa Millar, "Brooks, Coulson charged with phone hacking," *ABC News (AUS)* https://ab.co/2rTwjoQ

193 Tom Shine, "47 percent of Congress Members Millionaires," *ABC News (US)* https://abcn.ws/2Lvku14

194 Paul Krugman, *The Conscience of a Liberal* (W. W. Norton, New York, 2007)

195 N Gregory Mankiw, *Principles of Economics*, (Cengage Learning, Boston, 1997)

196 Justen Charters, "Barack Obama's Net Worth Has Risen 438 percent Since Running for President," *Independent Journal Review* http://bit.ly/2rT9VvL

197 Brian Montopoli, "Obama Signs Bill To Extend Bush Tax Cuts," *CBS* https://cbsn.ws/2rSfuKS

198 Cameron Reilly, "Who Does Obama Work For?," *CameronReilly.com* http://bit.ly/2rNTQaA

199 "Obama Top Contributors, 2008 Cycle," *OpenSecrets.org* http://bit.ly/2rRYowI

200 David A Graham, "Was Trump Fibbing About Buying Politicians Then or Now?," *The Atlantic*, http://bit.ly/2mLL7GL

201 Adam Chandler, "Larry Kudlow and the Return of Supply-Side Economics," *The Atlantic* http://bit.ly/2rQBJkn

202 "List of Presidents of the United States by net worth," *Wikipedia* http://bit.ly/2rP4mOR

203 "Cost of Election," *Open Secrets* https://www.opensecrets.org/overview/cost.php

204 "Political funding in Australia," *Wikipedia* http://bit.ly/2rThemU

205 "Can power be bought?," *The Age* http://bit.ly/2rOWP2u

206 Hamish Fitzsimmons, "Mysteries remain in political donations," *ABC Radio* https://ab.co/2rQ14uz

207 Sarah Thompson, Anthony Macdonald and Jake Mitchell, "Gina Rinehart sells out of Fairfax Media," *Sydney Morning Herald* http://bit.ly/2rRmmrN

208 Jack Shafer, "Trump Is Right It Is the Amazon Washington Post," *Politico* https://politi.co/2rThh24

209 Adam Johnson, "Washington Post Ran 16 Negative Stories on Bernie Sanders in 16 Hours," *FAIR*, http://bit.ly/2meoSsP

210 Amy Goodman, "Kucinich & Braun Blast ABC For Reducing Campaign Coverage," *Democracy Now!* http://bit.ly/2rSOiLU

211 Amy Goodman, "NBC Las Vegas Debate to Include Kucinich After NBC Wins Appeal to Exclude Him," *Democracy Now!* http://bit.ly/2rT9ZM1

212 Ben Norton, "Comparing Hillary Clinton's Top Donors to Bernie Sanders' Top Donors," *TruthOut*, https://truthout.org/articles/comparing-hillary-clinton-s-top-donors-to-bernie-sanders-top-donors/

213 Thomas E. Patterson, "Pre-Primary News Coverage of the 2016 Presidential Race: Trump's Rise, Sanders' Emergence, Clinton's Struggle," *Harvard Kennedy School* http://bit.ly/2rRyGZm

214 Joe Churcher, "Political donations rise by £1.9m," *Independent* https://www.independent.co.uk/news/uk/politics/political-donations-rise-by-19m-7778388.html

215 *The Podcast Network* http://www.thepodcastnetwork.com

216 "Marketing The Messiah," *Deep Dive Documentaries*, http://deepdivedocumentaries.com

217 Eric Bates, "Smoked Out," *Mother Jones*, http://bit.ly/2rSOKd4

218 Richard Behar, "The Thriving Cult of Greed and Power" *Time Magazine*, May 6, 1991 page 50.

219 "Death In The West," *Wikipedia*, https://en.wikipedia.org/wiki/Death_in_the_West

220 Adam Hochschild, "Shoot-Out in Marlboro Country," *Mother Jones*, http://bit.ly/2rQ1qBp

221 "Intelligence firm Black Cube apologizes for Harvey Weinstein work," *CBS News*, https://cbsn.ws/2rPgbEH

222 Nick Penzenstadler and Susan Page, "Exclusive: Trump's 3,500 lawsuits unprecedented for a presidential nominee," *USE Today*, http://bit.ly/2kUvAUk

223 Glenn Fleishman, "The People vs Donald Trump: Every Major Lawsuit and Investigation the President Faces," *Fortune*, https://fortune.com/2018/09/21/donald-trump-lawsuit-investigation-charges-news-update/

224 "McLibel case" , *Wikipedia* https://en.wikipedia.org/wiki/McLibel_case

225 Max Fisher, "How Saudi Arabia captured Washington," *Vox* http://bit.ly/2NH4CI9

226 Brian M Conley, "How Do Lobbyists Influence Bills in State Legislatures?," *Scholars.org* http://bit.ly/2LtDcWE

227 Eric Lipton, Brooke Williams "How Think Tanks Amplify Corporate America's Influence," *New York Times*, https://nyti.ms/2rRz3mI

228 "Lobbying Database," *Open Secrets*, https://www.opensecrets.org/lobby/

229 Lee Fang, "Where Have All the Lobbyists Gone?," *The Nation*, http://bit.ly/2rP2Xb9

230 Lee Drutman, "How Corporate Lobbyists Conquered American Democracy," *The Atlantic*, http://bit.ly/2rMvkGW

231 "What is Citizens United?," *Reclaim Democracy*, http://bit.ly/2rQufhb

232 Bill Allison and Sarah Harkins, "Fixed Fortunes: Biggest corporate political interests spend billions, get trillions," *Sunlight Foundation* http://bit.ly/2rQ1xgj

233 *Merchants Of Doubt* http://www.merchantsofdoubt.org

234 "Bad Science–A Resource Book," The Climate Change Law and Policy Project Blog, http://bit.ly/2rQyRDW

235 George Monbiot, "Just follow the money," *The Guardian*, http://bit.ly/2rQuhpj

236 Jane Mayer, "Covert Operations," *The New Yorker*, http://bit.ly/2rT5YHb

237 Anthony DePalma, "Fidel Castro, Cuban Revolutionary Who Defied U.S., Dies at 90," *New York Times*, https://nyti.ms/2rTaBkN

238 Cameron Reilly, "#29, Fidel Castro," *A Cold War Podcast* http://bit.ly/2rQ1BN5

239 I F Stone, *The Hidden History of the Korean War, 1950–1951*, (Little Brown & Co, Boston, 1952)

240 Seth Rosenfeld, *Subversives: The FBI's War on Student Radicals, and Reagan's Rise to Power* (Picador, London, 2013)

241 GE Theater, "Live Better Electrically," *YouTube* http://bit.ly/2rPgjEb

242 Thomas W. Evans, *The Education of Ronald Reagan: The General Electric Years and the Untold Story of his Conversion to Conservatism*, (Columbia University Press, New York, 2006)

243 Seth Rosenfeld, "Reagan's Personal Spying Machine," *New York Times*, https://nyti.ms/2rPgmjl

244 David Halperin, "Before Rubio, Before Luntz: Meet A Founding Father of Climate Change Denial," *Republic Report* http://bit.ly/2rSOWci

245 "Luntz Research Memo," *Mother Jones*, http://bit.ly/2rQyTf2

246 "Attacks on Renewable Energy Standards," *Energy & Policy Institute* http://bit.ly/2rRZlVO

247 Rebekah Wilce, "Kochs, Corps, and Monsanto Trade Group Have Bankrolled Group Attacking Dr Oz," *PR Watch* http://bit.ly/2rSglv4

248 "Institute of Public Affairs," *SourceWatch* http://bit.ly/2lv9GqY

249 Ben Cubby and Antony Lawes, "The benefit of the doubt," *Sydney Morning Herald* http://bit.ly/2rPgyPB

250 Matthew Knott, "Institute for Public Affairs true colours: under fire from scientists over Plimer book mail out," *ClimateShifts*, https://climateshifts.org/2012/04/05/institute-for-public-affairs-true-colours-under-fire-from -scientists-over-plimer-book-mail-out/

251 "The 97 percent consensus on global warming," *Skeptical Science* http://bit.ly/2rSgT46

252 Suzanne Goldenberg and Helena Bengtsson, "Biggest US coal company funded dozens of groups questioning climate change," *The Guardian* http://bit.ly/2rT6fKd

253 Ibid

254 Derek Thompson, "Google's CEO: The Laws Are Written by Lobbyists'," *The Atlantic* http://bit.ly/2rSP6jU

255 Erika Eichelberger, "House Passes Bill Written by Citigroup Lobbyists," *Mother Jones*, http://bit.ly/2rSuNTY

256 Matthew Yglesias, "Why Lobbyists Write Bills and Why You Shouldn't Worry Too Much About It," *Slate* http://bit .ly/2rTxoOY

257 Cameron Reilly, "Economics & War," *A Cold War Podcast* http://bit.ly/2rTaNR3

258 "List of recessions in the United States," *Wikipedia* http://bit.ly/2rP57HH

259 Peter T Leckie, *Economic Causes Of War*, (Socialist Party of Canada, Vancouver, 1920.) http://bit.ly/2rQCQ3F

260 William Appleman Williams, *The Tragedy Of American Diplomacy*, (W. W. Norton & Company, New York, 1959)

261 Lee Fang, "Google won't renew its military AI contract," *The Intercept* http://bit.ly/2rRZDfm

262 William D Hartung, "Only the Pentagon Could Spend $640 on a Toilet Seat," *The Nation* http://bit.ly/2rZZFSB

263 Ibid

264 David Vine, "Baseworld Profiteering," *TomDispatch* http://bit.ly/2rTx94Y

265 Angelo Young "And The Winner For The Most Iraq War Contracts Is... KBR ," *IBT* http://bit.ly/2rPZEAk

266 "KBR Controversy," *Wikipedia* http://bit.ly/2rPZDfK

267 Liam O'Donoghue, "The biggest Iraq War scandal that nobody's talking about," *Salon* http://bit.ly/2rZZIxL

268 "KBR Investor Presentation November 2015 ," *KBR*, http://bit.ly/2mpF7n6

269 "Killer Facts: The scale of the global arms trade," *Amnesty*, http://bit.ly/2rPhyDc

270 Melvin A Goodman, "Eisenhower's Neglected Warning," *Consortium News*, http://bit.ly/2rQuvwF

271 "Freedom In The World 2015," *Freedom House* http://bit.ly/2rPZE3i

272 Mark Mazzetti, "Claims of Saudi Role in 9/11 Appear Headed for Manhattan Court," *New York Times* https://nyti .ms/2rRFZ2V

273 Brett Wilkins, "Trump Touts $12.5B Saudi Arms Sale as US Support for Yemen War Literally Fuels Atrocities," *Counterpunch* http://bit.ly/2rQuxEN

274 Denver Nicks, "The U.S Is Still No.1 at Selling Arms to the World," *Time* http://bit.ly/2rRG6LT

275 "We have a record of Iraq's WMD," *Herald-Tribune* http://bit.ly/2rSuVmq

276 Michael Dobbs, "U.S. Had Key Role in Iraq Buildup," *Washington Post* https://wapo.st/2rQux7L

277 Zachary Cohen, "Amnesty report: ISIS armed with U.S weapons," *CNN* https://cnn.it/2LAWVUE

278 Cameron Reilly, "G'DAY WORLD #242—Vint Cerf," *cameronreilly.com* https://cameronreilly.com/gday-world -242-vint-cerf/

279 David Pallister, "How the U.S sent $12bn in cash to Iraq And watched it vanish," *The Guardian*, http://bit.ly/2rTb0nj

280 "Legality of the Iraq War," *Wikipedia* http://bit.ly/2LAjGIo

281 "Oversight of Funds Provided to Iraqi Ministries," *OSIGIR* http://bit.ly/2rShtyO

282 Michael Hirsh, "Hirsh: Blackwater And The Bush Legacy," *Newsweek* http://bit.ly/2rQvjBH

283 Donald L. Barlett and James B. Steele, "Billions Over Baghdad," *Vanity Fair* http://bit.ly/2rQvoW1

284 Wesley Lowery, "91 percent of the time the better-financed candidate wins. Don't act surprised." *The Washington Post* https://wapo.st/2rRnfR9

285 Samuel Burke, "The risk of daring to disagree with the NRA," *CNN* https://cnn.it/2rP3tpB

286 Mark Davis, "A snip at $22m to get rid of PM," *Sydney Morning Herald* http://bit.ly/2n5kv49

287 Mitchell Hobbs, David McKnight, " 'Kick this mob out': The Murdoch media and the Australian Labor Government (2007 to 2013)," *Global Media Journal* http://bit.ly/2rRGnyp

288 Bruce Hawker, *The Rudd Rebellion*, (Melbourne University Publishing, Melbourne, 2013)

289 Kevin Rudd, "Cancer eating the heart of Australian democracy," *Sydney Morning Herald* http://bit.ly/2rT6zIV

290 Bill Curry, "Rahm Emanuel's moment of reckoning: How he ended up in a fight for his political life," *Salon*, https://www.salon.com/2015/03/01/rahm_emanuels_moment_of_reckoning_how_he_ended_up_in_a_fight_for _his_political_life/

291 "Goldman Sachs," *Wikipedia*, http://bit.ly/2rPhL9s

292 Louise Story And Eric Dash, "Goldman Settles With S.E.C for $550 Million," *New York Times*, https://nyti.ms/2rSPlLQ

293 Louise Story And Eric Dash, "Bankers Reaped Lavish Bonuses During Bailouts," *New York Times*, https://nyti.ms/2rQvA7H

294 "9 Wall Street Execs Who Cashed In on the Crisis," *Mother Jones*, http://bit.ly/2rPZSYc

295 William F. Buckley, *God and Man at Yale: The Superstitions of "Academic Freedom"* , (Henry Regnery, Chicago, 1951)

296 "Powell Memorandum" aka "Attack on the American Free Enterprise System" (PDF), *Washinton and Lee University School Of Law*, http://bit.ly/2rMvcaq

297 "Not what it used to be," *The Economist* https://econ.st/2rP2PZd

298 Mark Gongloff, "You Need A College Degree To Get A Job (And Crushing Debt To Get A Degree)," *Huffington Post* http://bit.ly/2rP2R3h

299 Jaison R. Abel and Richard Deitz, "Working as a Barista After College Is Not as Common as You Might Think," *New York Fed* https://nyfed.org/2rT5Ozz

300 Judith Ohikuare, "What Really Happens When You Default On Your Student Loans," *Refinery29* https://r29.co/2rOX5Po

301 TomP, "Koch Buys Econ Dept at Florida State," *Daily Kos* http://bit.ly/2rRmFmr

302 Ronald Evans, *Schooling Corporate Citizens: How Accountability Reform has Damaged Civic Education and Undermined Democracy*" (Routledge, Abingdon, 2014)

303 David Horowitz, *The Professors: The 101 Most Dangerous Academics in America*, (Regnery Kids , Washington DC, 2006)

304 "Blackwater aka Academi," *Wikipedia* https://en.wikipedia.org/wiki/Academi

305 Chris Weller, "New education secretary Betsy DeVos champions vouchers and charter schools—here's what that means," *Business Insider* http://bit.ly/2rPh9Rc

306 Emmanuel Felton, "'It's like a black and white thing': How some elite charter schools exclude minorities," *The Hechinger Report / NBC News* https://nbcnews.to/2rRFt4Z

307 *The National Alliance for Public Charter Schools* http://bit.ly/2rMvfTE

308 The British-American coup that ended Australian independence https://www.theguardian.com/commentisfree /2014/oct/23/gough-whitlam-1975-coup-ended-australian-independence

309 Ibid

310 Ibid

311 John Pilger, *A Secret Country*, (Random House, New York, 1989)

312 Steve Straub, "Thomas Jefferson, Men by their constitutions are naturally divided into two parties," *The Federalist Papers* http://bit.ly/2oKsHad

313 Ole Helby Petersen, Ulf Hjelmar, Karsten Vrangbæk & Lisa la Cour, "Effects of contracting out public sector tasks: A research-based review of Danish and international studies from 2000-2011," *VIVE–The National Research and Analysis Center for Welfare*, http://bit.ly/2rPZXuY

314 "In Sex Scandals, GOP Trumps Democrats," *The Daily Beast* https://thebea.st/2rPhdR5

315 "List of American federal politicians convicted of crimes," *Wikipedia* http://bit.ly/2rPhjbp

316 Peter Olsen-Phillips, Russ Choma, Sarah Bryner and Doug Weber, "The Political One Percent of the One Percent in 2014: Mega Donors Fuel Rising Cost of Elections," *Open Secrets*, http://bit.ly/2rPhmE7

317 François Petry and Benoît Collette, "Measuring How Political Parties Keep Their Promises: A Positive Perspective from Political Science," *ResearchGate* http://bit.ly/2rPhpjh

318 Nic Fleming, "Voters view tall people as better suited for leadership," *The Guardian* http://bit.ly/2rQ3463

319 "Meet the Press Transcript August 23, 2015," *NBC* https://nbcnews.to/2rRzHRa

320 To prevent American readers trying to argue that the Mueller report did find evidence of collusion but just couldn't convict due to DOJ rules, here's the key quote from page 181 of the report "...the investigation did not establish that the contacts.. amounted to an agreement to commit any substantive violation of federal criminal law-including foreign-influence and campaign-finance laws…," *cameronreilly.com* https://cameronreilly.com/my -thoughts-on-mueller-and-russiagate/

321 Michelle Crouch, "13 Secrets Reality TV Show Producers Won't Tell You," *Reader's Digest*, http://bit.ly/2rOXWzc

322 Mark Leibovich, "The Politics of Distraction," *New York Times* https://nyti.ms/2rQ36Ld

323 Noam Chomsky and David Barsamian, "Noam Chomsky Diagnoses the Trump Era," *The Nation* http://bit.ly/2rPhtj1

324 Paul Farhi, "One billion dollars profit? Yes, the campaign has been a gusher for CNN," *Washington Post* https://wapo.st/2rQDgaf

325 "Public Trust in Government: 1958-2017," *Pew Research* https://pewrsr.ch/2rSB3uW

326 Alexis Carey, "Australian institutions among the world's least-trusted, global survey finds," *News.com.au*, http://bit.ly/2NJnmXw

327 "World Values Survey" http://www.worldvaluessurvey.org

328 Kit Yarrow, "The Science of How Marketers (and Politicians) Manipulate Us," *Money.com* http://bit.ly/2rP86Qv

329 *Motherlode Marketing Agency*, http://www.motherlode.com.au

330 Briony Harris, "These are world's most democratic countries, according to the Economist," *WeForum*, http://bit.ly/2rPmMPk

331 Eugene Volokh, "Is the United States of America a republic or a democracy?," *The Washington Post* https://wapo.st/2rQBaXH

332 "Standard of living in China," *Wikipedia* http://bit.ly/2rO13HG

333 "What's gone wrong with democracy," *The Economist* https://econ.st/2rQIMJZ

334 Ian Vasquez and Tanja Porcnik, *The Human Freedom Index 2017* http://bit.ly/2NOoIgU

335 "Majority of Americans Support Campaign Finance Reform," *Ipsos* http://bit.ly/2rMByqi

336 Jocelyn Kiley, "Public support for 'single payer' health coverage grows, driven by Democrats," *Pew Research*, https://pewrsr.ch/2rPmO9U

337 Christine Filer, "Two-thirds say large corporations pay too little in federal taxes (POLL)," *ABC News* https://abcn.ws/2rS6Z2s

338 Colleen Cartwright, "FactCheck Q&A: do 80 percent of Australians and up to 70 percent of Catholics and Anglicans support euthanasia laws?," *The Conversation* http://bit.ly/2rPoal9

339 Matt McDonald, "Lowy Institute Poll shows Australians' support for climate action at its highest level in a decade," *The Conversation* http://bit.ly/2rQIR07

340 Jarryd Bartle, "Most Australians support decriminalising cannabis, but our laws lag behind," *The Conversation* http://bit.ly/2rSB7uG

341 "John Gotti," *Wikipedia* http://bit.ly/2rRMgM1

342 Christopher Achen and Larry Bartels, *Democracy for Realists: Why Elections Do Not Produce Responsive Government*, (Princeton University Press, New Jersey, 2017)

343 Thomas Piketty, *Capital in the Twenty-First Century*, (The Belknap Press of Harvard University Press, London, 2014)

344 John Cassidy, "Piketty's Inequality Story in Six Charts," *New Yorker* http://bit.ly/2NJoqea

345 "Robert Yates's Version, 18 June 1787," *US National Archies* http://bit.ly/2NHdBsU

346 Peter H Lindert and Jeffrey G Williamson, *Unequal gains: American growth and inequality since 1700*, Princeton University Press, New Jersey, 2016)

347 Claudia Patricolo, "New Report Claims Czech Republic Has Lowest Inequality in EU," *Emerging Europe* http://bit.ly/2NJdcX5

348 "Czech Republic," *World Inequality Database* http://bit.ly/2rQIRNF

349 Amanda Reiman, "75 Years of Racial Control: Happy Birthday Marijuana Prohibition," *Huffington Post* http://bit.ly/2AsKeqp

350 Indian Hemp Drugs Commission https://en.wikipedia.org/wiki/Indian_Hemp_Drugs_Commission

351 "Kills Six In A Hospital: Mexican, Crazed by Marihuana, Runs Amuck With Butcher Knife–February 21, 1925," *New York Times* https://nyti.ms/2rSEhLa

352 "Mexican Family Go Insane; Five Said to Have Been Stricken by Eating Marihuana–July 6, 1927," *New York Times* https://nyti.ms/2GJAbD5

353 Rudolph Joseph Gerber , *Legalizing Marijuana : Drug Policy Reform and Prohibition Politics*, (Greenwood Publishing Group, Westport, Connecticut, 2004)

354 "Shafer Commission," *Wikipedia* https://en.wikipedia.org/wiki/Shafer_Commission

355 G. G. Nahas and A Greenwood, "The first report of the National Commission on marihuana (1972): signal of misunderstanding or exercise in ambiguity," *US National Library of Medicine National Institutes of Health*, https://www.ncbi.nlm.nih.gov/pmc/articles/PMC1749335/

356 Dan Baum, *Smoke and Mirrors: The War on Drugs and the Politics of Failure*, (Little, Brown, Boston, 1996)

357 Leon Trotsky, "Whither France?," *Marxists.org* http://bit.ly/2B41vXE

358 Robert O. Paxton, *The Anatomy Of Fascism*, (Alfred A Knopf, New York, 2004) 218

359 Jeff Nesbit, "The Secret Origins Of The Tea Party," *Time* http://bit.ly/2rQ4Yni

360 Umberto Eco, "Ur-Fascism," *New York Review Of Books* http://bit.ly/2B2W5Ms

361 Robert Paxton, "Five Stages of Fascism," *The Journal of Modern History*, Vol 70, No 1 (Mar., 1998)

362 Rosie Gray, "Trump Defends White-Nationalist Protesters: 'Some Very Fine People on Both Sides'," *The Atlantic* https://www.theatlantic.com/politics/archive/2017/08/trump-defends-white-nationalist-protesters-some-very -fine-people-on-both-sides/537012/

363 Lis Power & Rob Savillo, "Cable news applies "far-left" framing 6 times more often than "far-right" framing," *Media Matters For America* https://www.mediamatters.org/cnn/cable-news-applies-far-left-framing-6-times-more-often-far-right-framing

364 Justin Sink and Jonathan Levin, "Trump pressures Maduro with new Venezuela gold sanctions," *The Mercury News* https://bayareane.ws/2GLAaOY

365 Glenn Greenwald, Andrew Fishman, "The Most Misogynistic, Hateful Elected Official in the Democratic World: Brazil's Jair Bolsonaro " *The Intercept* http://bit.ly/2mq5md5

366 Jake Johnston, "How Pentagon Officials May Have Encouraged a 2009 Coup in Honduras," *The Intercept* http://bit.ly/2EGj6rO

367 Roque Planas, "Hillary Clinton's Response To Honduran Coup Was Scrubbed From Her Paperback Memoirs," *Huffington Post* https://www.huffingtonpost.com.au/entry/hillary-clinton-honduras-coup-memoirs_n_56e3 4161e4b0b25c91820a08

368 Peter Tinti, "Inside the Corruption and Repression Forcing Hondurans to Flee to the US," *VICE*, http://bit.ly/2EGIBJv

369 Sandra Cuffe, "U.S.-Trained Police Are Hunting Down and Arresting Protesters Amid Post-Election Crisis in Honduras," *The Intercept* http://bit.ly/2EHE1e7

370 Sarah Kinosian, "Crisis of Honduras democracy has roots in US tacit support for 2009 coup," *The Guardian* http://bit.ly/2ECsWu0

371 "Warren Buffett shares his opinion on China, Costco, Elon Musk, College, and more," *Yahoo Finance*, https://youtu.be/uddpWu5-1Uk?t=950

372 Tim Weiner, *Enemies: A History of the FBI*, (Penguin, London, 2012)

373 "Australian Communist Party v Commonwealth," *Wikipedia* http://bit.ly/2K0tTwA

374 "A Cold War podcast, Episode 91 "Marshall Plan Part I" ," *acoldwar.com* http://bit.ly/2VTybvF

375 James E. Pool III and Suzanne Pool, *Who Financed Hitler*, (Macdonald and Jane's Publishers Limited, London, 1979) 281-282

376 Ben Aris and Duncan Campbell, "How Bush's grandfather helped Hitler's rise to power," *The Guardian* http://bit.ly/2EJhUUC

377 Jane Mayer, *Dark Money: The Hidden History of the Billionaires Behind the Rise of the Radical Right*, (Doubleday, New York, 2016)

378 Charles Higham, *Trading With the Enemy*, (Delacorte Press/New York, 1983)

379 "The Business Plot," *Wikipedia* https://en.wikipedia.org/wiki/Business_Plot

380 McCormack–Dickstein Committee, *Wikipedia* http://bit.ly/2rQzUnt

381 Charles Higham, Trading With the Enemy, (Delacorte Press/New York, 1983)

382 Michael Dobbs, "Ford and GM Scrutinized for Alleged Nazi Collaboration," *Washington Post* https://wapo.st/2rTsbVD

383 Anthony C Sutton, *Wall Street and the Rise of Hitler*, (Clairview Books, London, 2010)

384 "Kevin Rudd a 'psychopathic narcissist' ," *The New Daily* http://bit.ly/2rP8nD1

385 John Pinsker, "The Pointlessness of the Workplace Drug Test," *Salon* http://bit.ly/2rSmG9Q

386 *QAV Investing Podcast*, http://qavpodcast.com.au

387 Tim Smith, "10 Top Performing Ethical Investment Funds in 2018," *Canstar* http://bit.ly/2VVRXqn

388 *B Corp website* http://bcorporation.com.au

389 *YourMorals.org* http://www.yourmorals.org

390 "In-home TV Still Tops Aussie Screening Habits," *Nielsen*, http://bit.ly/2rQ8zBJ

391 Steve Henn, "Online Marketers Take Note Of Brains Wired For Rewards," *NPR* https://n.pr/2rP8oXB

392 "G'Day World #336—The Sammartino Method," *cameronreilly.com* http://bit.ly/2s05nE1

393 Benjamin Graham, *The Intelligent Investor* (Collins Business, New York, 1949)

394 Burton G. Malkiel, *A Random Walk Down Wall Street*, (W. W. Norton & Company, New York, 1973)

395 "Bullshit Filter Checklist," https://thebullshitfilter.com/the-bullshit-checklist/

396 "List of fallacies," *Wikipedia* http://bit.ly/2rTCN7a

397 Rudyard Kipling, *Rewards and Fairies*, (Doubleday, Page & Company, New York, 1910)

INDEX